STILL LIFE

DOAN LY

CHRONICLE CHROMA

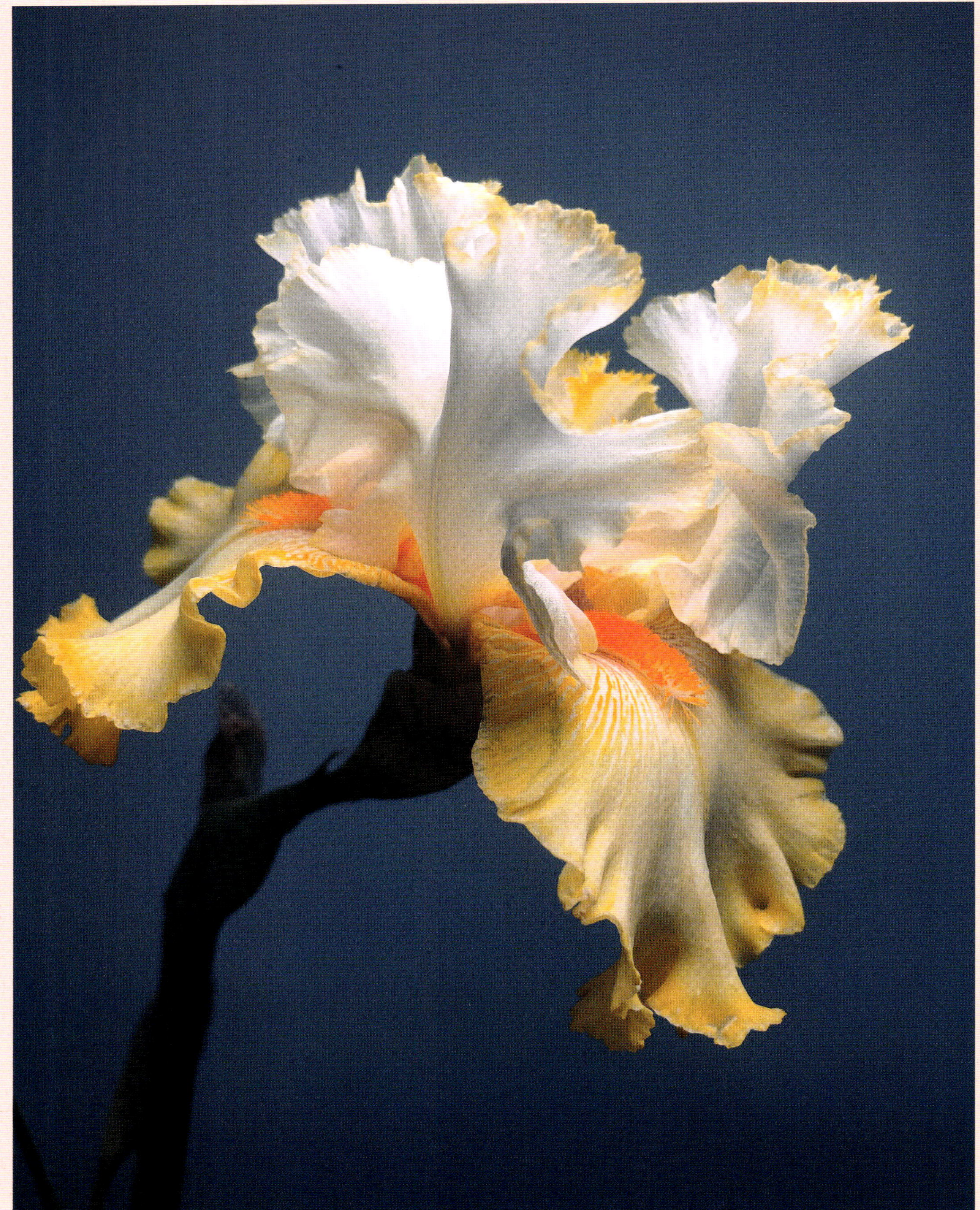

*"I want to be caught off guard.
I want to see anew.*

*I want to experience a quiet
moment that is larger than life.*

*I want to learn something, but
mostly, I want to share beauty
and bring joy."*

Doan founded her design studio, a.p. bio, in 2015. A nerdy play on Advanced Placement Biology—flowers being the sex organs of plants—a.p bio is, as you'll see in the coming pages, less a flower shop than a flower think tank.

INTERVIEW WITH DOAN LY

by Rose Courteau

I first met Doan Ly in 2021. It was late summer, and I'd been assigned to write about her for *T Magazine* as one of "12 Talents Shaping the Design World." At that time, I was unfamiliar with the intricacies of floral design and nervous about interviewing an artist who used flowers as a primary medium. What would we talk about?

So much, it turned out. At a vaguely Italian restaurant a short walk from her studio—then located near Brooklyn's Navy Yard—we ordered too much food and I quickly became enamored of Doan's vibrant, unassuming demeanor and her life story, which contains many unpredictable turns. Born in Saigon, Vietnam, at age five, she escaped the country by boat with her parents, spending a year at a refugee camp in Indonesia before settling in Minnesota in the 1980s. In Vietnam, her mother had been a secretary and her father a postman. (He also served as a translator for US forces during the Vietnam War, earning their family asylum.) In America, they scraped by on the low-paying jobs available to them. At times, Doan recalls, her mother collected cans to supplement their income.

Though admitted to Stanford for college—"it seemed very promising!" Doan says with a laugh—she didn't follow the safe trajectory her parents had hoped she would. (Given what they'd endured, she doesn't "blame them at all for wanting me to go a very safe route.") Instead she got involved in campus theater, and after graduating with a degree in English, earned her MFA in acting at New York University's Tisch School of the Arts. She spent a few subsequent years in Los Angeles, waiting tables and working at a bowling alley while picking up minor screen parts—one of the most notable and strange being a recurring role on *CSI: Crime Scene Investigation*, playing a herpetologist.

It wasn't until she returned to New York that Doan took up floristry initially as a side hustle, moonlighting at a popular, now-shuttered plant store in the Brooklyn neighborhood of Williamsburg while managing a Quaker intentional community house in Manhattan. Though flowers may seem like a simple pleasure to most of us, the business of flowers is a grueling one for those who work in it. Florals are expensive and have inflexibly short shelf lives, while arrangements require picture-perfect presentation. Days in the shop can be long. ("Valentine's Day was a bitch," she says.) During that time, "I was just wishing that I could watch something of my own grow, that I had the capital or confidence to start my own business, says Doan. Finally:

> My mom just wouldn't have it anymore. She was like, "You have to [open your own business]." She said that she and my father would support me, if I needed it, that they would help me. My dad worked in a factory. He's retired, but my parents are poor. . . . [After acting] I didn't give myself permission to take any more risks. And it wasn't until my mother said, "Let's do this. We'll be a team. We're okay. We can take care of you, and you can pay us back." It meant a lot to me just to have that permission, even though I knew they didn't have the means to support me. I just needed that blessing from them. Once my mind started opening up to it, I found all sorts of ways to imagine what struggling as a small business owner would be. And it seemed worth it.

And so Doan founded her design studio, a.p. bio, in 2015. A nerdy play on Advanced Placement Biology—flowers being the sex organs of plants—a.p bio is, as you'll see in the coming pages, less a flower shop than a flower think tank that. Needing to present her work to prospective clients, she taught herself how to use a camera—a Canon 5D Mark III—and developed a distinct photographic aesthetic using continuous and natural light that often lends her subjects an ethereal, even painterly, quality. (She also uses her iPhone to capture moments on the fly.) And there are the flowers themselves, of course, which in Doan's hands take on a Technicolor, sometimes anthropomorphic, quality. (Doan intersperses her arrangements with few greens, opting instead for vibrant, high-contrast compositions.) There are also props: fruit, gloves, socks, fake foods. Some of these objects are products, styled and shot for the likes of Veuve Clicquot, *Kinfolk* magazine, *Vogue Italy*, *Spain* and *China*, Comme Si, Vintner's Daughter, Sephora, Victoria's Secret, and *Gossamer* magazine. Some aren't props at all, but women, usually her assistants, whom she conscripts in front of the camera, occasionally for short videos. "The trope that I'm drawn to is sisterhood," she says:

When I photograph people, it's a lot of Asian sisterhood or sisterhood within my designers. This very feminine world that's supportive and very loving and playful. I like capturing women in a place of strong beauty and softness. I don't know how to define it because I'm not super conscious when I do it. I'm more drawn to color and group dynamics. But I think when I see it, there is a strong sense of femininity. It's a lot of women loving each other.

If there's a vibrance to Doan's photos, there's also frequently a pulpy evocation of time's passage. This awareness is foundational to the tradition of still life, which dates back centuries and encompasses the genre of memento mori—derived from the Latin phrase meaning "remember you must die"—symbolized most ubiquitously by a painting of a skull. While you won't find bones within the pages of this book, flowers, which deteriorate rapidly, illustrate exquisitely what we know about life more generally: that we are all in a state of decay. If we don't acknowledge this consciously on a daily basis, we tacitly recognize it in our attempts to hold onto things, to make things permanent. Case in point, of course, is the photograph. This book, which collects many of Doan's most beautiful (often whimsical) still lifes, is itself an attempt at object permanence and a record of Doan's singular perspective and her celebration of life.

Though Doan's work is unabashedly stylized—so different from the "woke up like this" aesthetic that continues to populate many a Pinterest board—her artistic process is largely intuitive. While working together on the introduction for this book, we considered including an instructional component to accompany some of the book's images—a sort of primer for those wishing to emulate her style. But this approach felt at odds with the desire for discovery that guides Doan, and so—over the course of several weeks in the fall of 2022—we chose to embrace the unfixed nature of creativity and to focus instead on what's Doan's mind, now: her current challenges as an artist and business owner, what it means to be "aspirational," the proliferation of mood boards, and more. Our conversations have been edited and condensed.

"This book, which collects many of Doan's most beautiful (often whimsical) still lifes, is itself an attempt at object permanence and a record of Doan's singular perspective and her celebration of life."

I thought I would start by asking you what you've been thinking about the last year, since we first spoke.

I think the challenge is just finding the next inspiration. I don't want to repeat myself. I want to find what more I have to say. And that's scary because I don't know if I have more to say. I don't know what that sounds like or looks like or feels like. When I started [a.p. bio], what I had to say was kind of unique in terms of my small realm of niche floral design and floral expression. But since then, through social media, it has been reflected back at me and it feels like this kind of never-ending mood board that repeats itself and is copied and regurgitated. I'm trying to find what I have to say that's distinct, that's uniquely my own. Nothing's original, nothing's that unique. But I'm trying to challenge myself.

You mentioned mood boards and Instagram and the Internet reflecting your work back at you. Up until pretty recently, artists might get copied, but [their work wasn't being disseminated] at such scale and so rapidly. At the same time, you've talked in the past about how Instagram enabled you to reach an audience that you wouldn't have [otherwise] reached. It just seems really complex.

It is, it's a mixed blessing. There's a really interesting article I read about art directors and mood boards and everything sort of feeling the same. Art directors pull from all the same imagery and there's no surprise. Everything has to be predetermined, proven and then executed exactly to what has already been put on a mood board. So everything that's created has already existed. It's like, "We found this, so we wanna recreate this in this way," so everything gets into this blender.

I'm often told that [my work is included] in mood boards. Like someone will say, "Oh, we did this [ad] campaign," and send me a mood board [of the images used for inspiration.] And it's my images. While I don't have the confidence to say that my work is influential, I have had proof presented to me in this form that people are replicating it, people are using it.

The other big challenge is that what has been my audience is no longer my audience. Instagram has changed significantly. The still image doesn't resonate or get rewarded in the way [it used to]. I don't relate to the cacophony of TikTok. I think it'll be interesting to see if there is a place for me that's uniquely mine with those parameters, with those kinds of rules. How can I have my own conversation within this environment?

It's interesting because you love making these short, whimsical films. I think some people would assume that would be great for TikTok.

It's funny, I think TikTok is very personal-presenting. I always present [my work] in a more formalized, controlled way. It's wacky, but it has its own kind of stiffness. Whereas I think TikTok is very creator-focused. That's not compelling to me. But I wonder if there is a way to have fun with that. I want to keep exploring making short, kind of surrealist videos and seeing where that leads me, where my imagination can go and how I can sort of break that stiffness a little bit and make it even weirder or make it even looser. I think that would be really fun.

Do you have specific new work in mind? Do you have images in your head right now?

I always have ideas. I don't know necessarily how it will look or how it will end up, but I always have a million ideas. I want to make films, I want to cast body parts. I wanna have people do zany things, even if they're a failure. I'm actually very forgiving of myself, in all my failures. I bring people together and I say, "Let's film this," [or], "Will you model for me? Will you do this thing?" And a lot of times it's mediocre.

There's never a lack of things that I want to try. There's just a lack of money and a lack of time. The reality is I have to pay the rent, and I have to make my business-earning side sustainable, so that I can have money to fund the zany part. That takes up a huge chunk of time.

If you weren't constrained by money at all, if some kind of benefactor came along, what would you do?

I would figure out how to make a whole kind of Greek ruin out of Jello. Like, do a bust and legs and arms and torsos and photograph it. And then I would have people come and interact with it and film it. What I do now [for previous series, such as a collection of molded breasts and gloves] is made out of agar. Agar is a huge part of Vietnamese desserts. All the jelly things are made of agar and beans and coconut milk. The jello boobs and hands that I make are from that, so they're ostensibly edible, but I don't add any flavoring or sugar just because it makes it easier to handle without the stickiness. But it would be so fun to have a feast that's actually super delicious and have a feast film.

I also love photographing women and having human subjects and not just object subjects, beyond the realm of the still life world. But it all is sort of connected in that world of feasting and rejoicing. On the other side is a bit of loneliness and loss and nostalgia. You know, they're all kind of next to each other, reverberating.

"When I photograph people, it's a lot of Asian sisterhood or sisterhood within my designers. This very feminine world that's supportive and very loving and playful. I like capturing women in a place of strong beauty and softness. I don't know how to define it because I'm not super conscious when I do it. I'm more drawn to color and group dynamics. But I think when I see it, there is a strong sense of femininity. It's a lot of women loving each other."

That question of how to keep sustaining yourself financially while also saving enough time and energy to make mistakes and pursue new ideas is a classic conundrum. Does that affect your relationship to the kind of work that you [do] for money?

I always feel very lucky that I get to do what I do. I feel so lucky that I get to choose the team that I work with and to create beautiful installations, centerpieces, whatever, that bring people joy. And I get to make a living out of that. That's such a dream. I make enough to be self-employed and travel and enough that I'm not worried paycheck to paycheck. So I feel incredibly blessed with that, and I don't resent having to do that work at all.

I haven't made enough to be able to hire enough admin and production help. That part gets super stressful because, in the end, I don't actually get to design that much. So that is the part that I resent, just having to wear so many hats. But that's part of having a business. I just need to figure out how to scale enough so that I have enough support. That magical balance might never come. But I work with what I have. So if I have a team doing an event and we have thirty minutes, I make them do a video. And people might never see that video, but it's part of my creative regeneration. It keeps me fueled, and it keeps my muscles flexed and warmed, and it reminds me that playing for the sake of playing has value. And it keeps this sense of ensemble. I think on a subconscious level, I'm treating my team as performers in [a] way. I value whatever mechanisms that have been put in place in the context of studio work that makes [us] not boxed in [to] what we do, who we are, or what our roles are. It's like I'm making invisible theater.

It's interesting to think of a studio as giving you permission to do all sorts of things that may not be the explicit purpose of the studio's business.

Yes. [We] talk about office culture, but it's built into a.p. bio studio culture that a sense of play is a part of how we work, just to be silly. This sense of invisible theater—I come back to that word—this sense of performance, of fluidity. Maybe in the end I'll be like, this is my art. I made lots of invisible performances.

I love that term of invisible theater, that there are these things that are in motion and of the moment. You can record them, but it's so different from the work of still lifes. It seems like there's almost this tension in your work of, "How much can I bring from behind the scene, and make that the scene itself, without sacrificing the stylization and the formality?" It feels like it gets a little bit to the heart of "art versus life," and how to integrate those two or not integrate them, and how much satisfaction you can get from having something be seen versus how much having something be seen kind of ruins it a little bit.

I love the idea of art versus life. I think I find kind of nuggets of art in the moment, the way maybe a street photographer walks around and sees these little compositions everywhere. I find little moments of play and theater and movies or scenes in the moment. It's fun to capture them in video or in still life, or even to direct them and have a funny little stylized interaction between two people that's clearly staged. It's a moment that we step away from what we're actually doing right now.

Someone commented once, "Your work teaches me to see flowers. I've learned to see flowers through your images." That's such a gift to be able to connect to people in that way.

Especially in the age of Instagram, art often becomes an object of lifestyle aspiration. I'm wondering if you have anxieties about that, or what gets lost when people only focus on the image or the end result [of an artistic process]?

I actually don't. I understand the aspirational aspect of it completely. And I think it's actually really nice because people find joy. I think people relate to it, and that's what is aspirational. Like if someone's a photographer or a stylist, then they're going to [try to] recapture a palette or a sensibility. But if you are talking about "aspirational" from a larger audience of non-artists,

I think that aspirational sense is just a connection of seeing something that is familiar, like a flower, captured in a way that moves you, that sparks your imagination or makes you think differently. I don't think people are necessarily trying to go out and take still lifes, but someone commented once, "Your work teaches me to see flowers. I've learned to see flowers through your images." That's such a gift to be able to connect to people in that way.

What's been your journey with putting this book together?

In my head, I'm hoping it's a survey of the different stylistic worlds that my photography touches. My colors are super bright, but joy for me is not saccharine. Joy for me doesn't come from cosmetic vibrancy. There is a longing and achiness to it, and a playfulness. It's not necessarily subversive, but it's not the joy of cupcakes.

I think that is what flowers are. They're delicate. But in spite of how small and fragile they are, they can have a larger-than-life aspect. It's the delicacy and fragility and finite moment of flowers that's very powerful. It's mortality; it's funerals and birthdays and all these celebrations and quiet moments. When you think about it in that kind of sociological way, their function [has] all these metaphors behind it.

The images are linked together as a loose story, often connected by color. I can remember where I was when I took each picture—how I was feeling, who I was with or wasn't with. Some were taken on dark and lonely days, late at night, desperate to capture something or feel visible. Some were taken with friends and of friends, or assistants, in a moment of luxurious and ridiculous play. Some of that playfulness was during Covid lockdown. Some were accidental.

I like to break the process and the expectations a little just for fun. In the end, it's just for fun. And I never thought my "just for fun" would resonate. It's really life-affirming to know that you can just create art in a way that is meaningful to you, just to find that sparkle that makes life a little magical in its complete ordinariness. And so I hope the book brings joy, and that someone enjoys picking it up and flipping through it, and having that physical sensation that makes books feel special. It's different from scrolling Instagram. Books have weight to them. They have gravitas.

"I hope the book brings joy, and that someone enjoys picking it up and flipping through it, and having that physical sensation that makes books feel special. It's different from scrolling Instagram. Books have weight to them. They have gravitas."

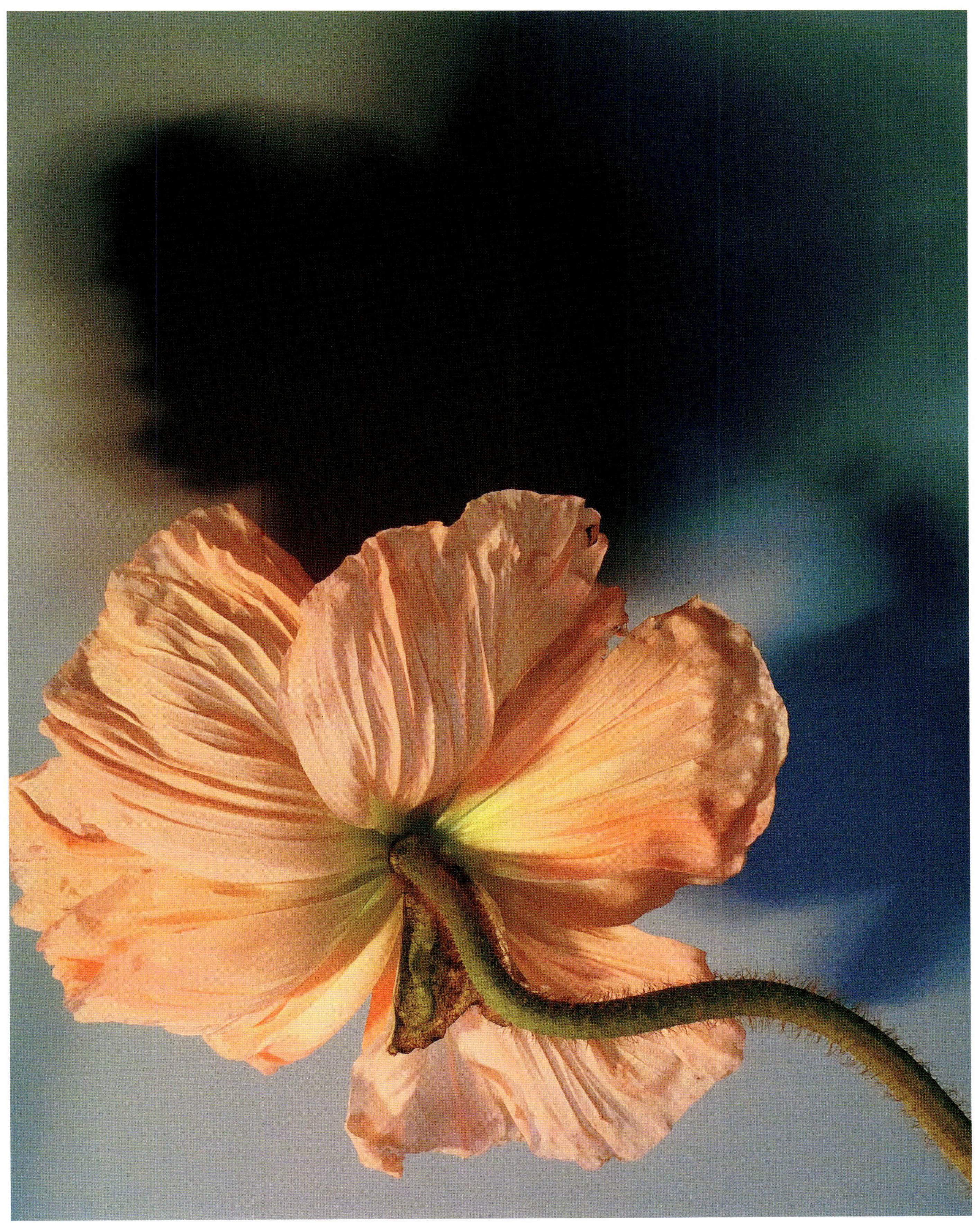

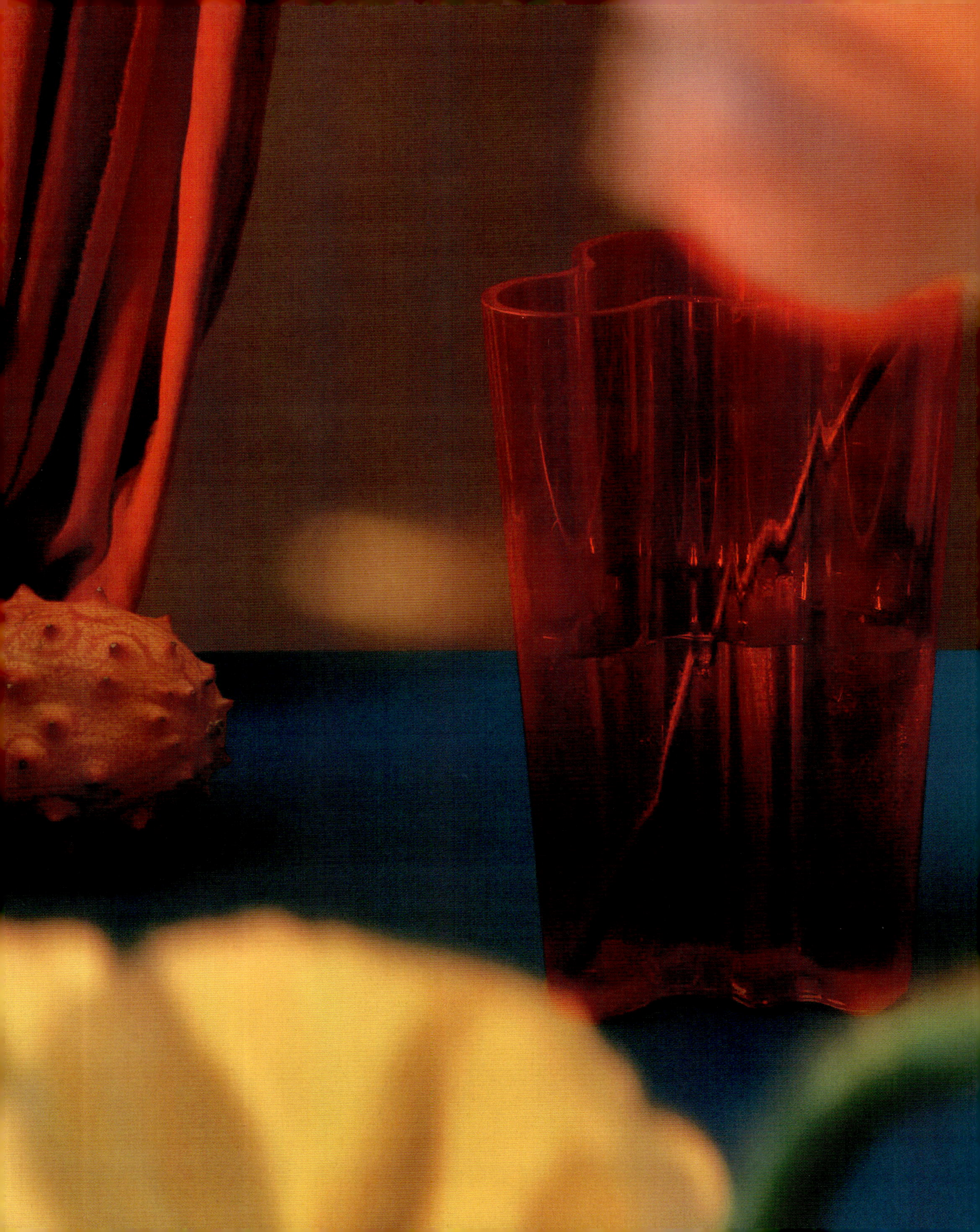

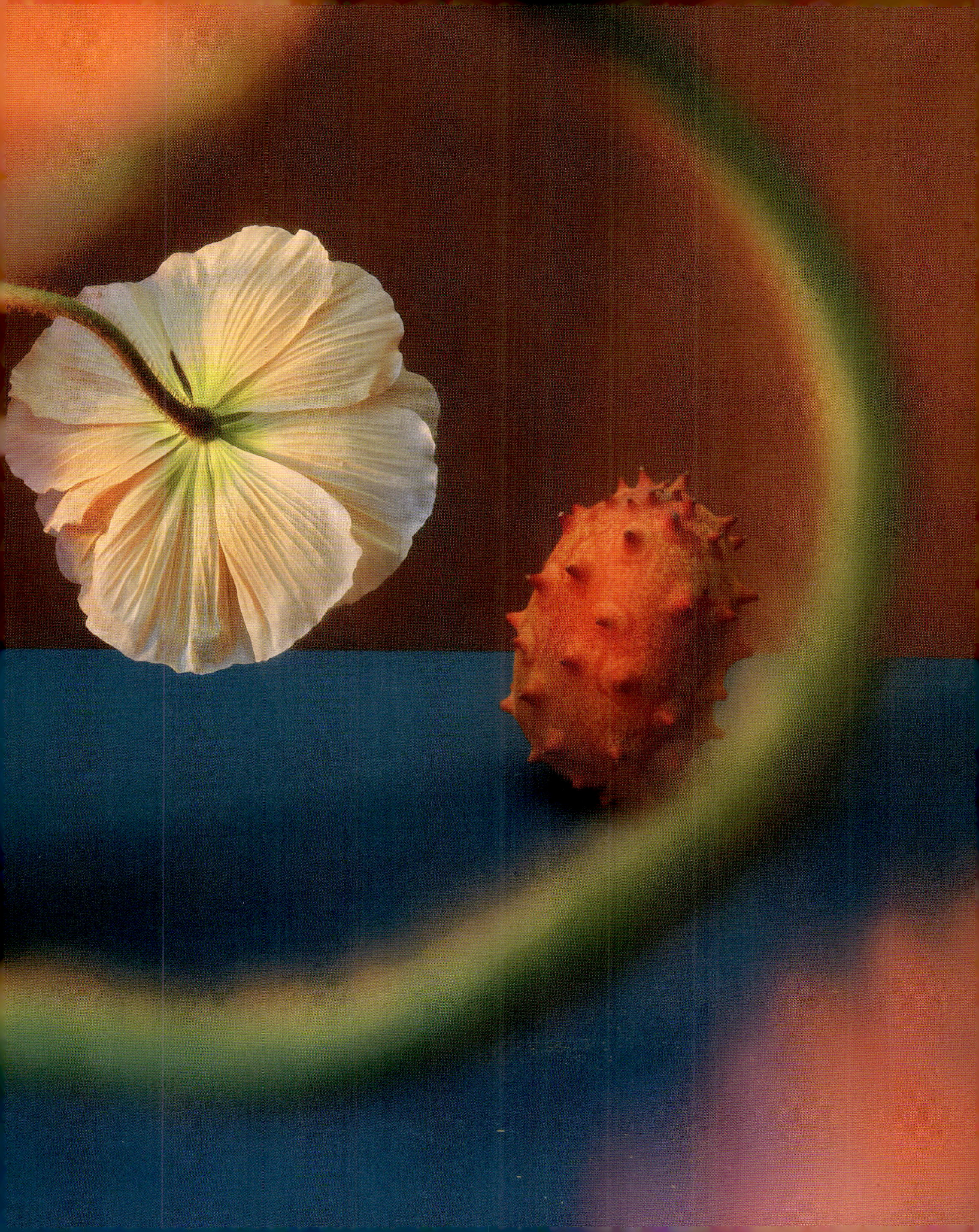

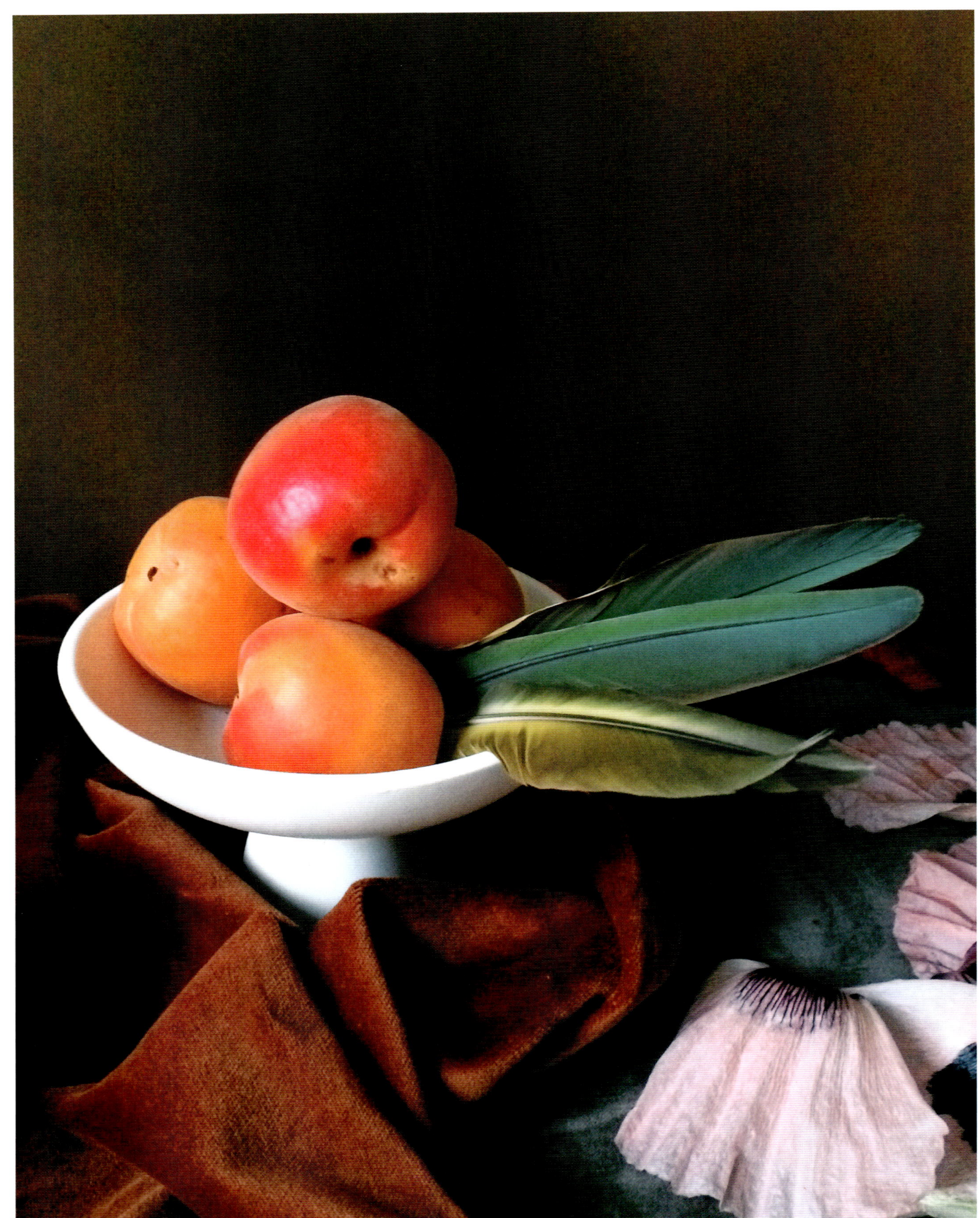

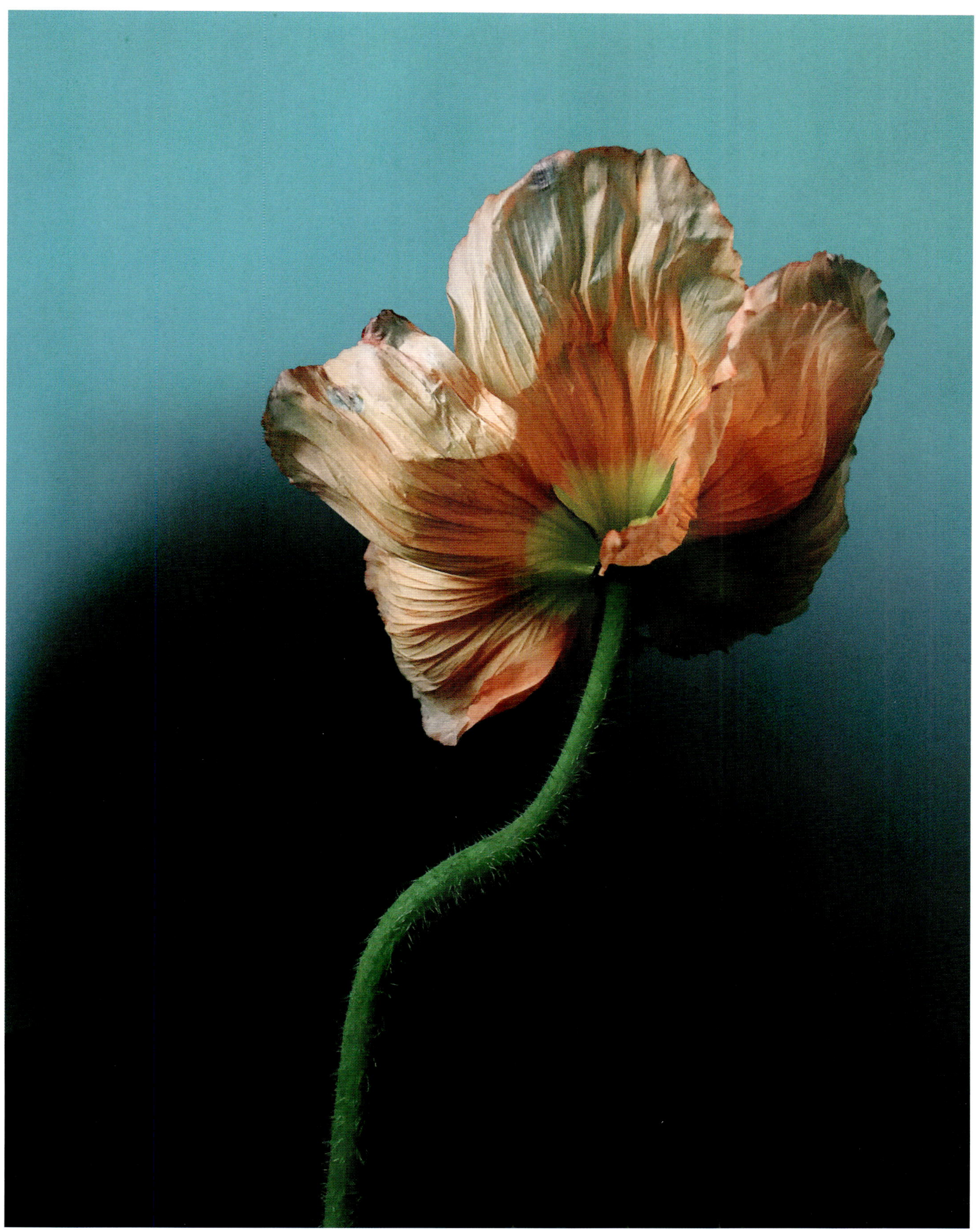

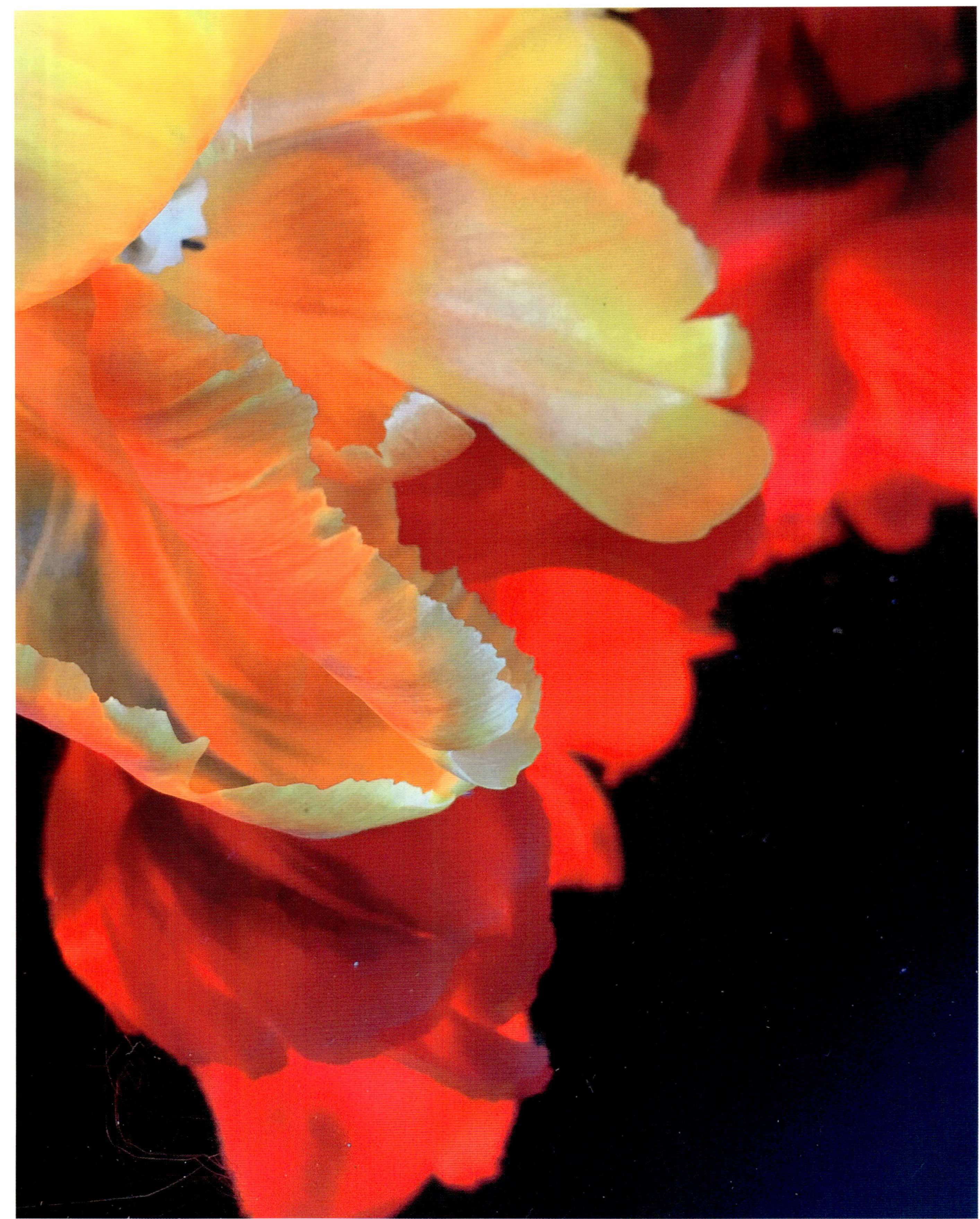

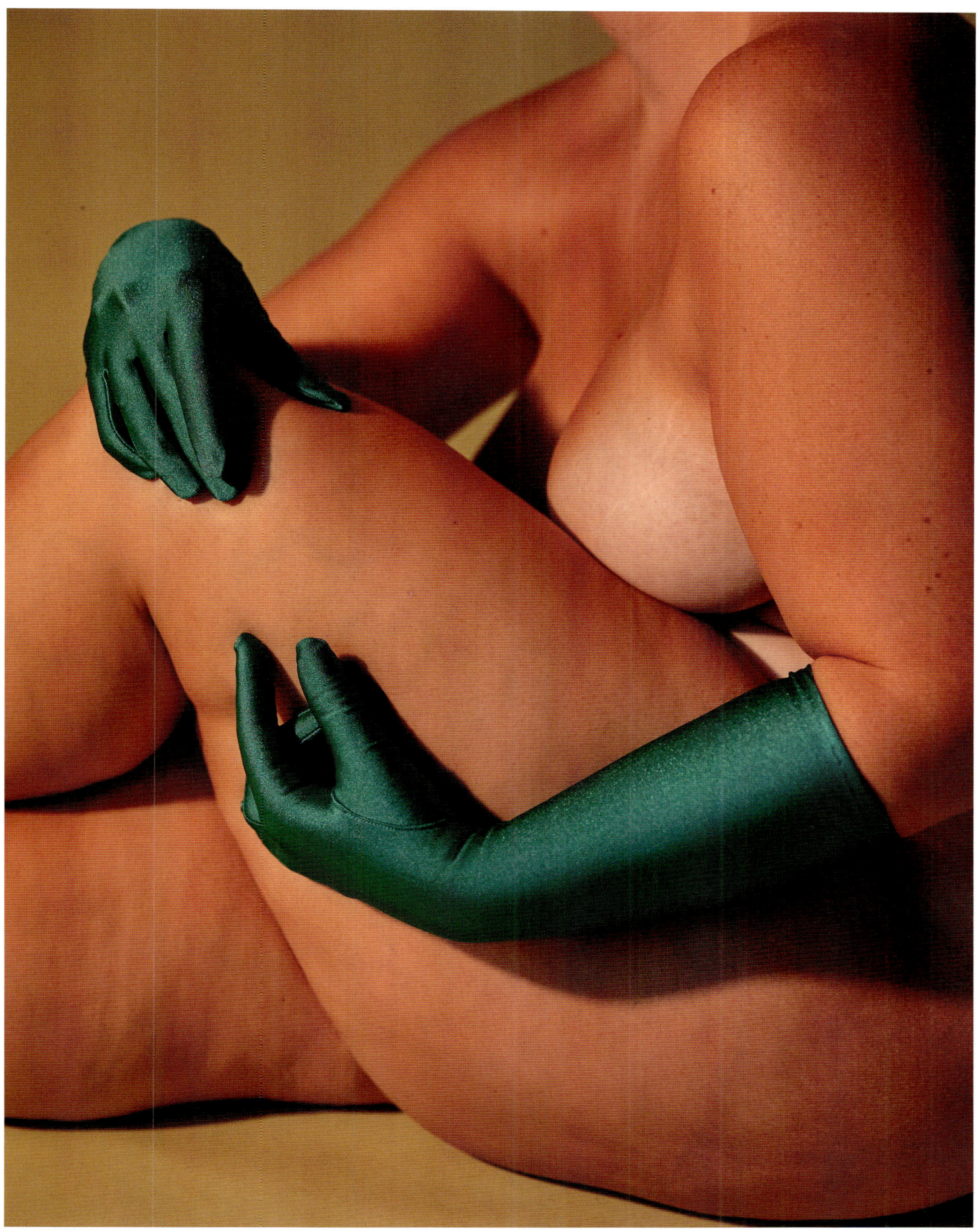

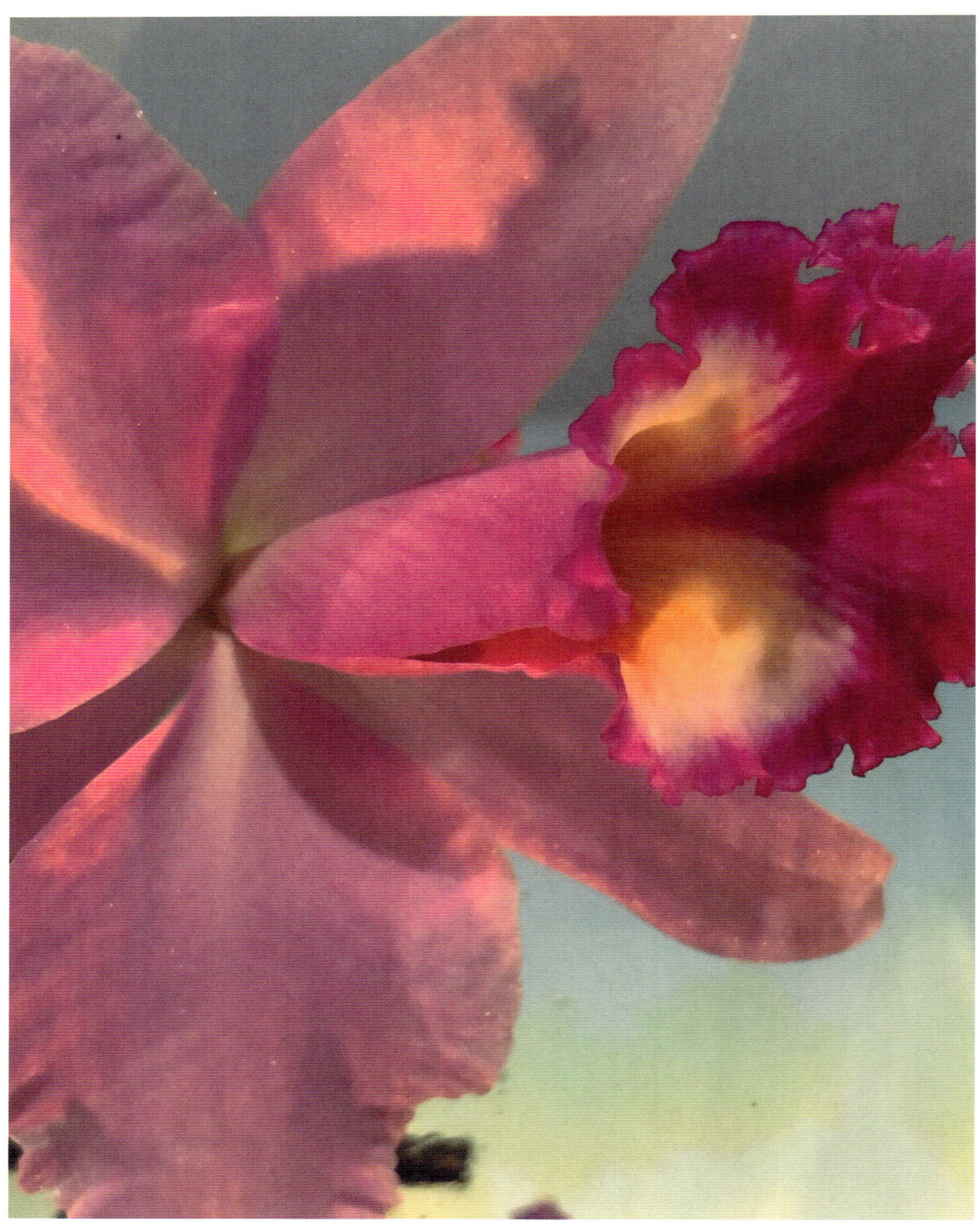

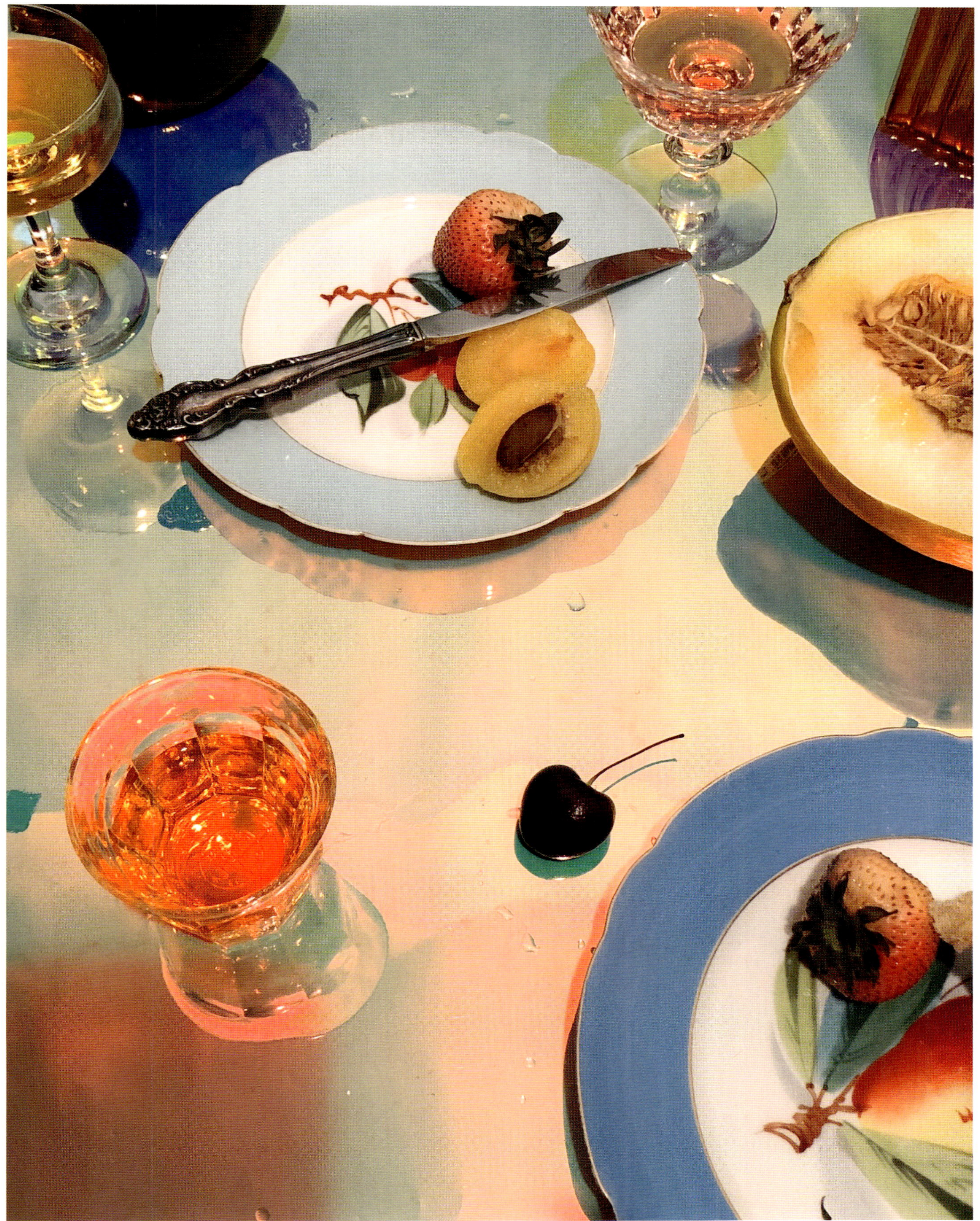

WHAT A LITTLE MOONLIGHT

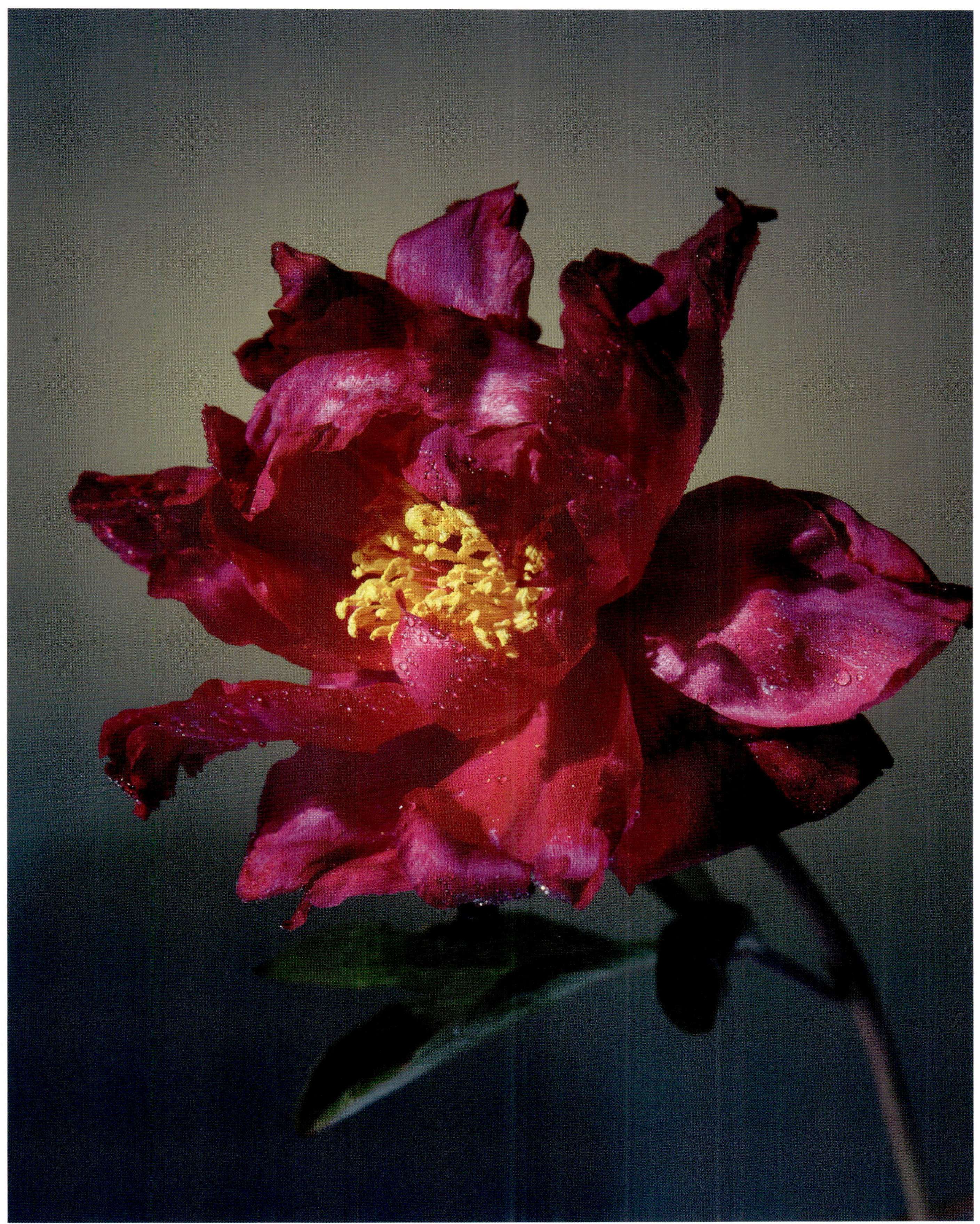

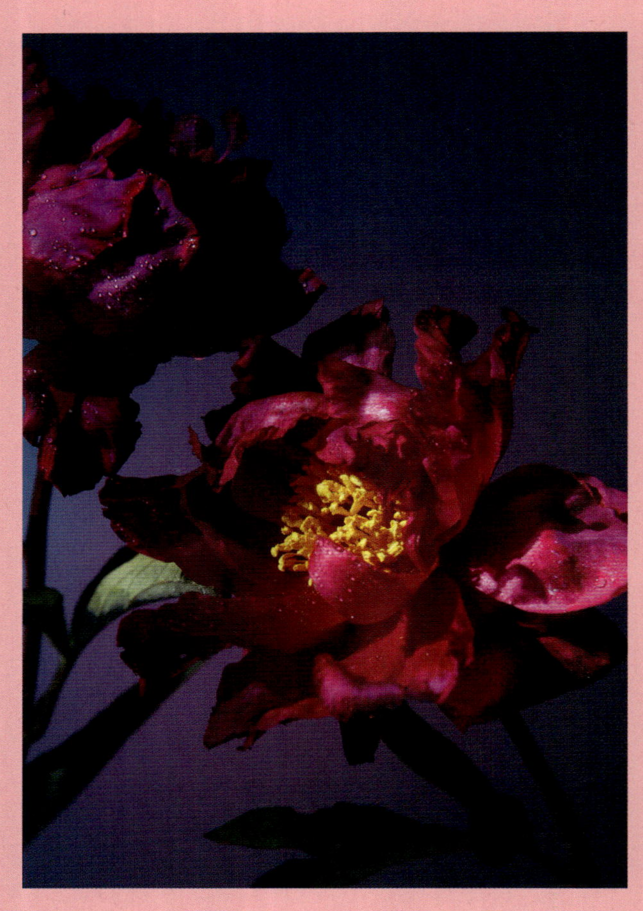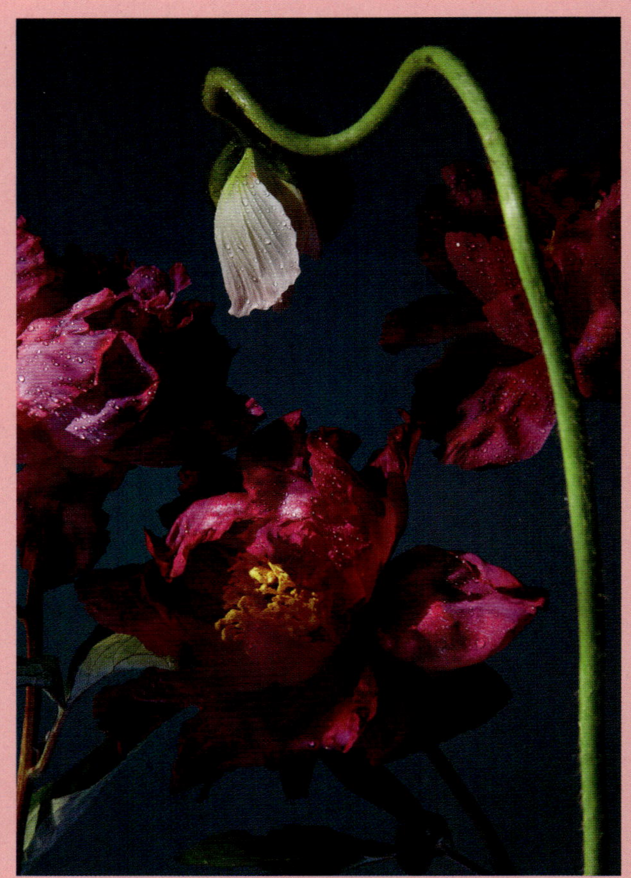

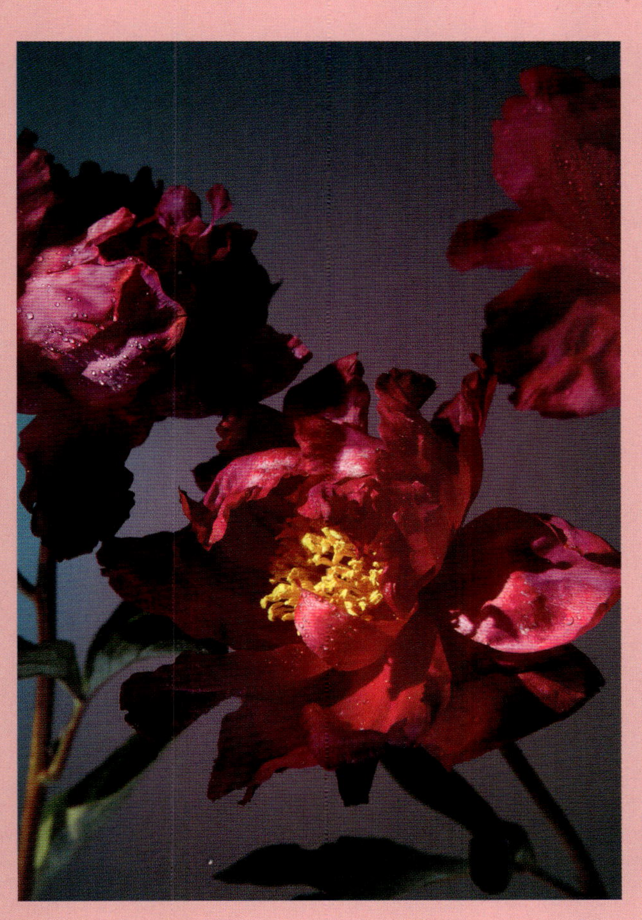
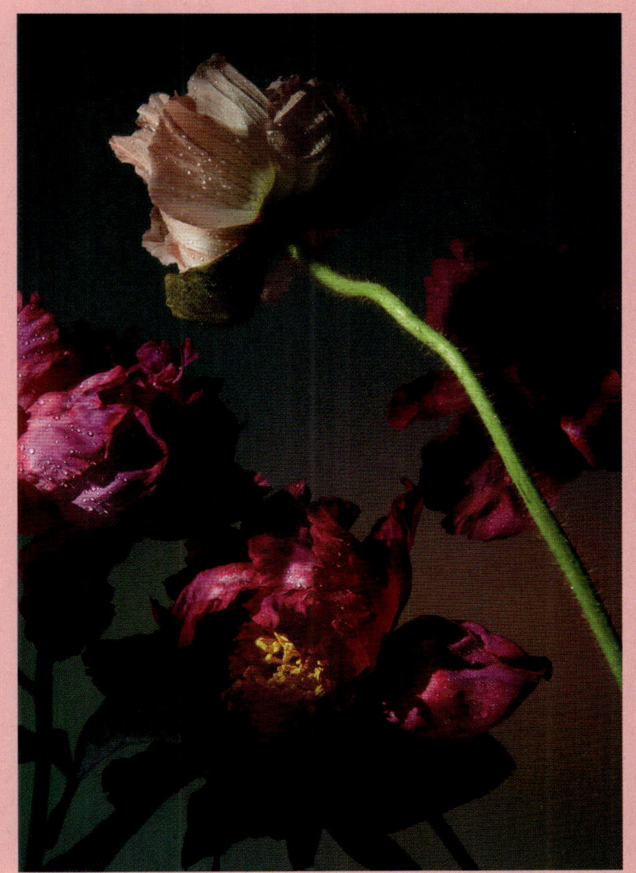

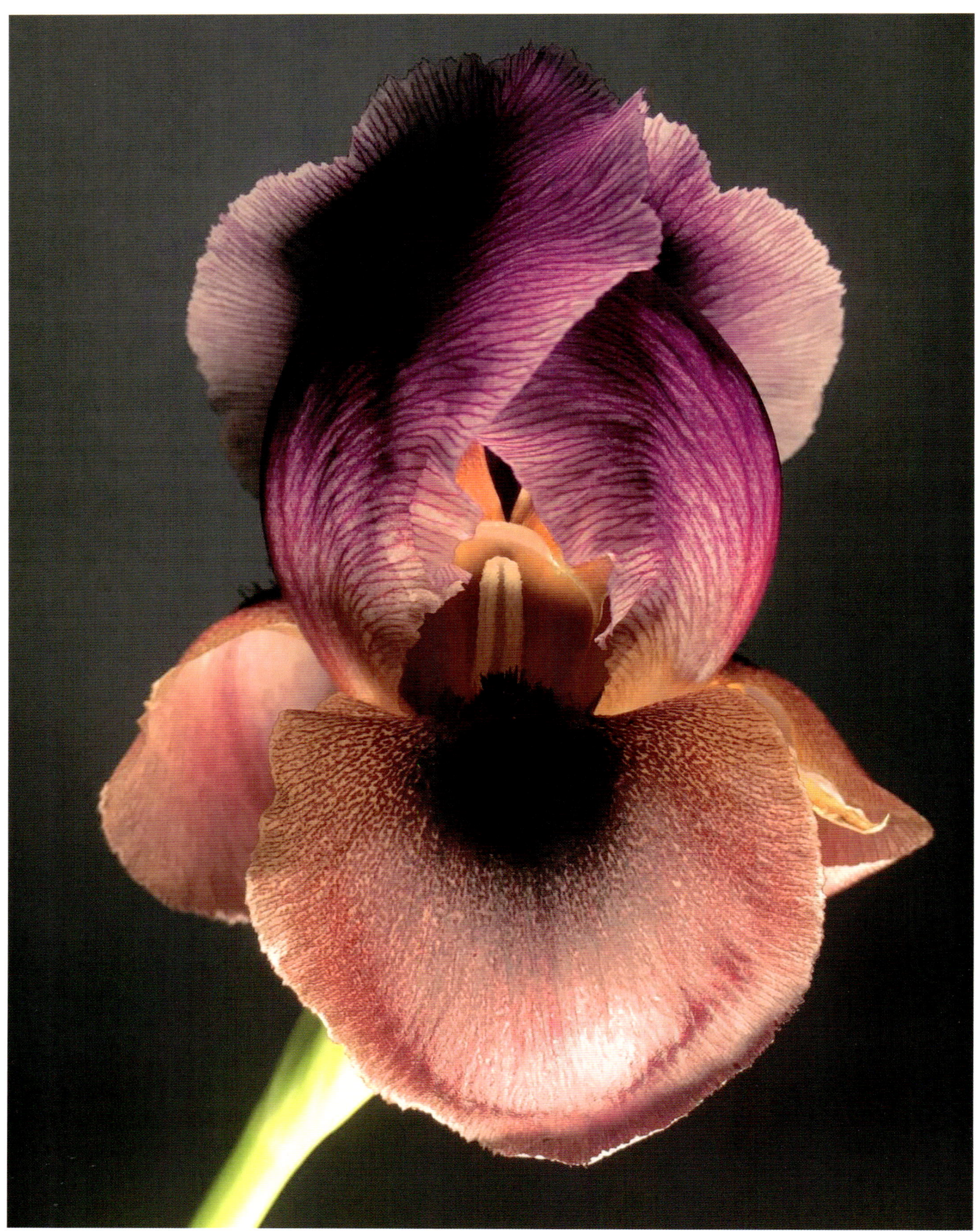

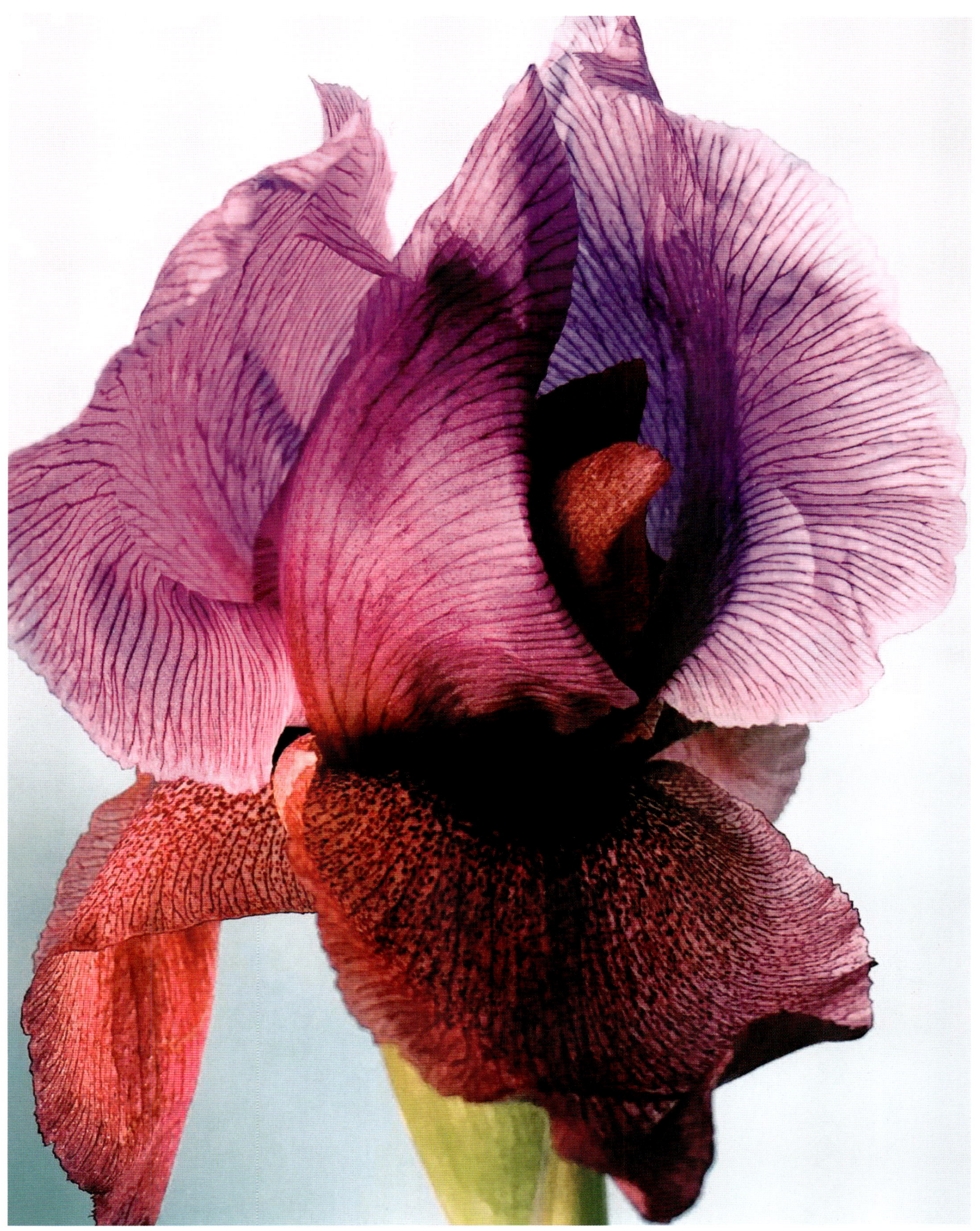

MY LUCKY DAY

A CHANCE ENCOUNTER LED TO THIS FIRST PHOTO.
SHE WAS MY DRIVER ON THE WAY TO A SHOOT.

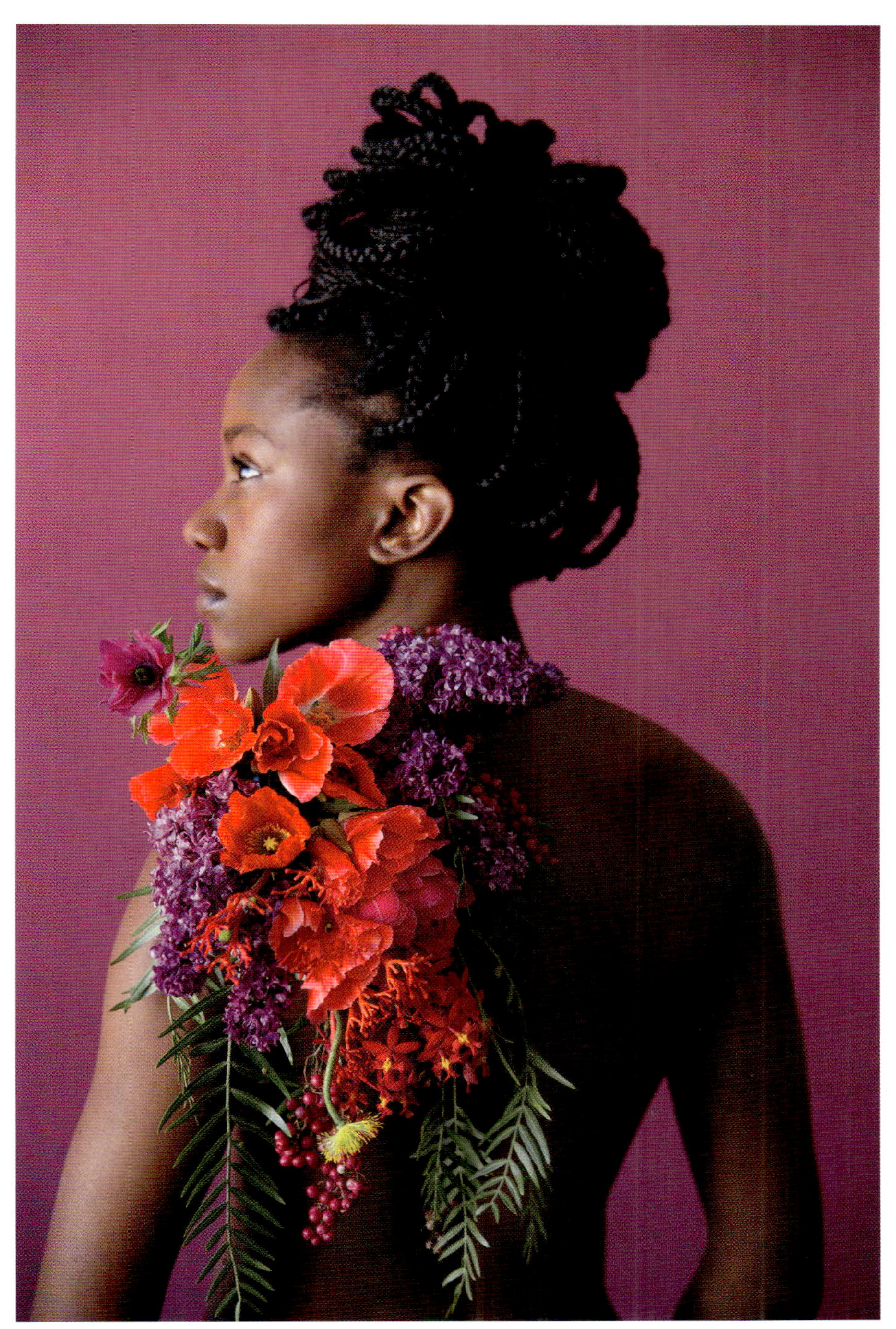

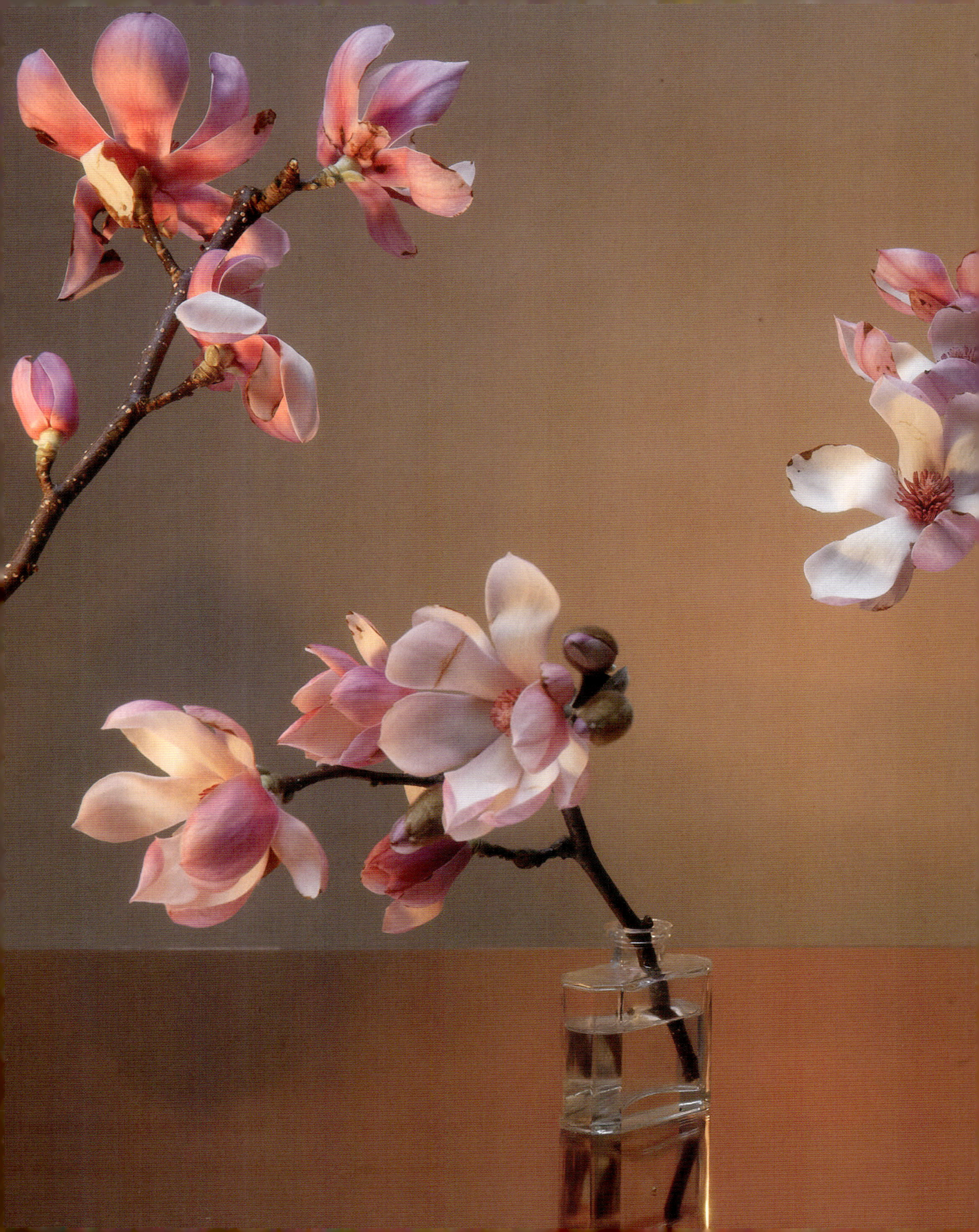

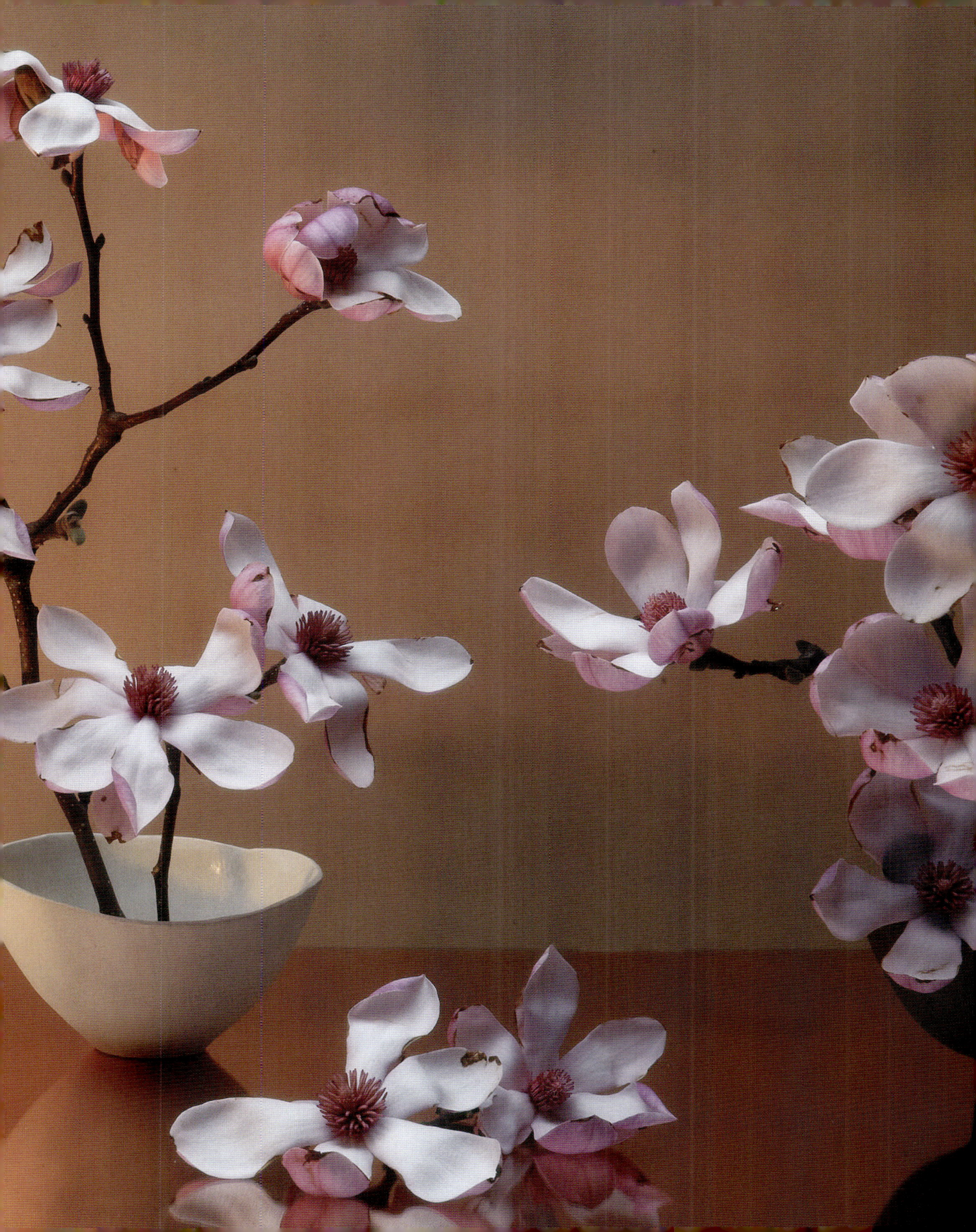

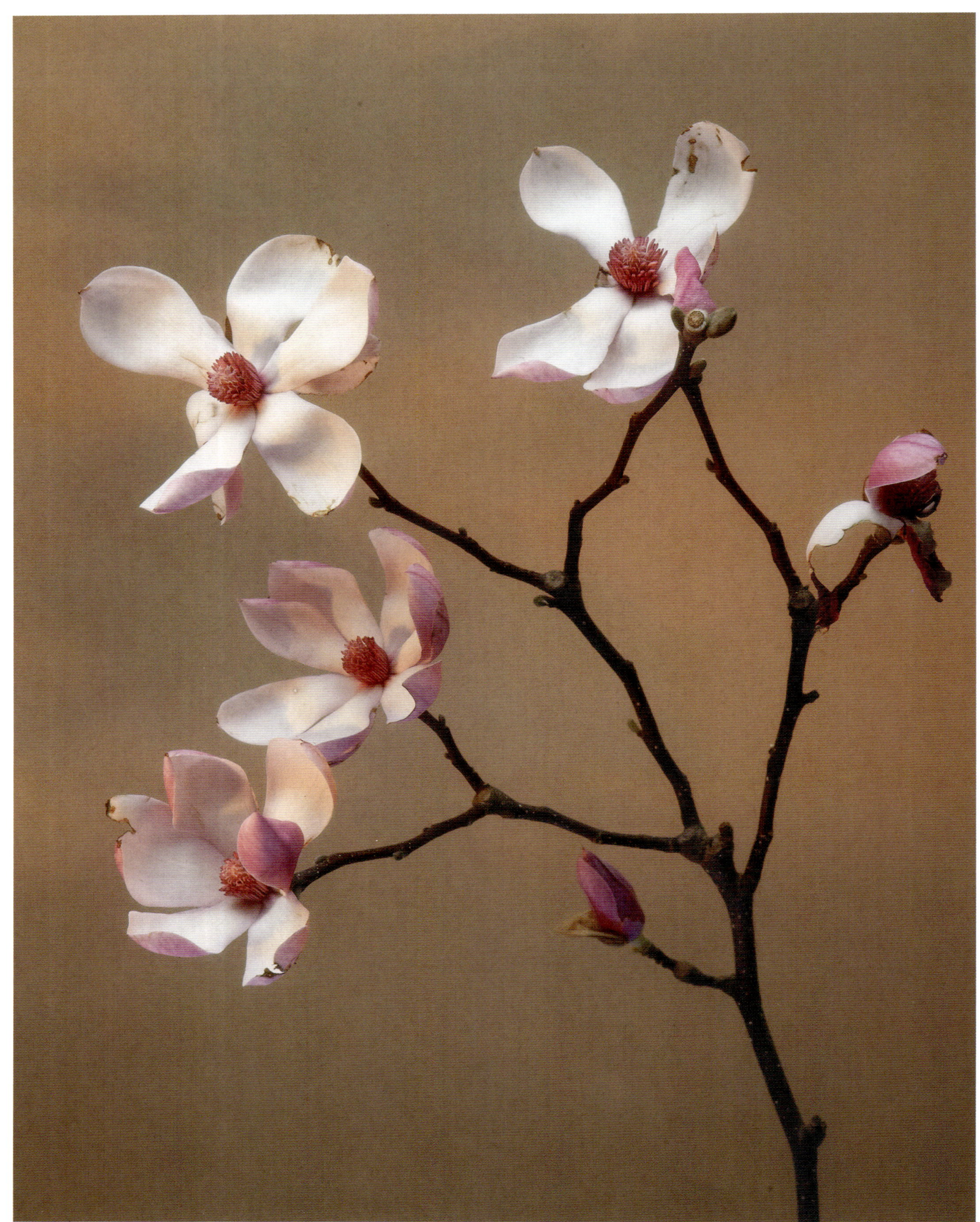

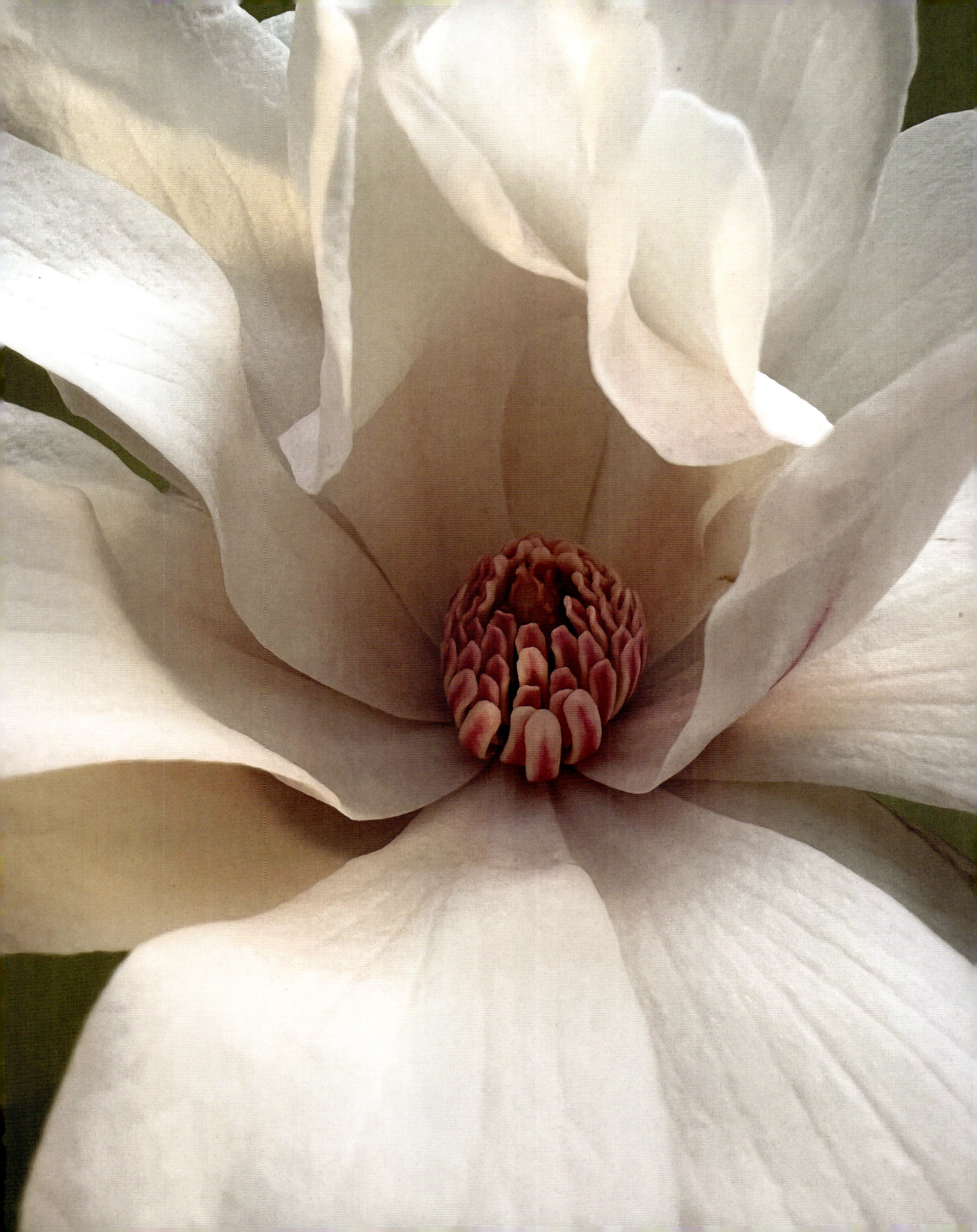

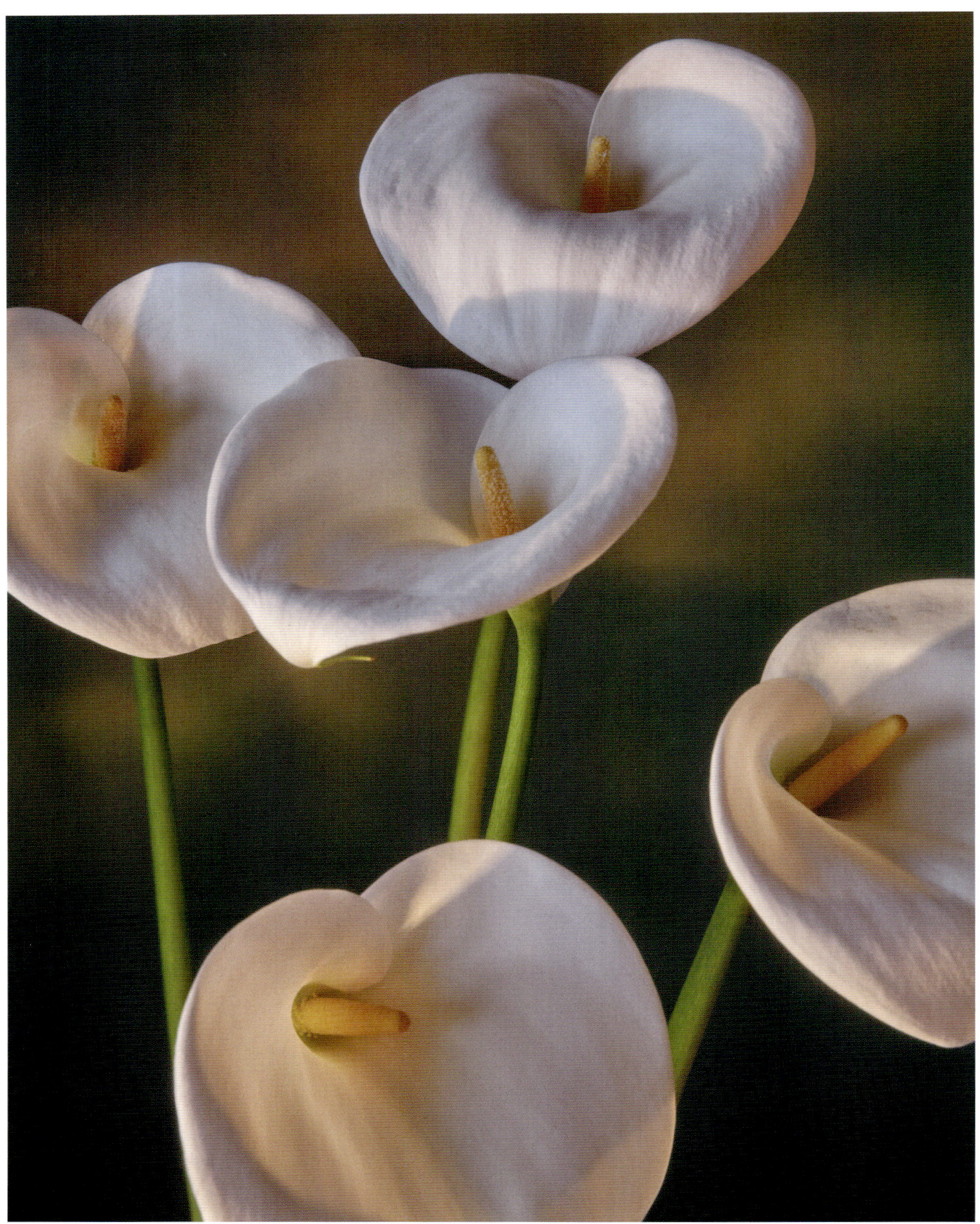

SO BEFORE THE LIGHT

GLACIER

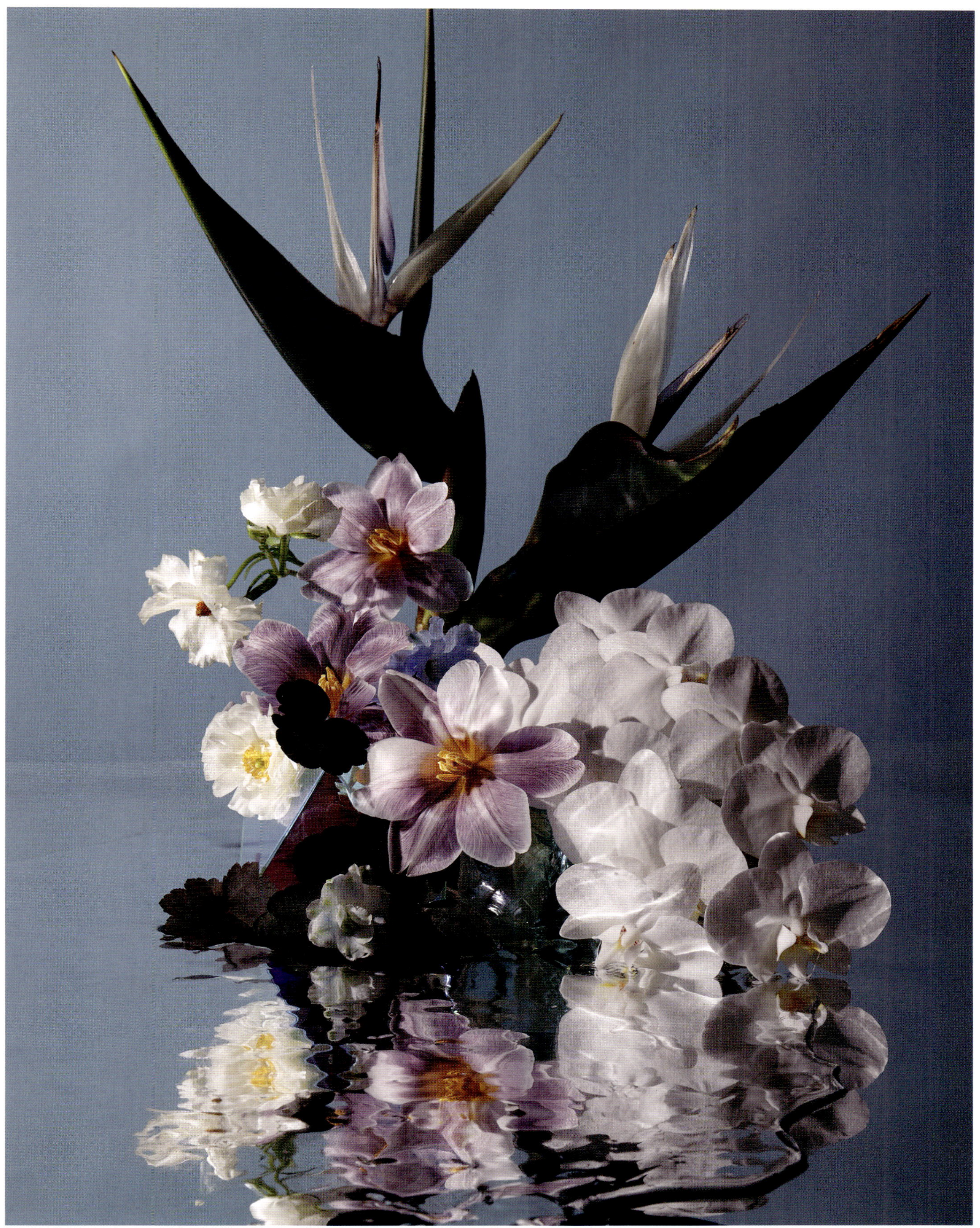

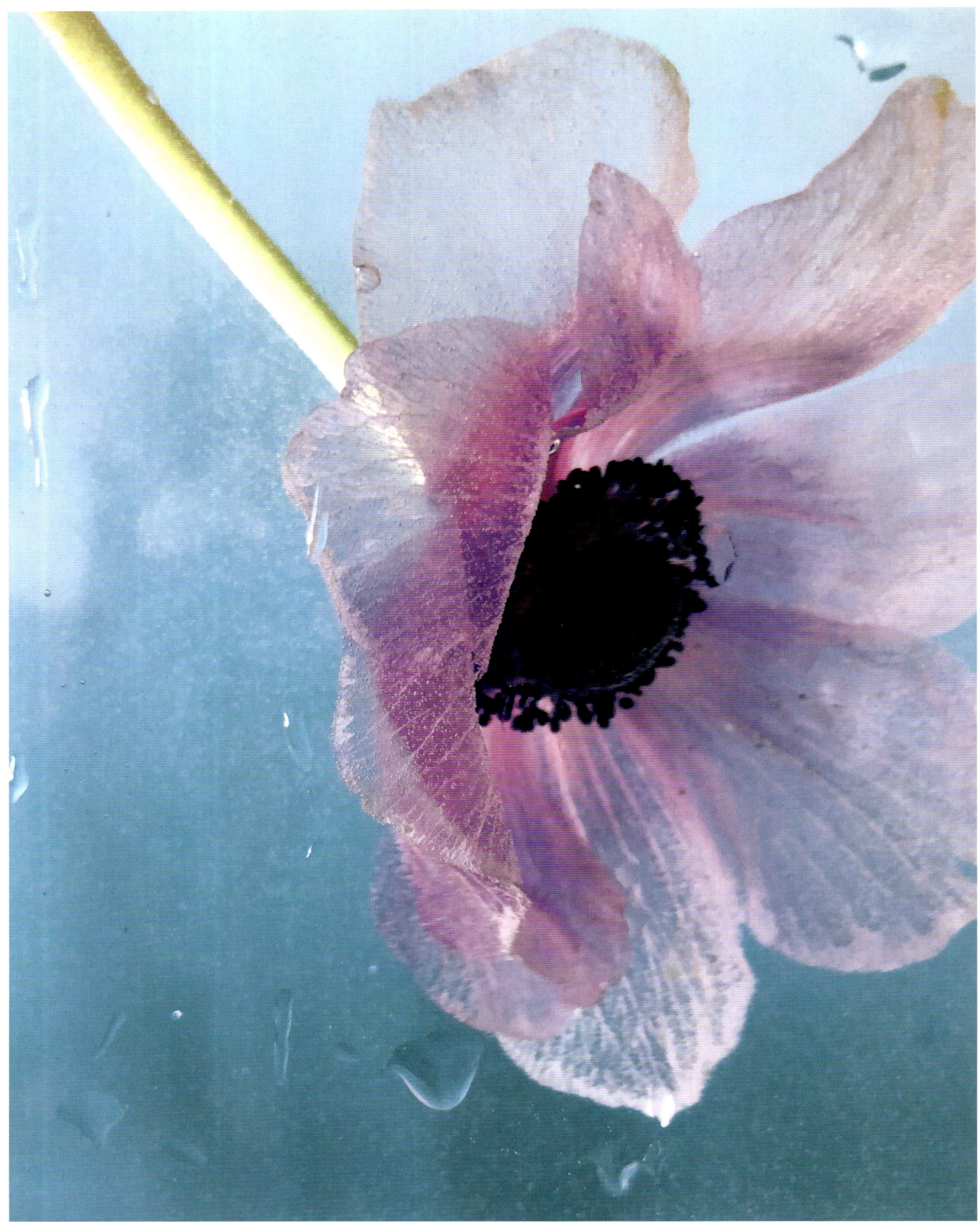

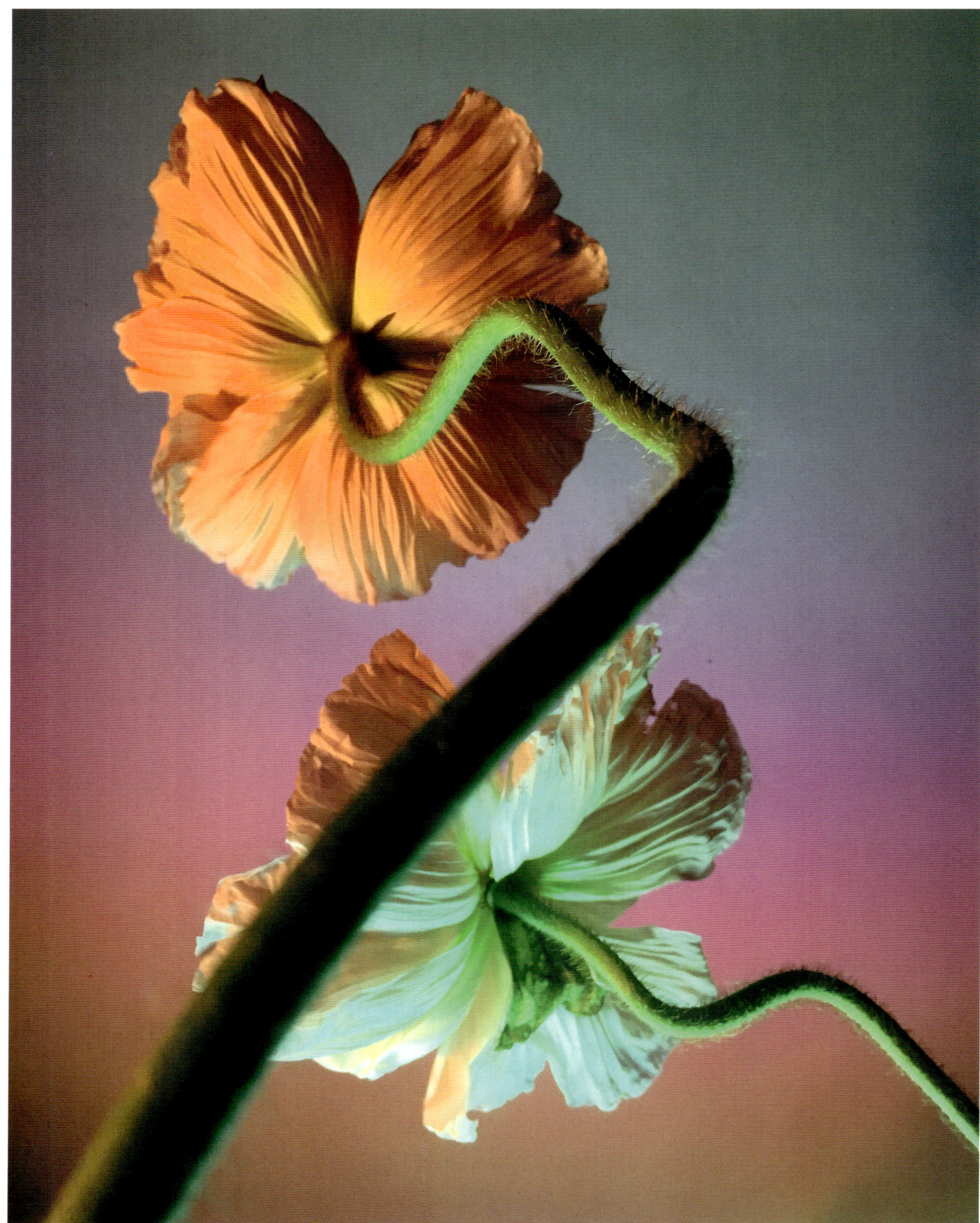

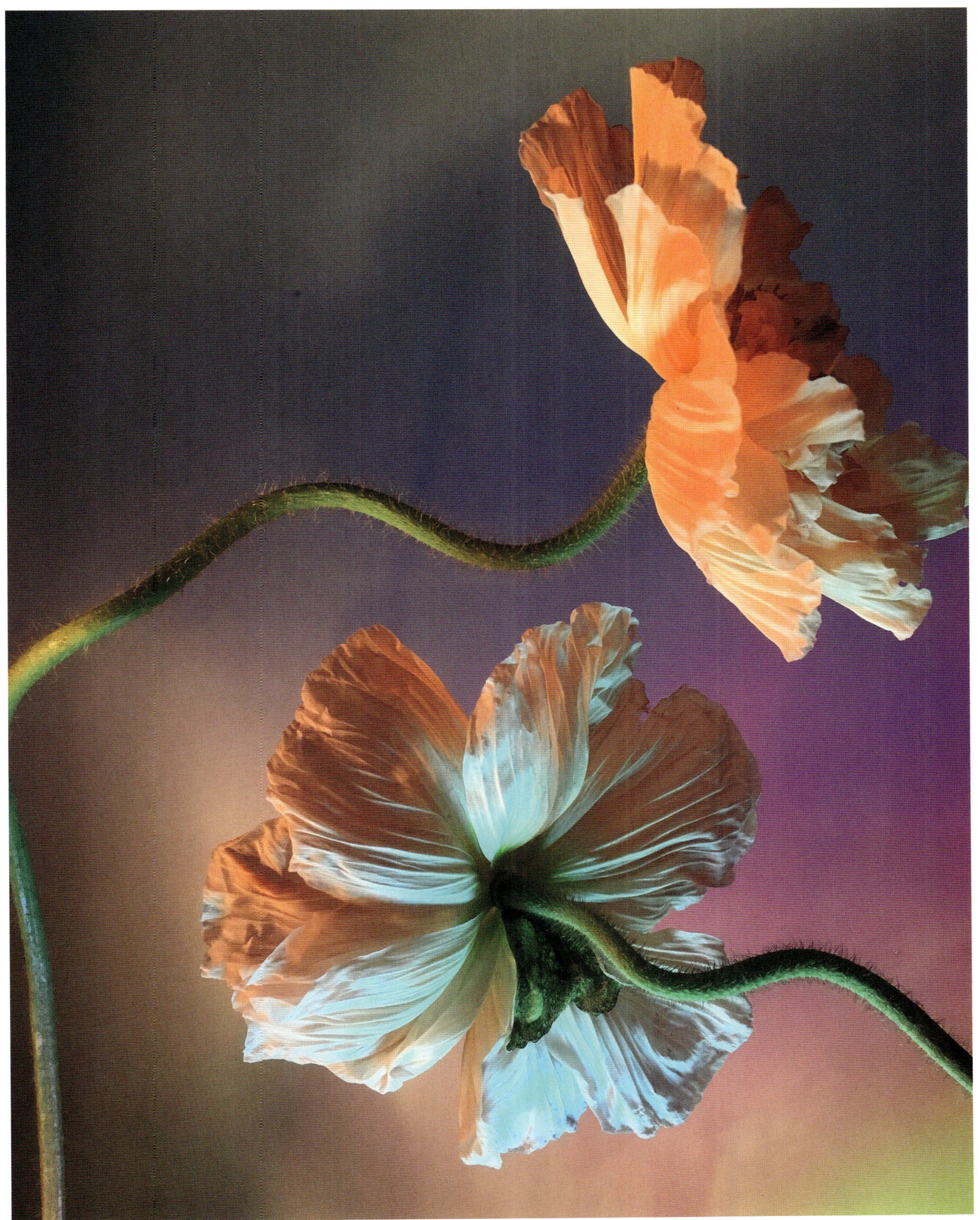

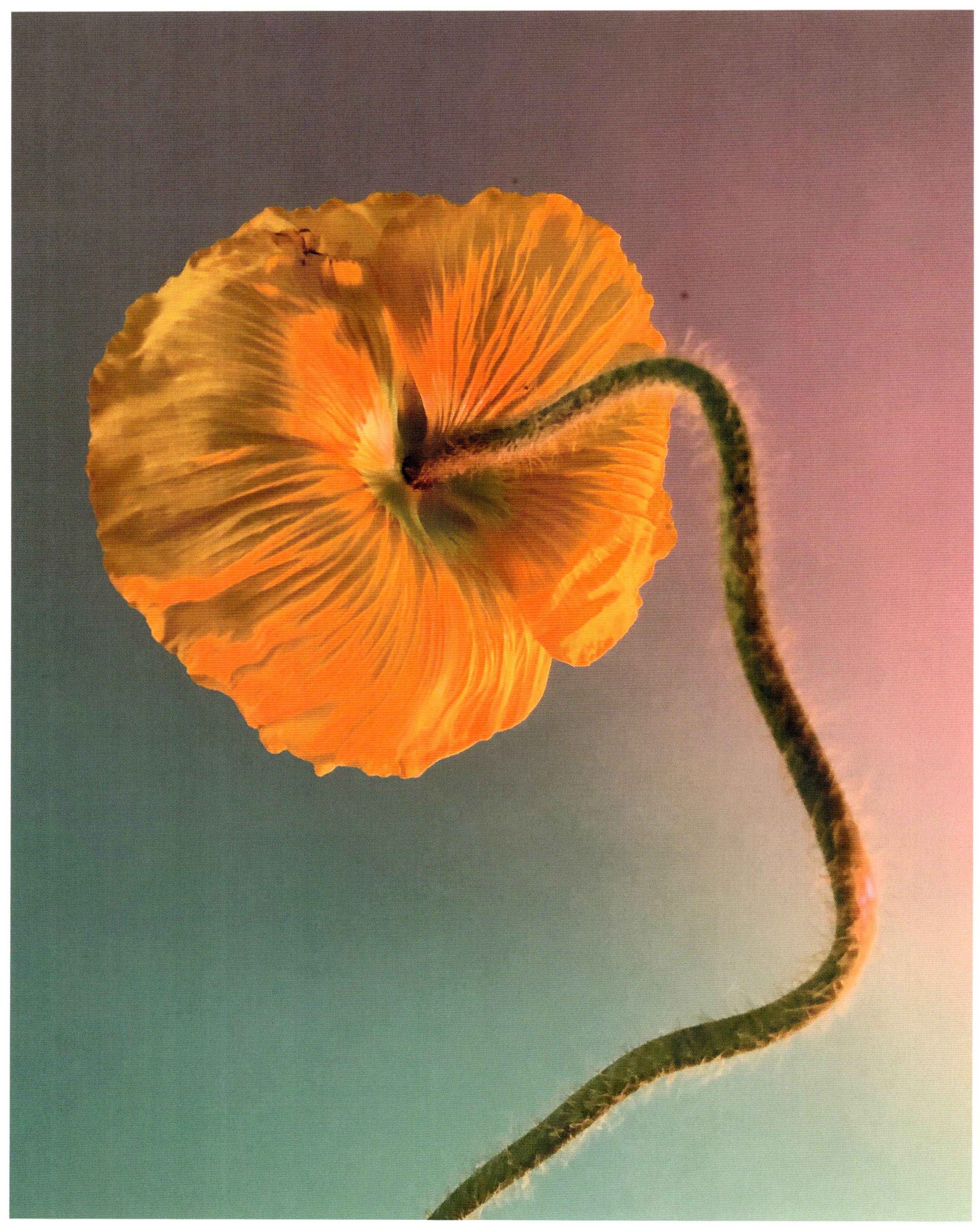

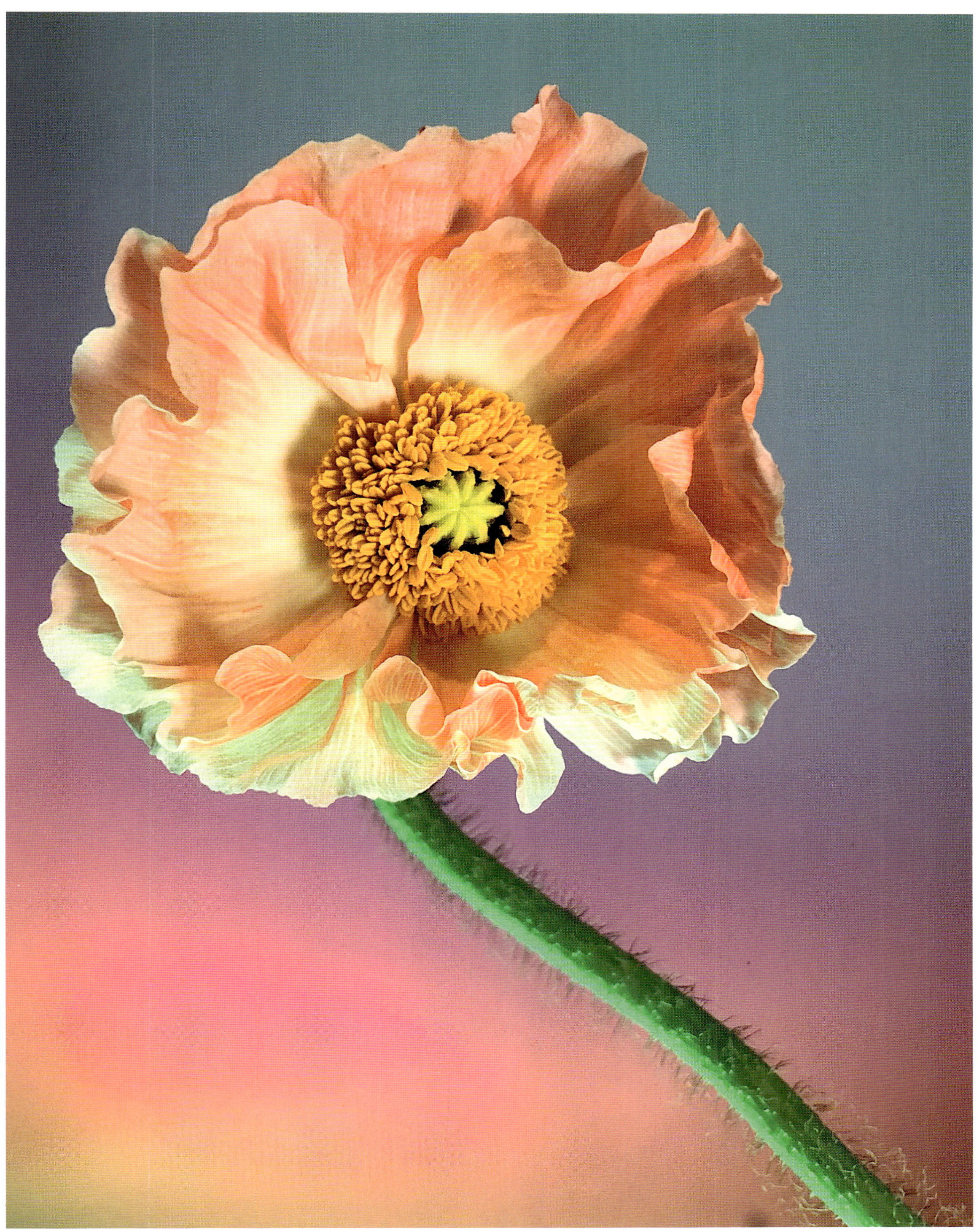

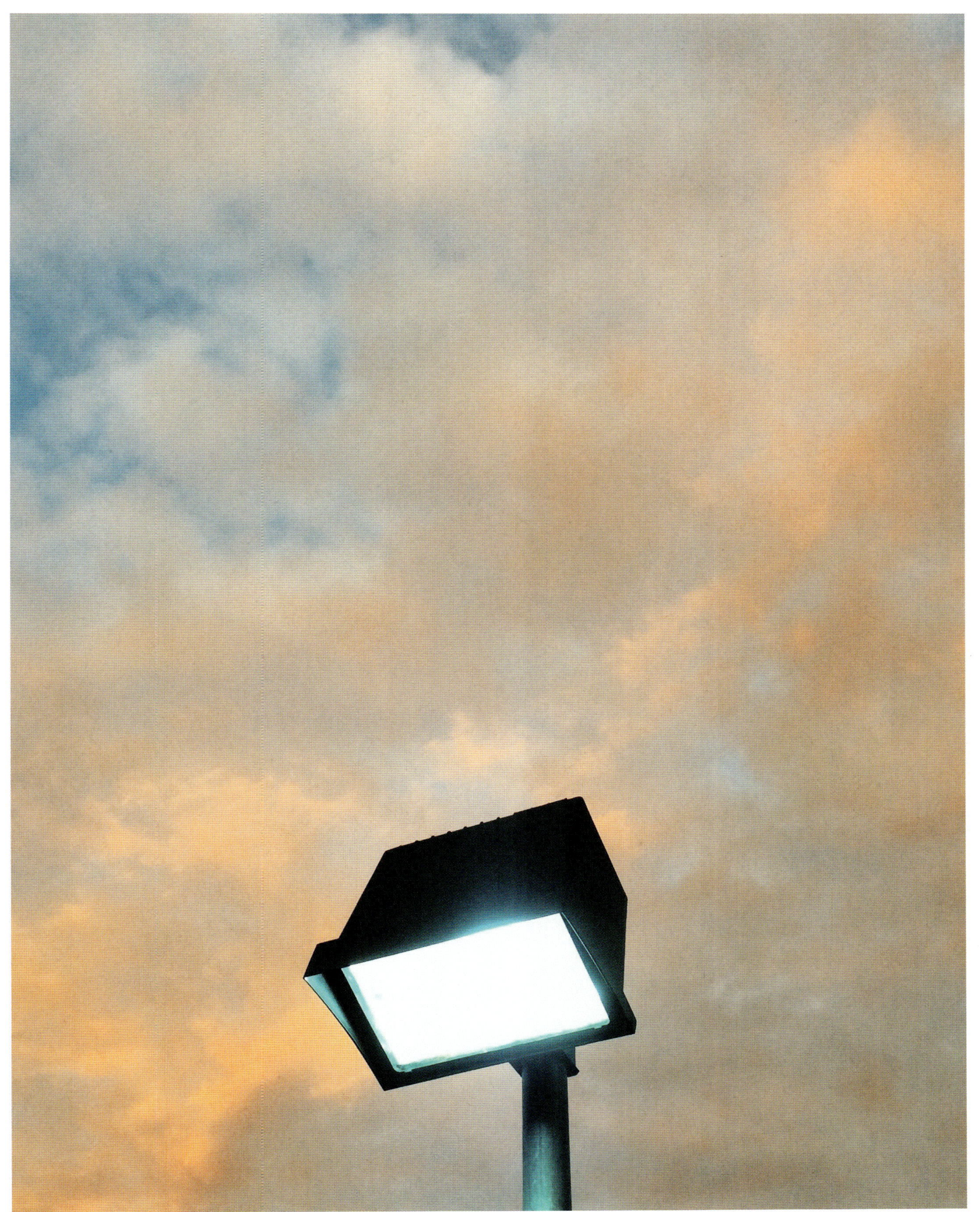

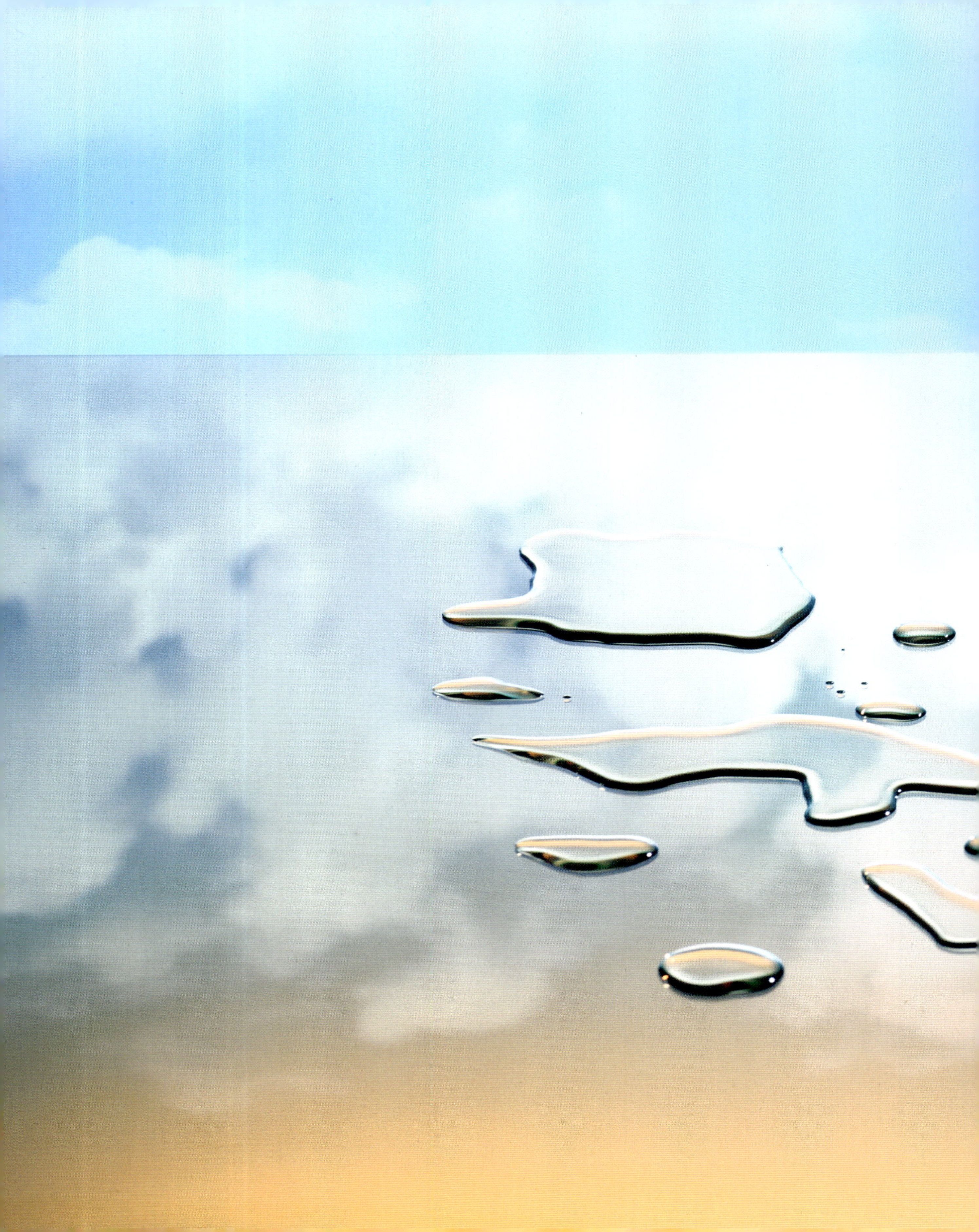

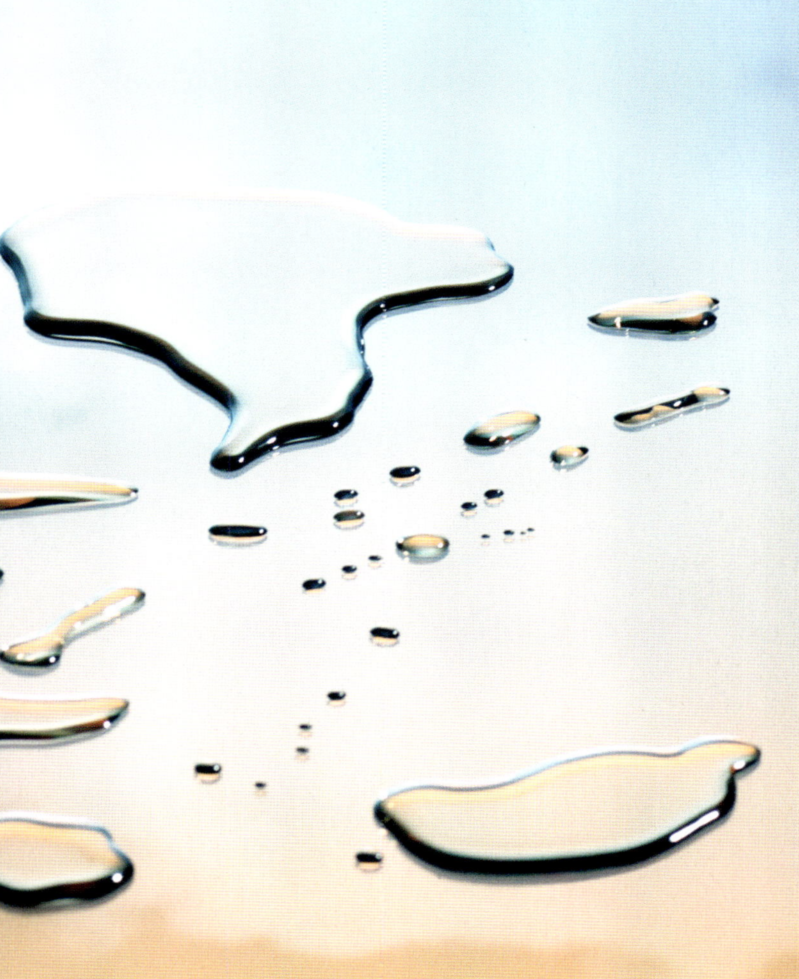

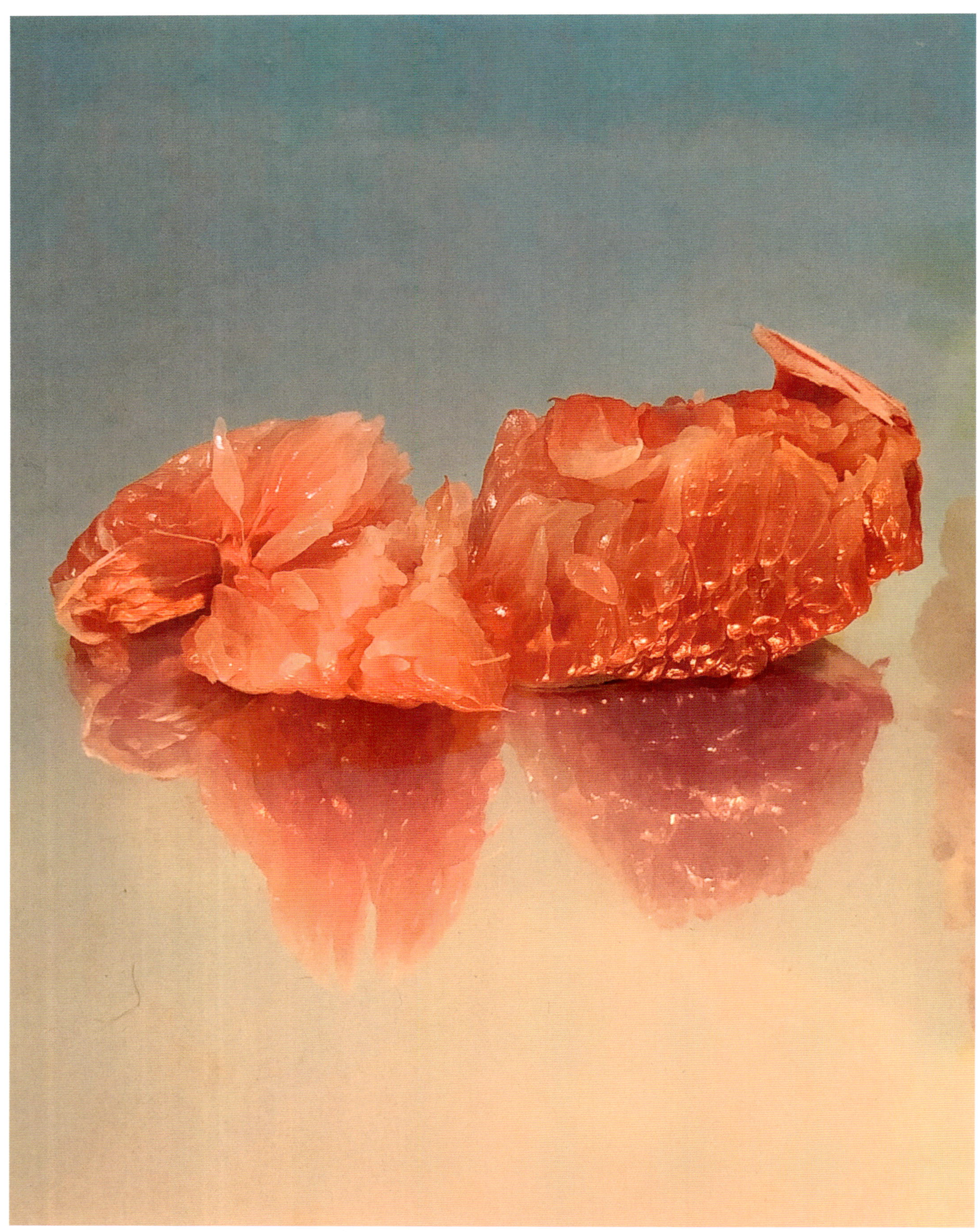

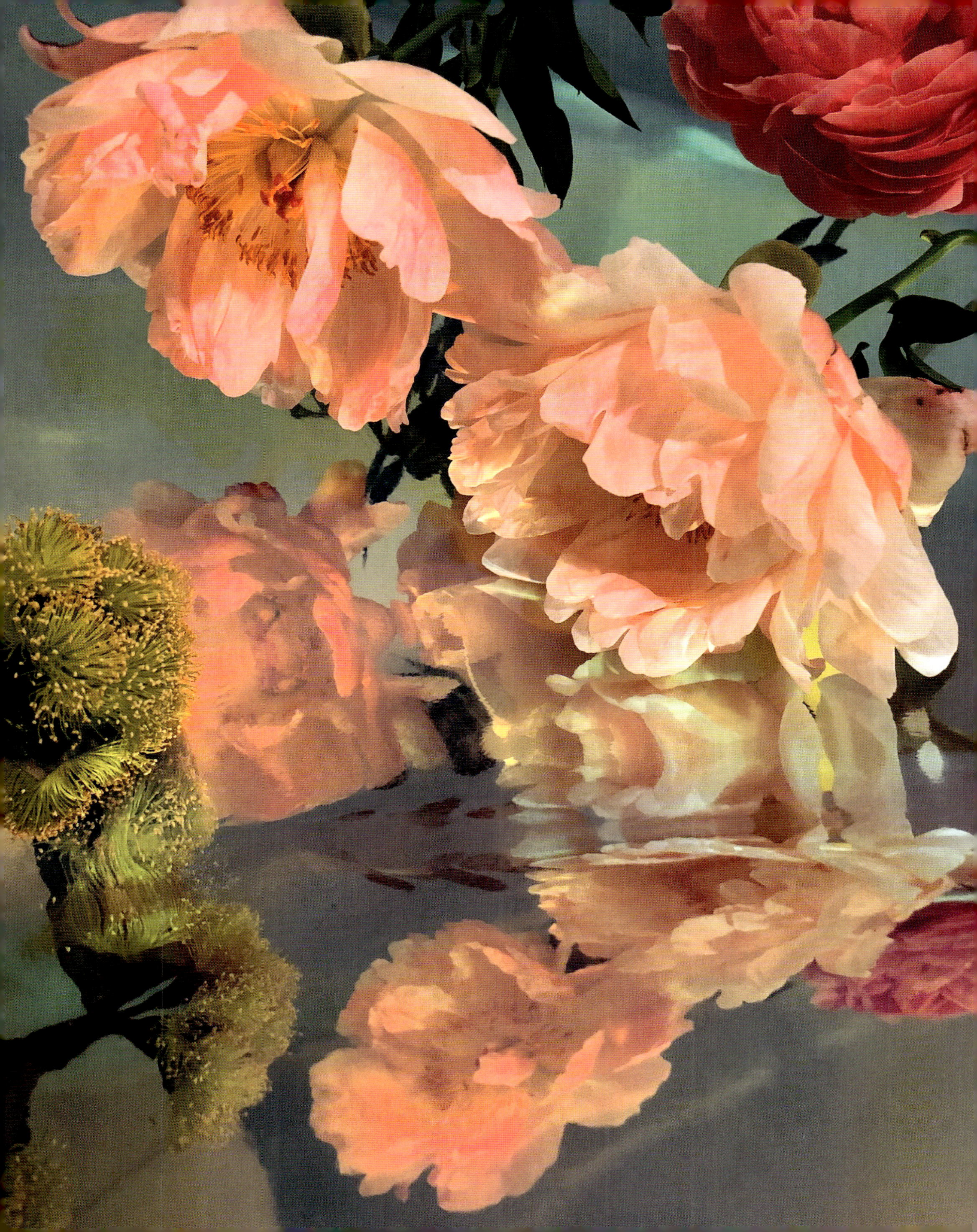

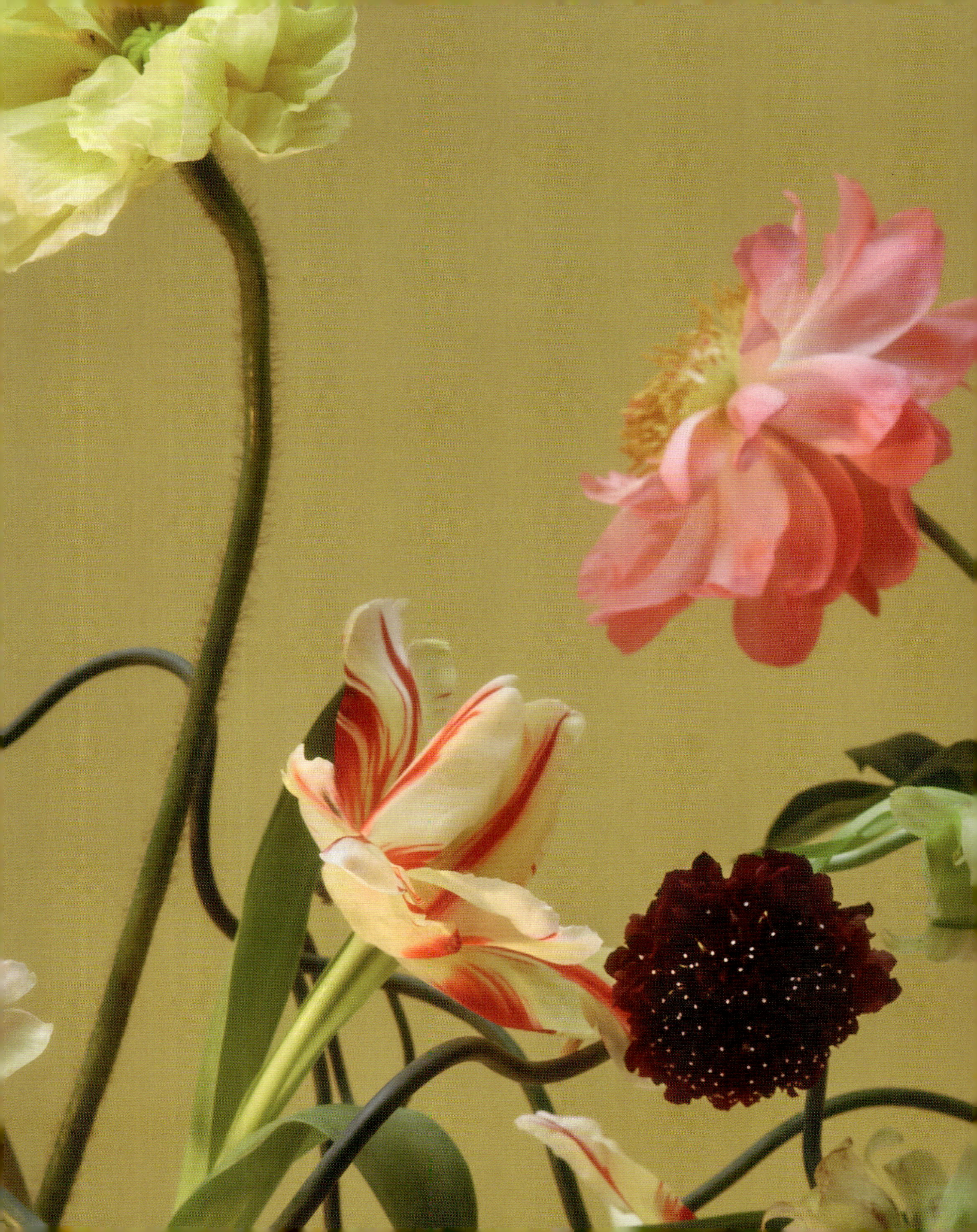

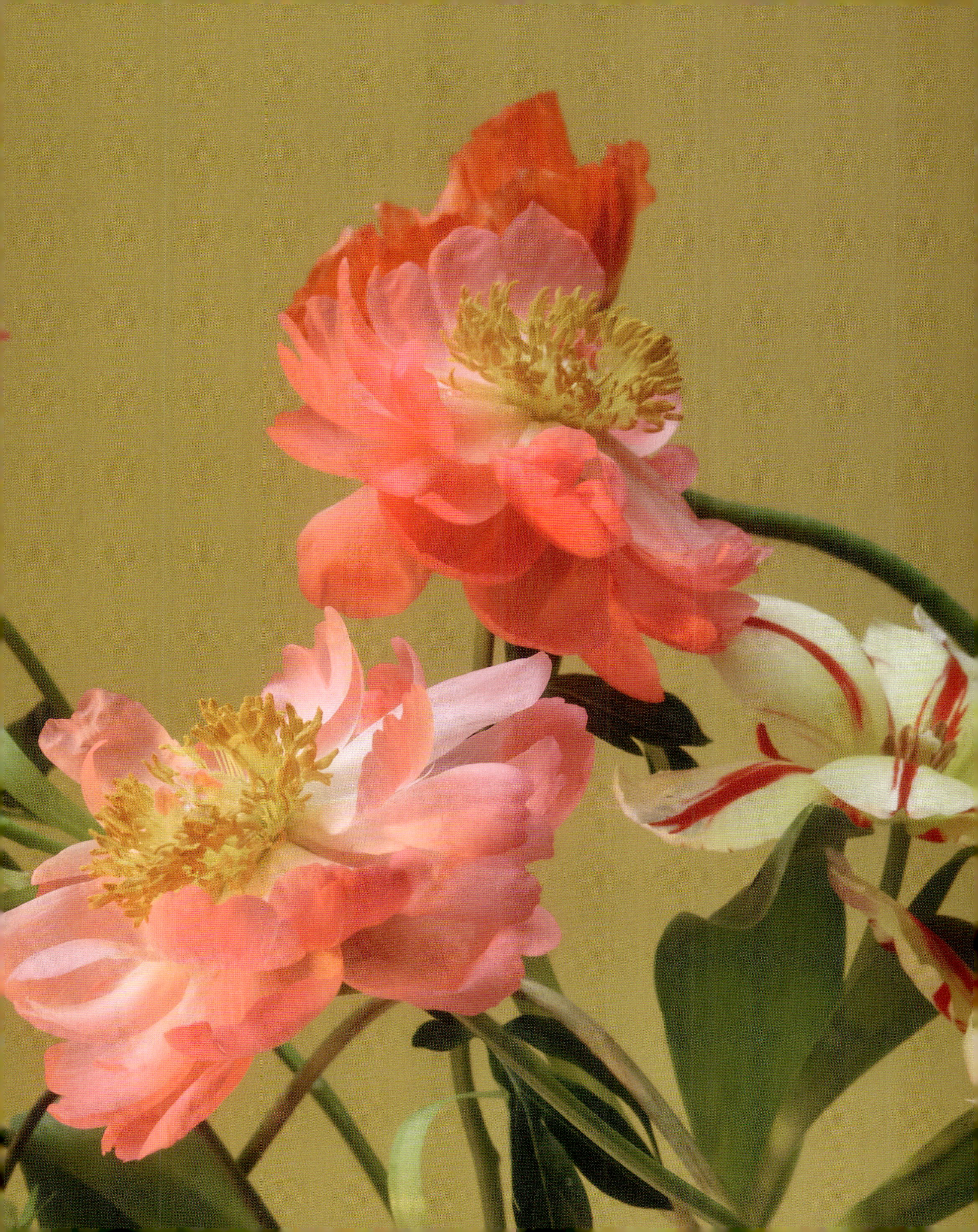

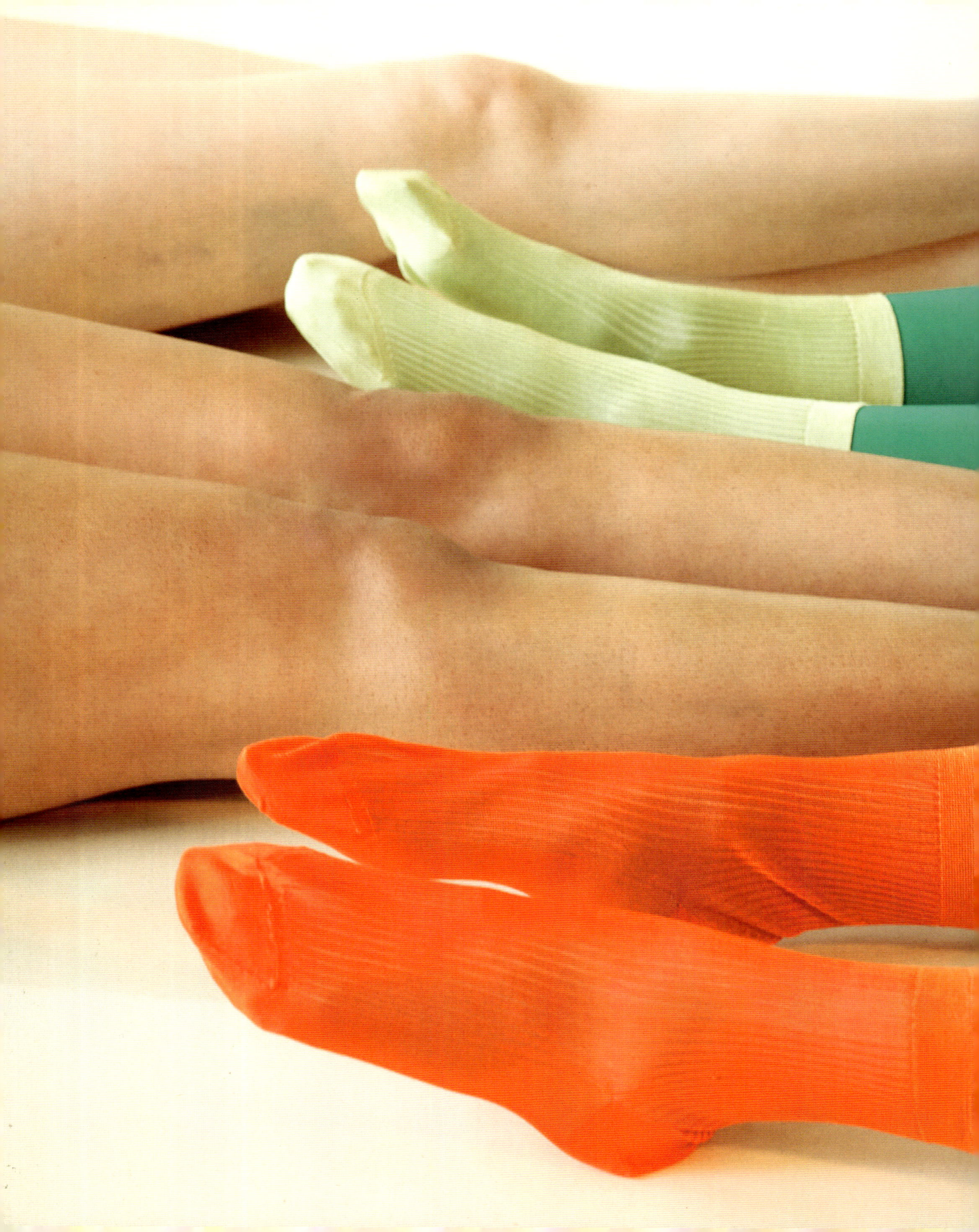

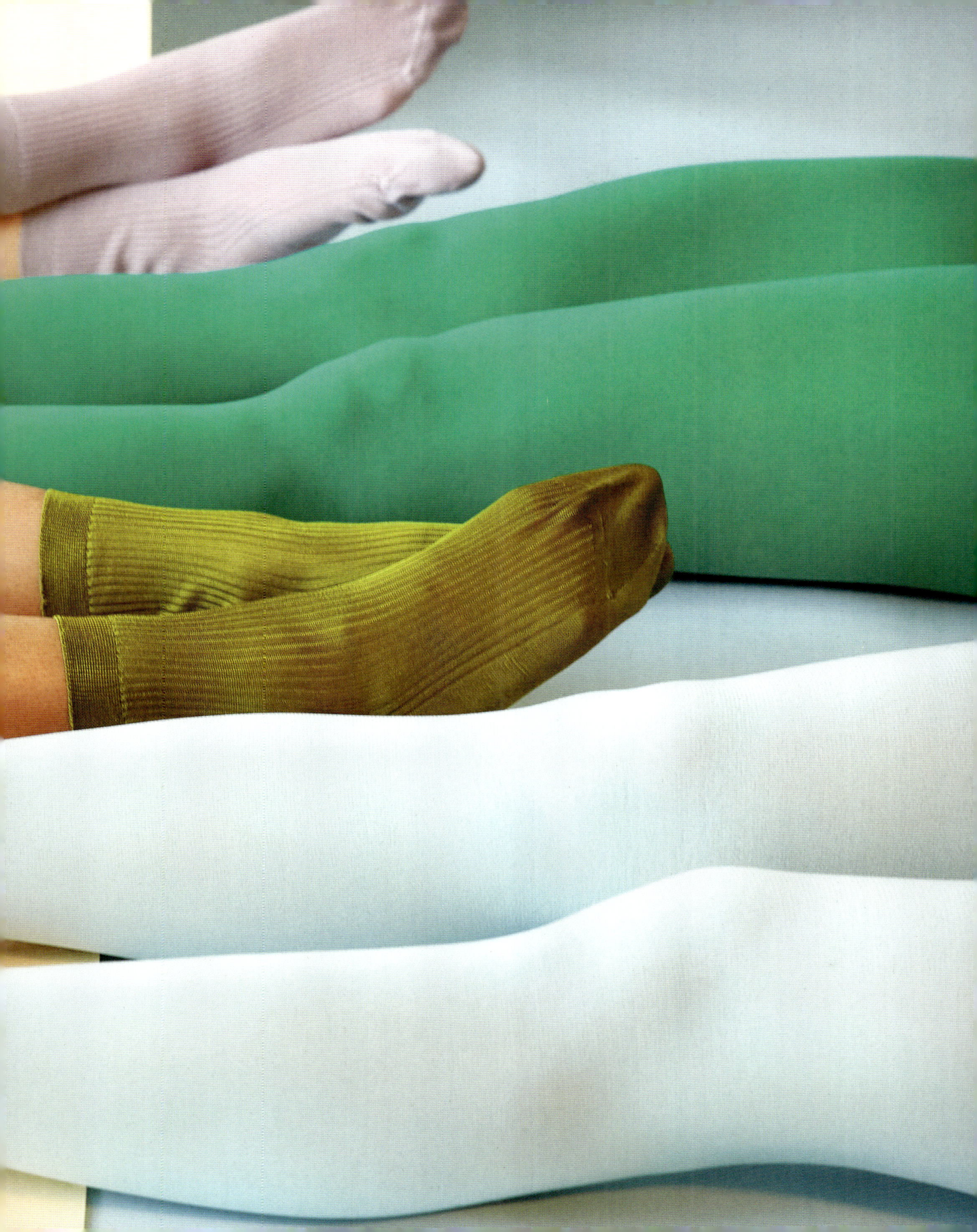

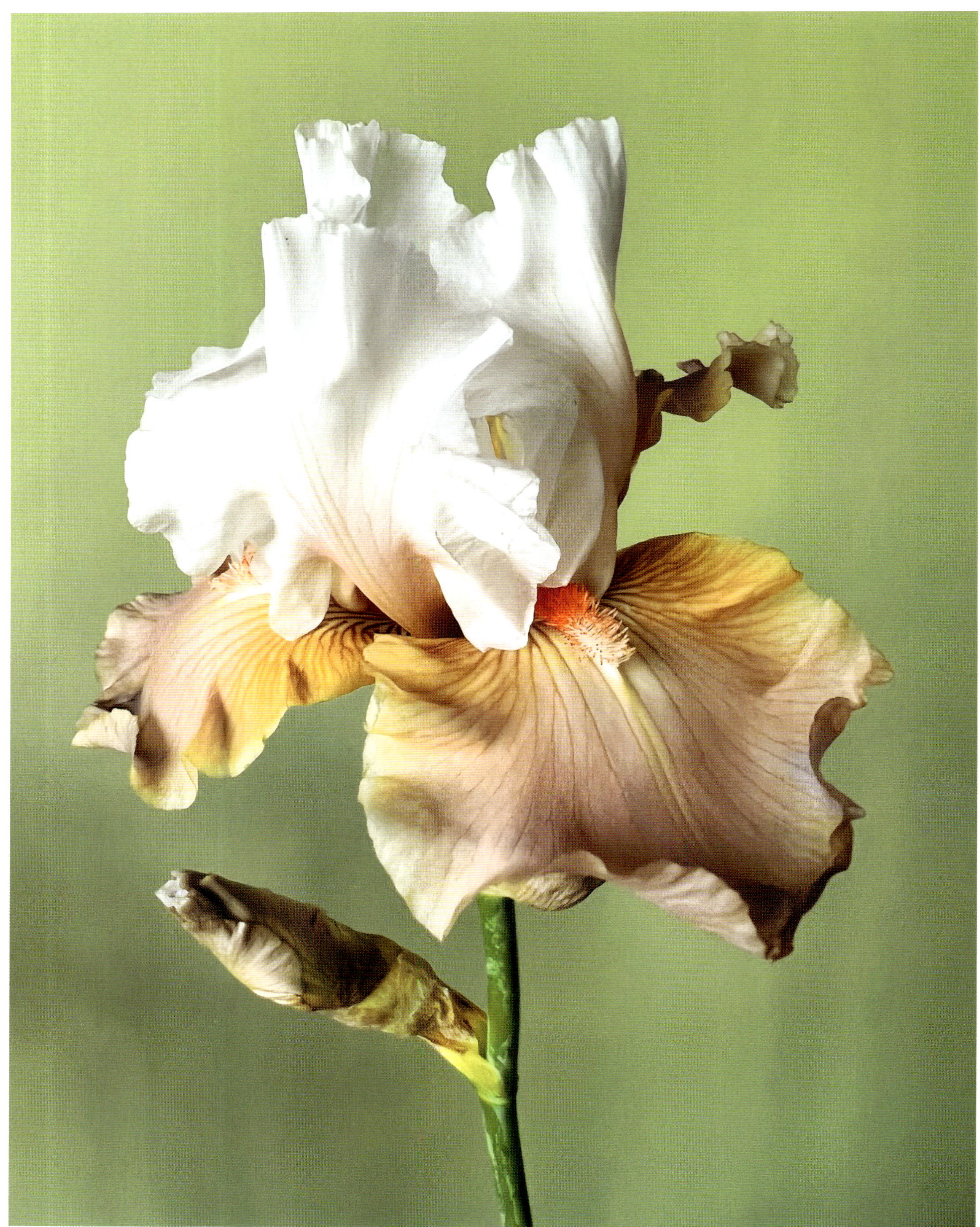

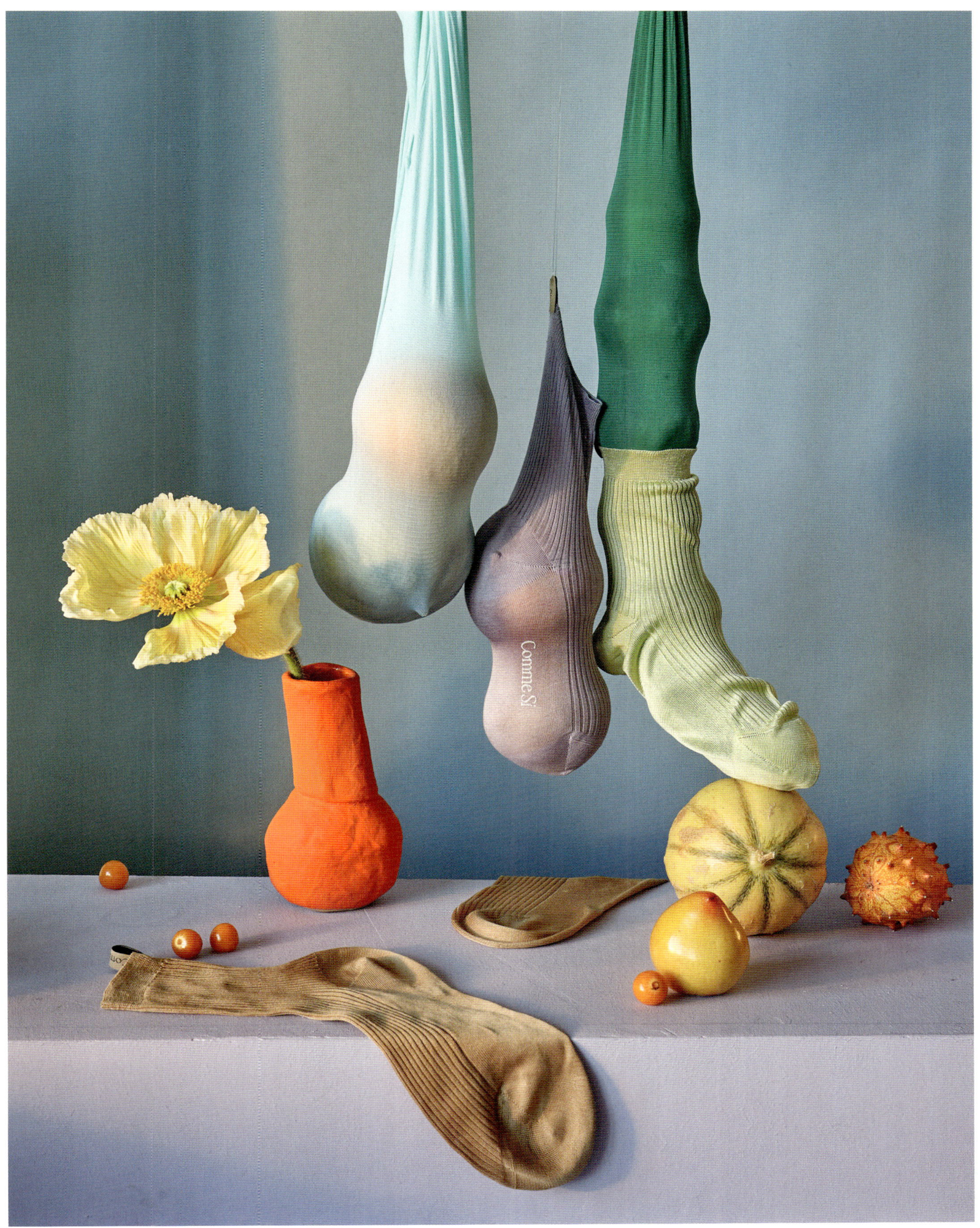
Comme Si

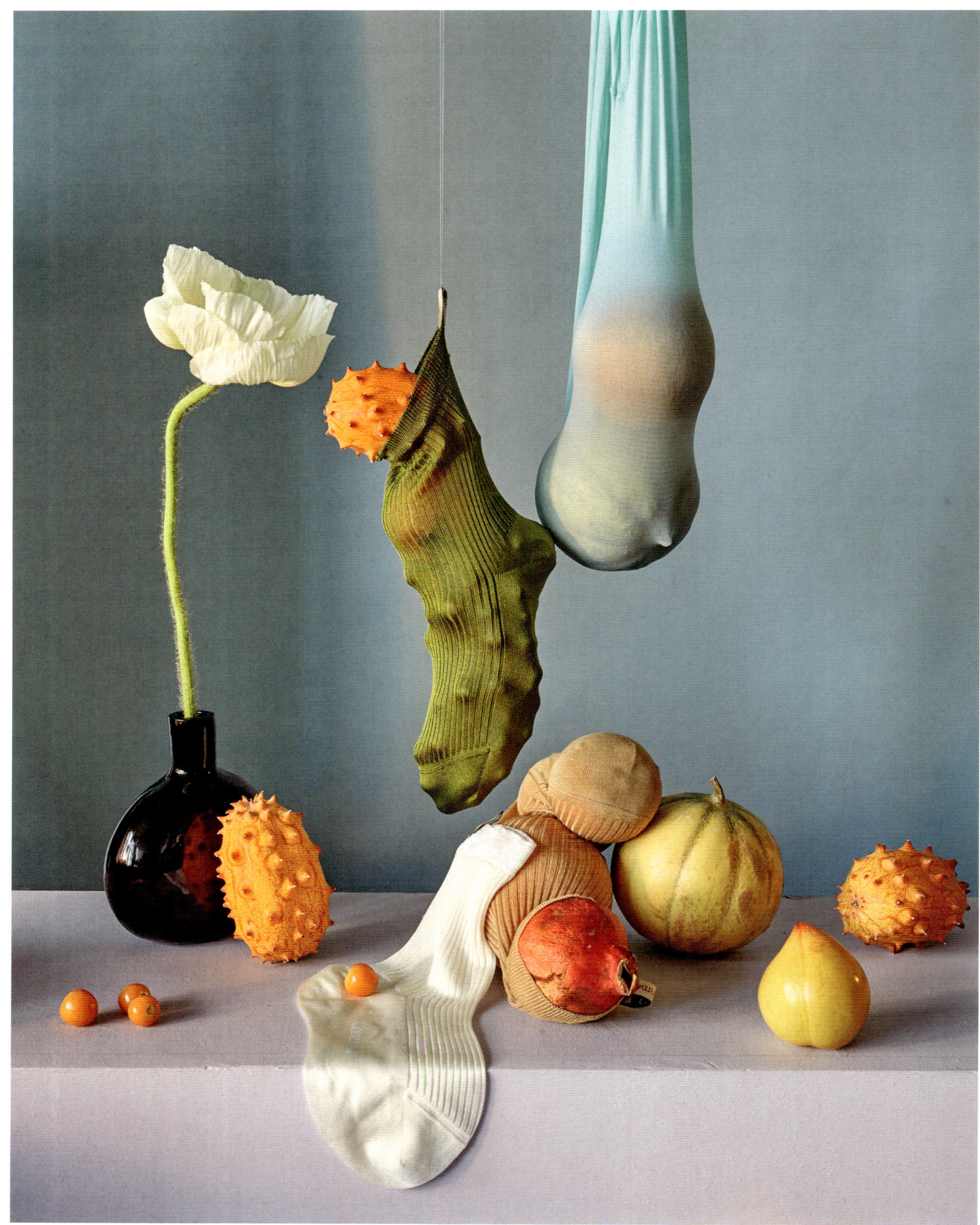

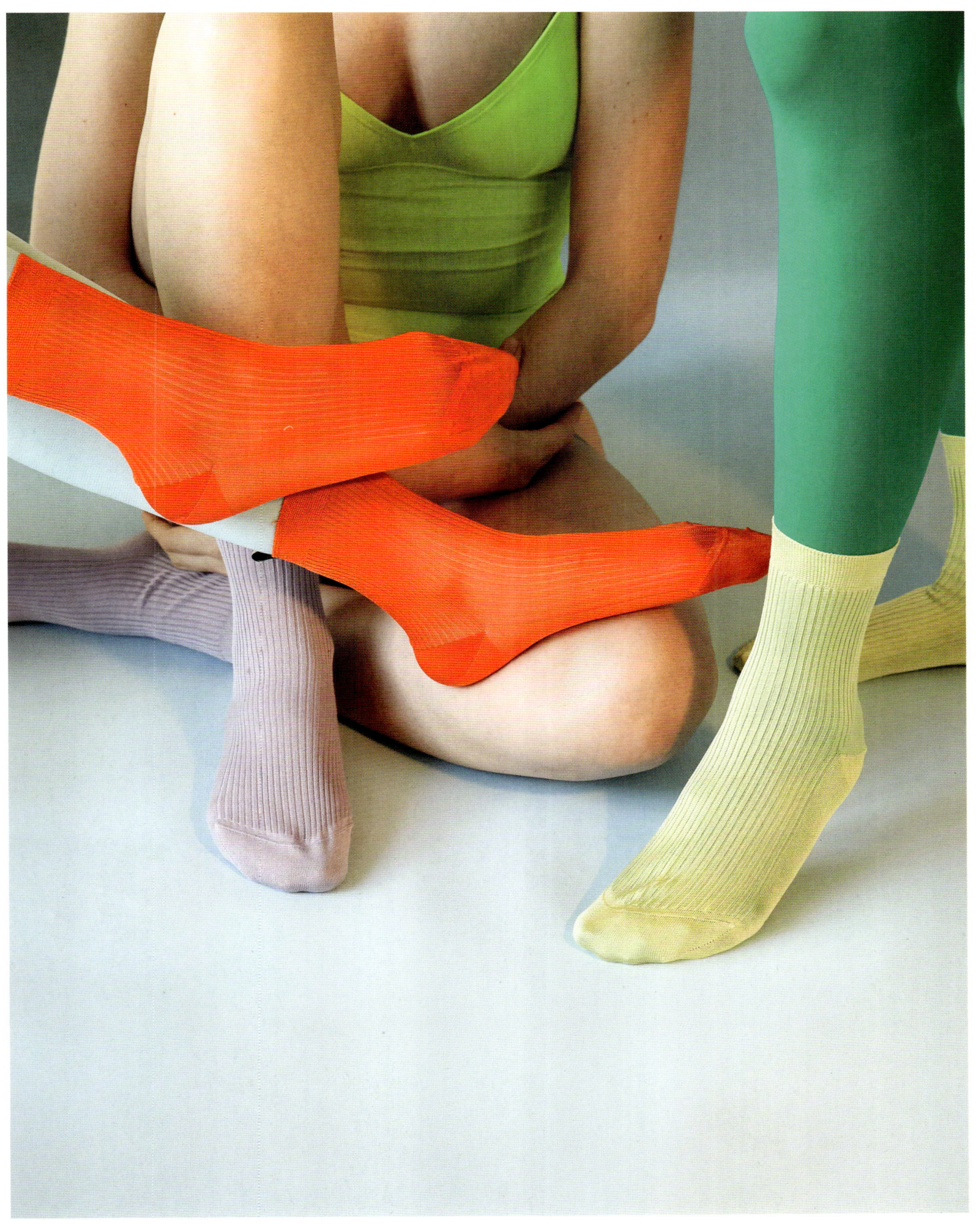

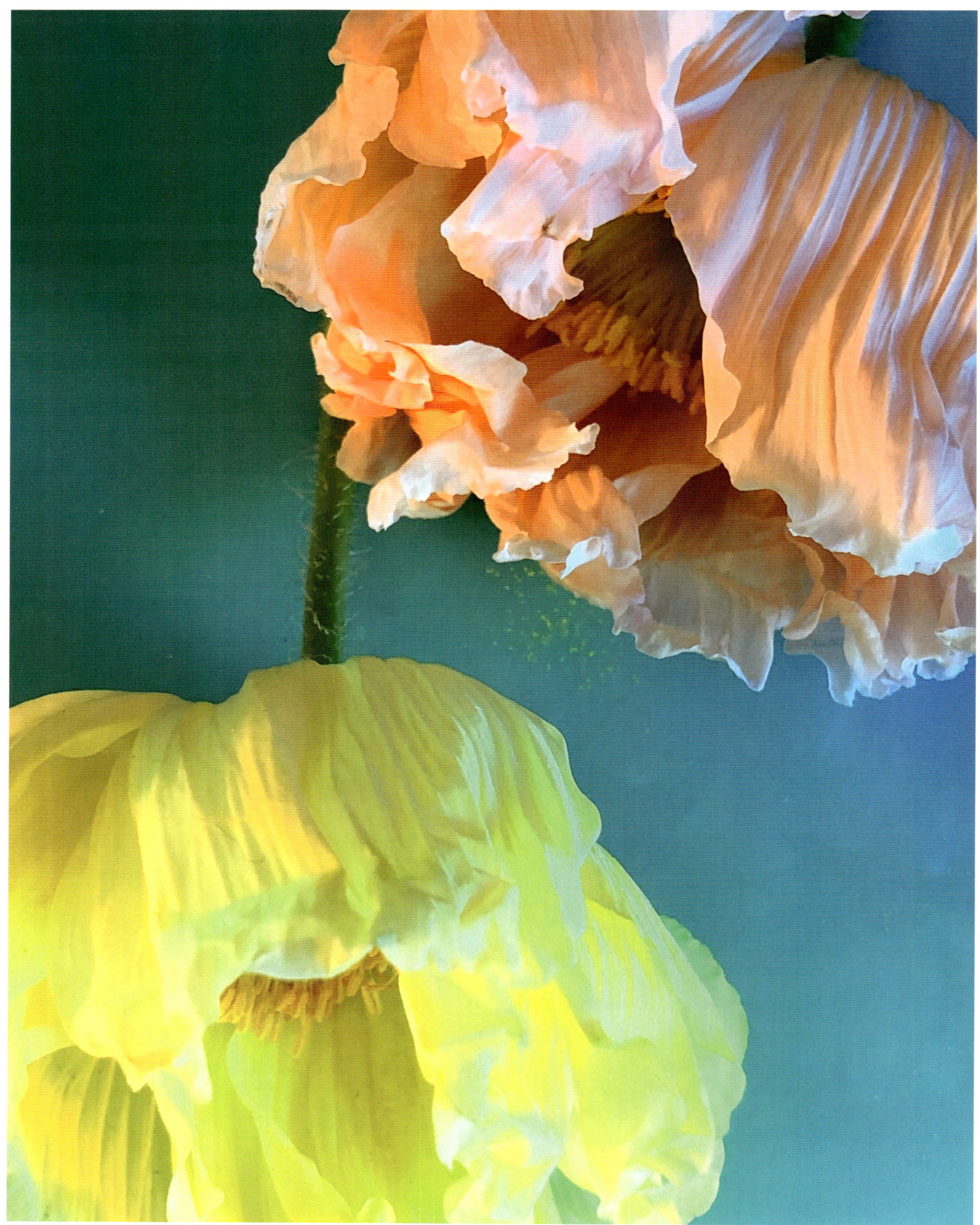

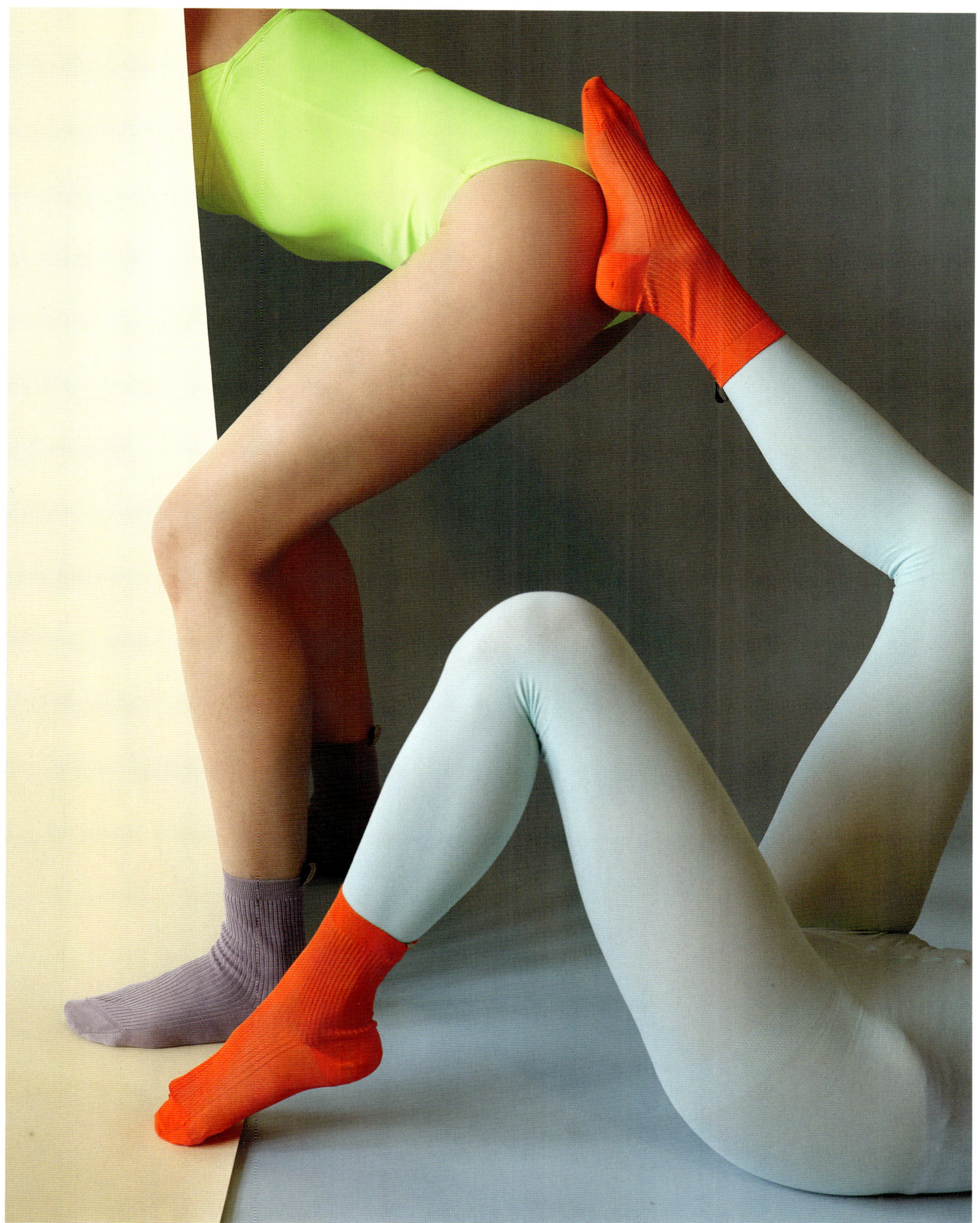

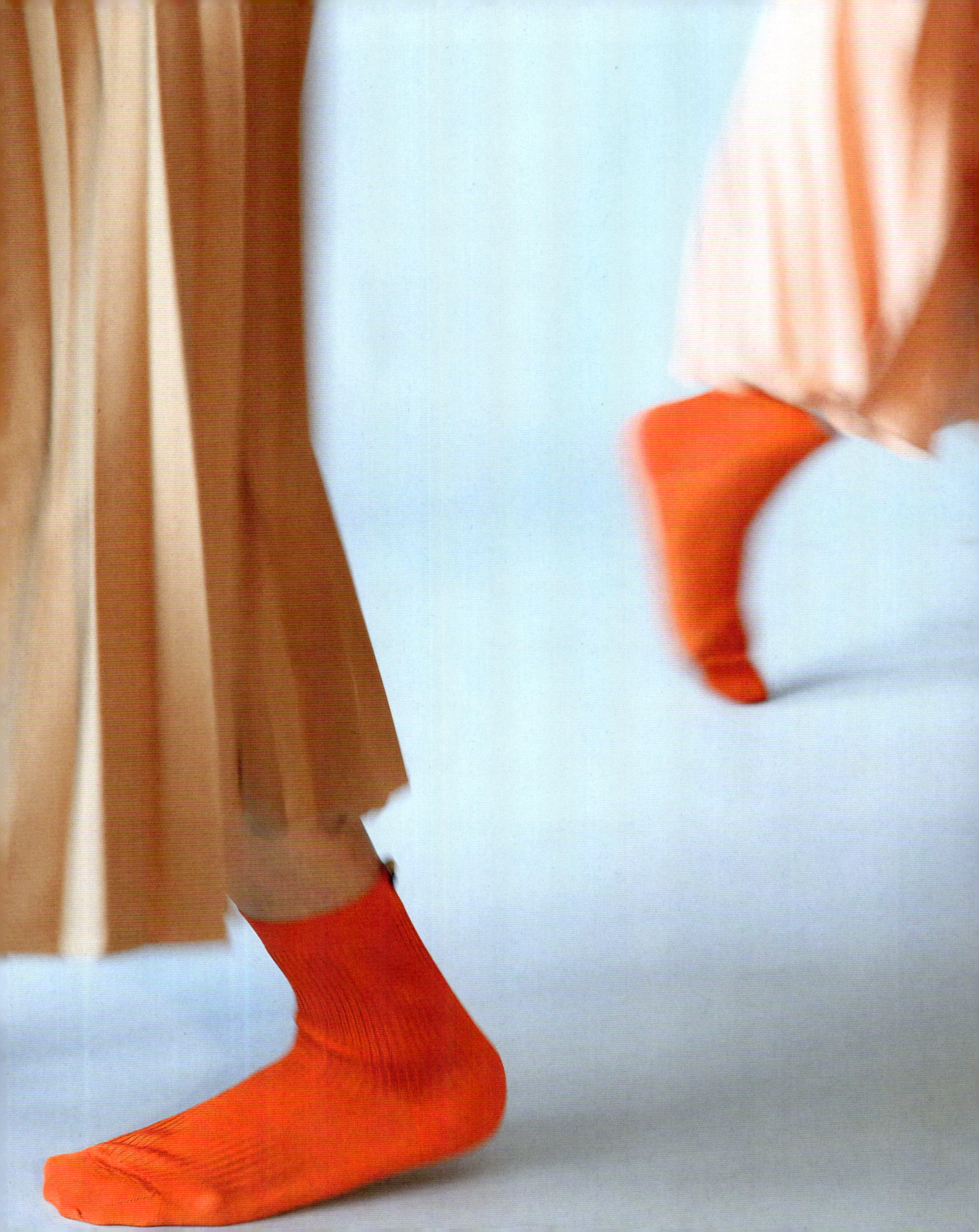

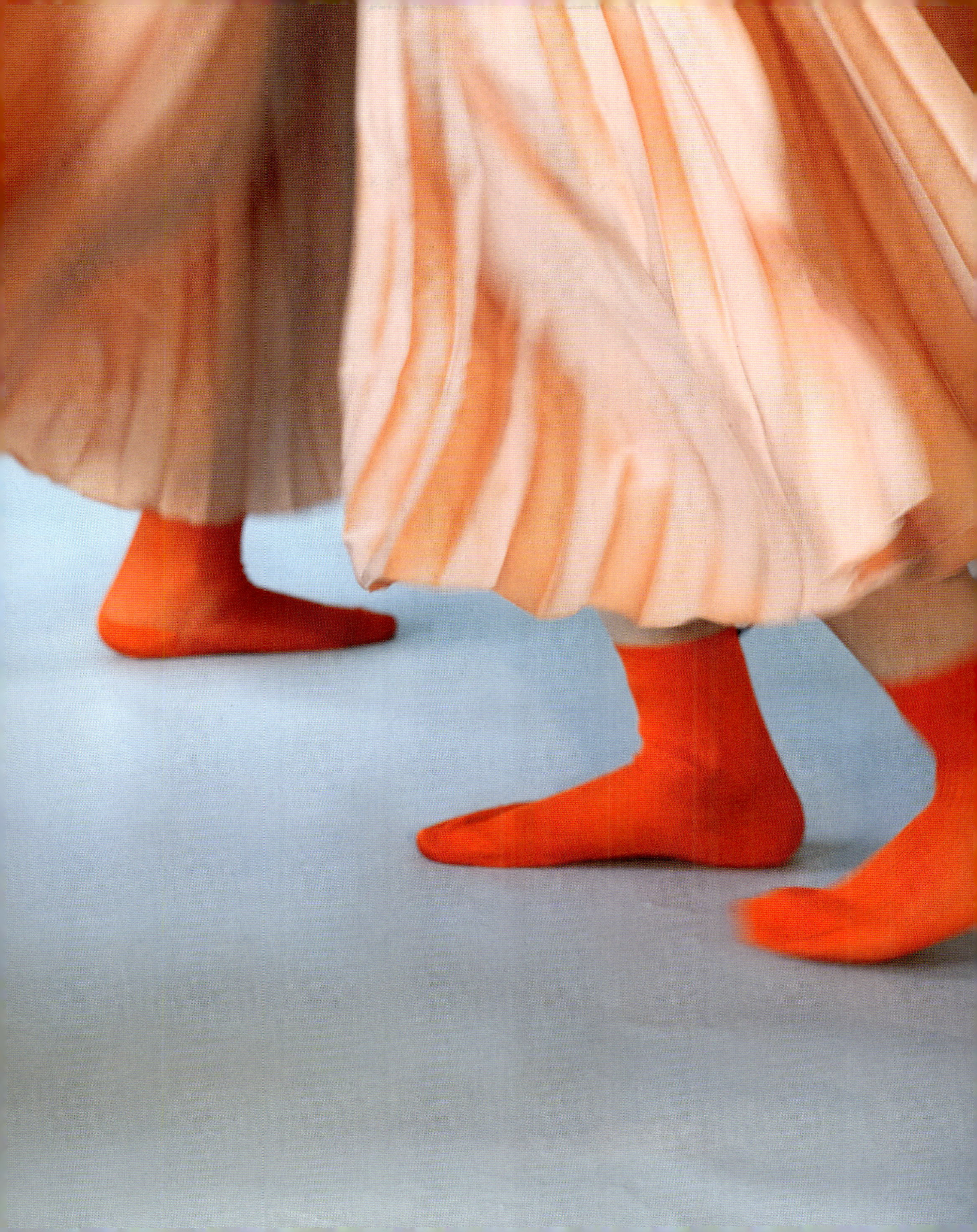

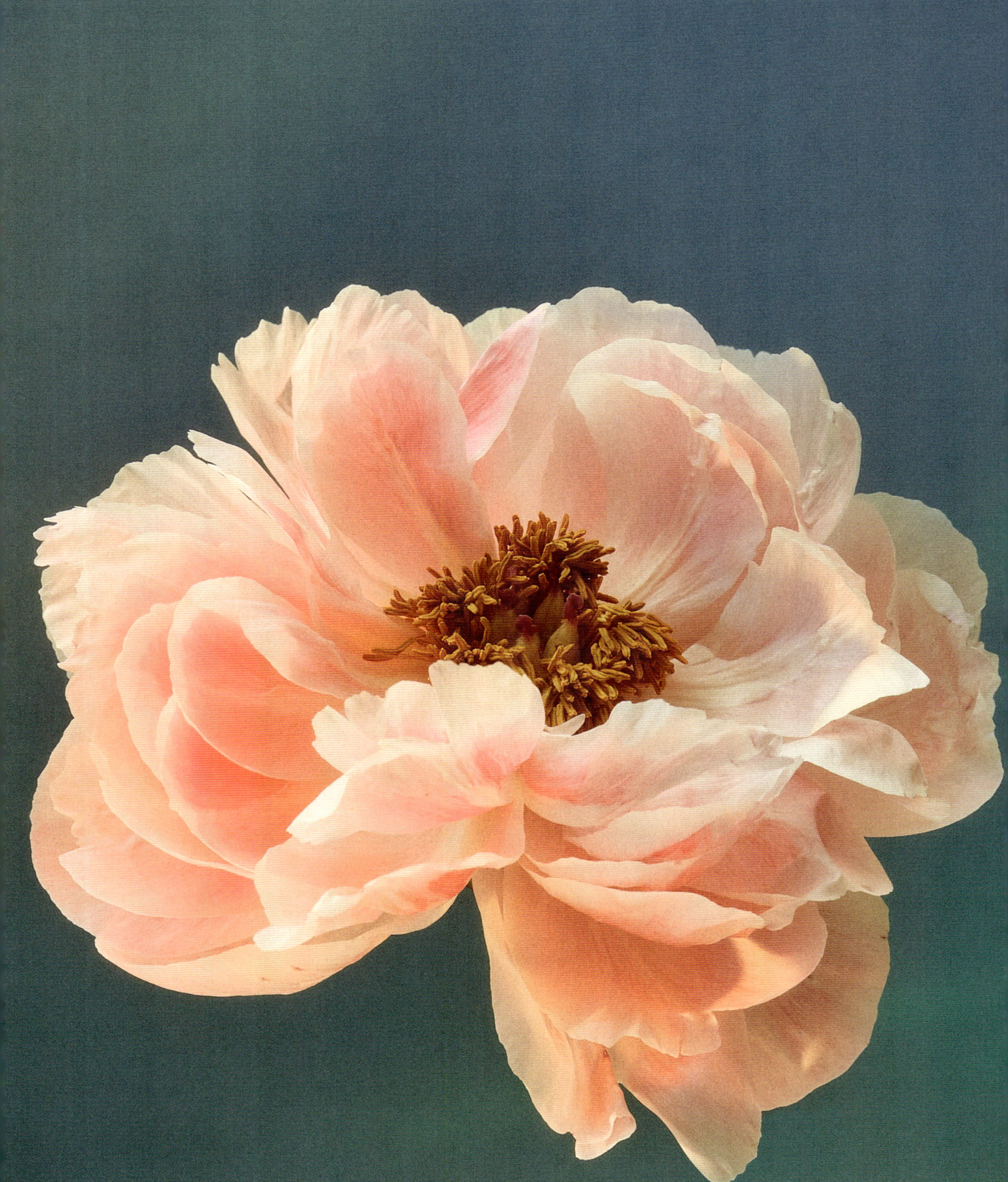

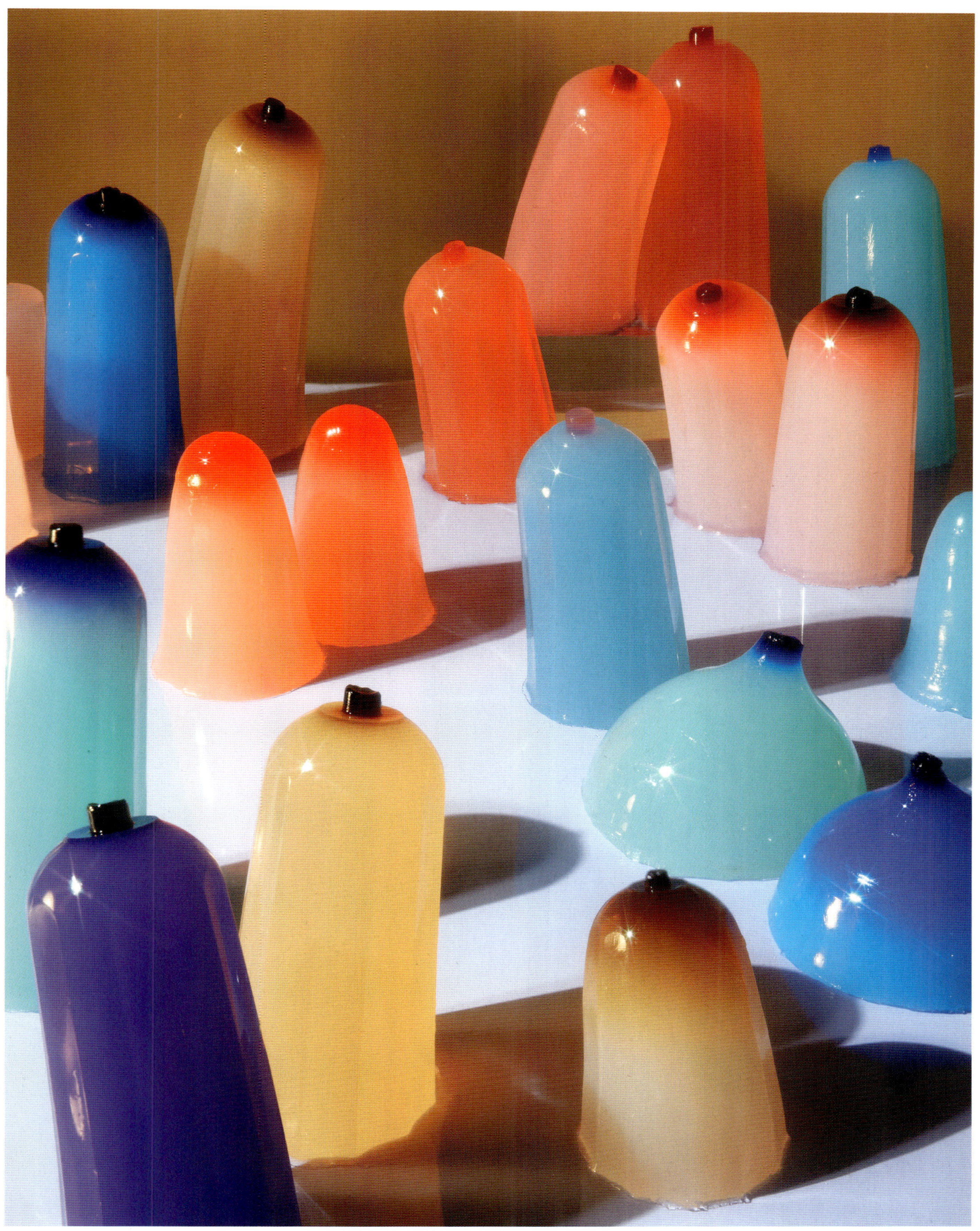

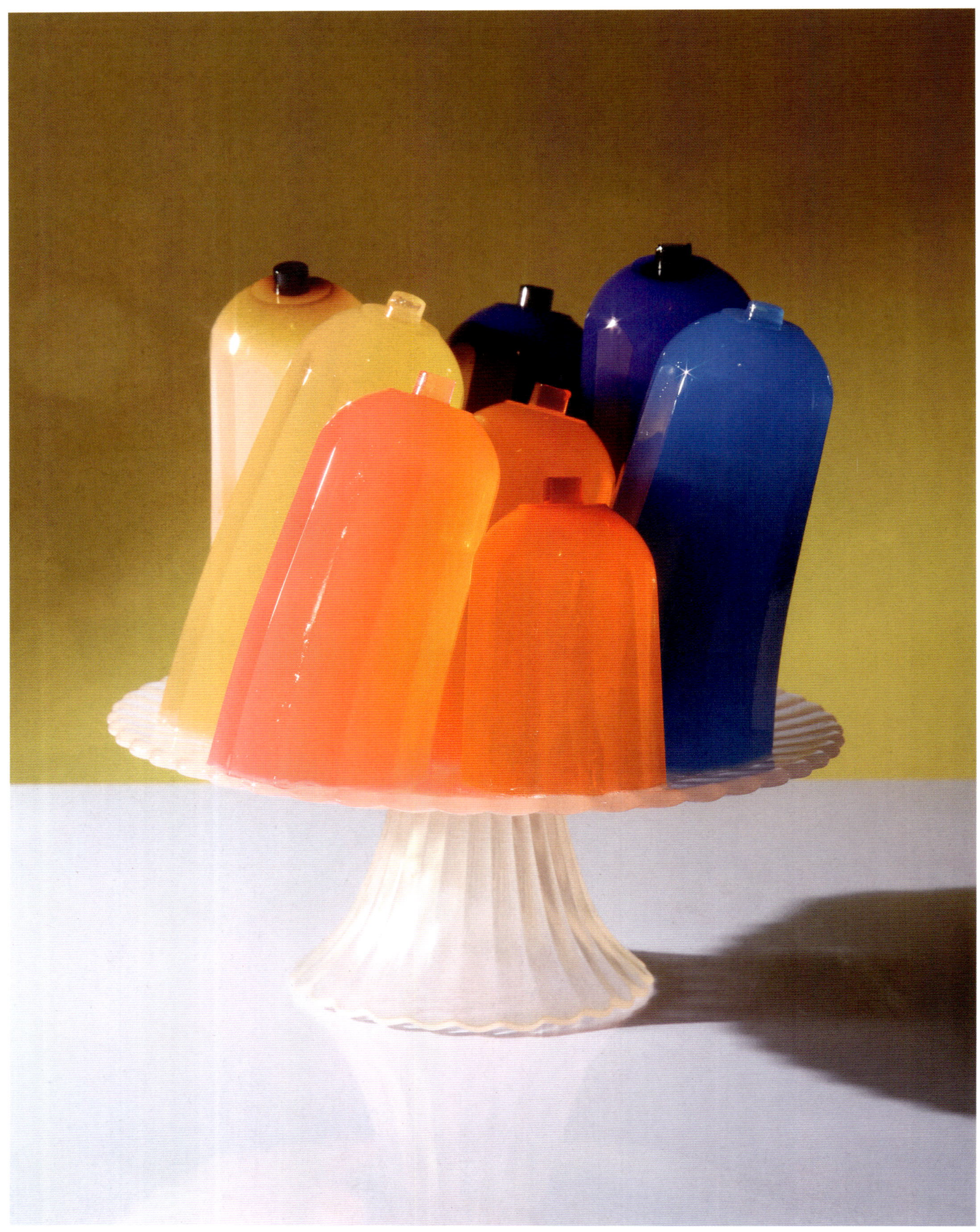

MAKING THE MOST OF IT

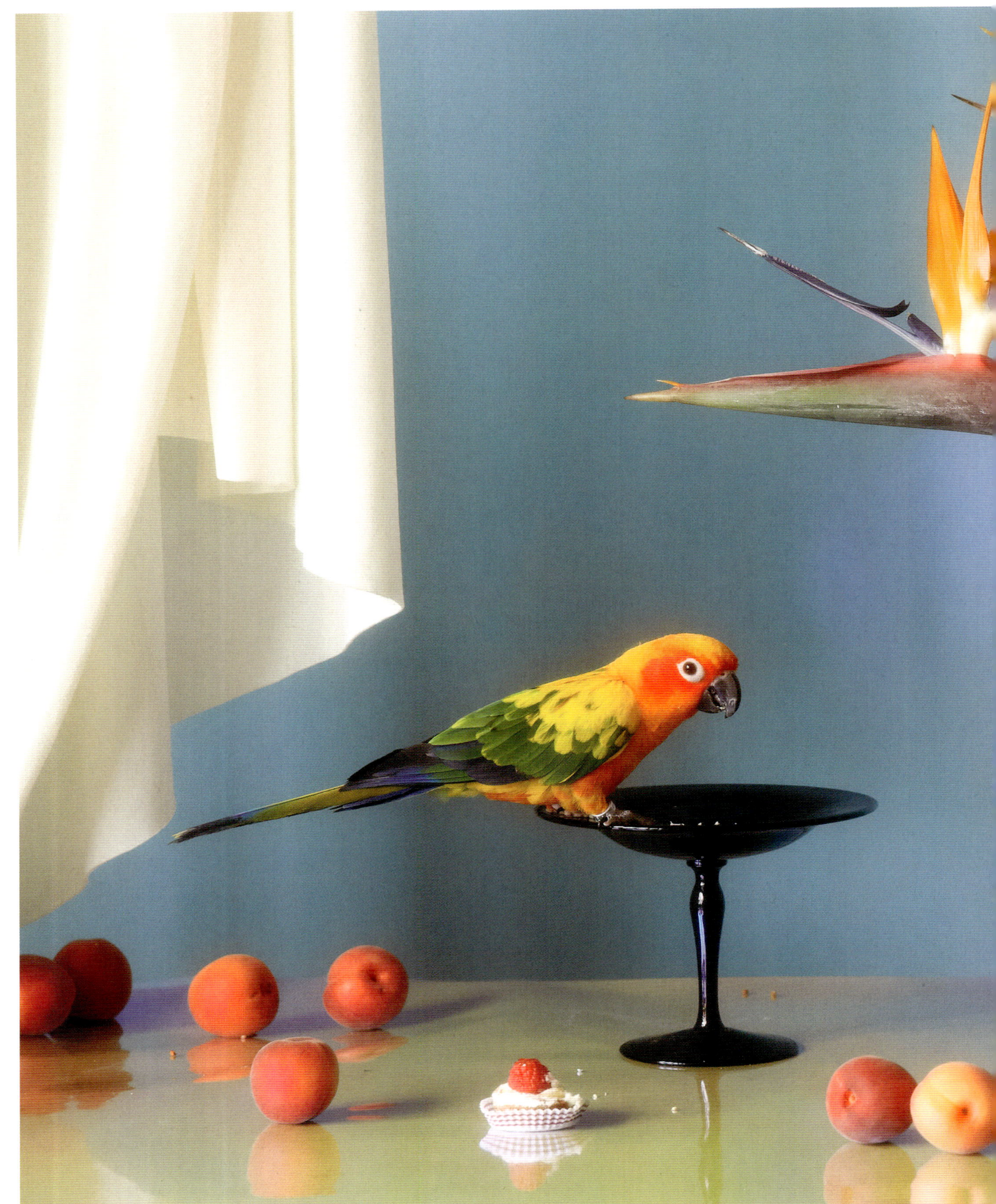

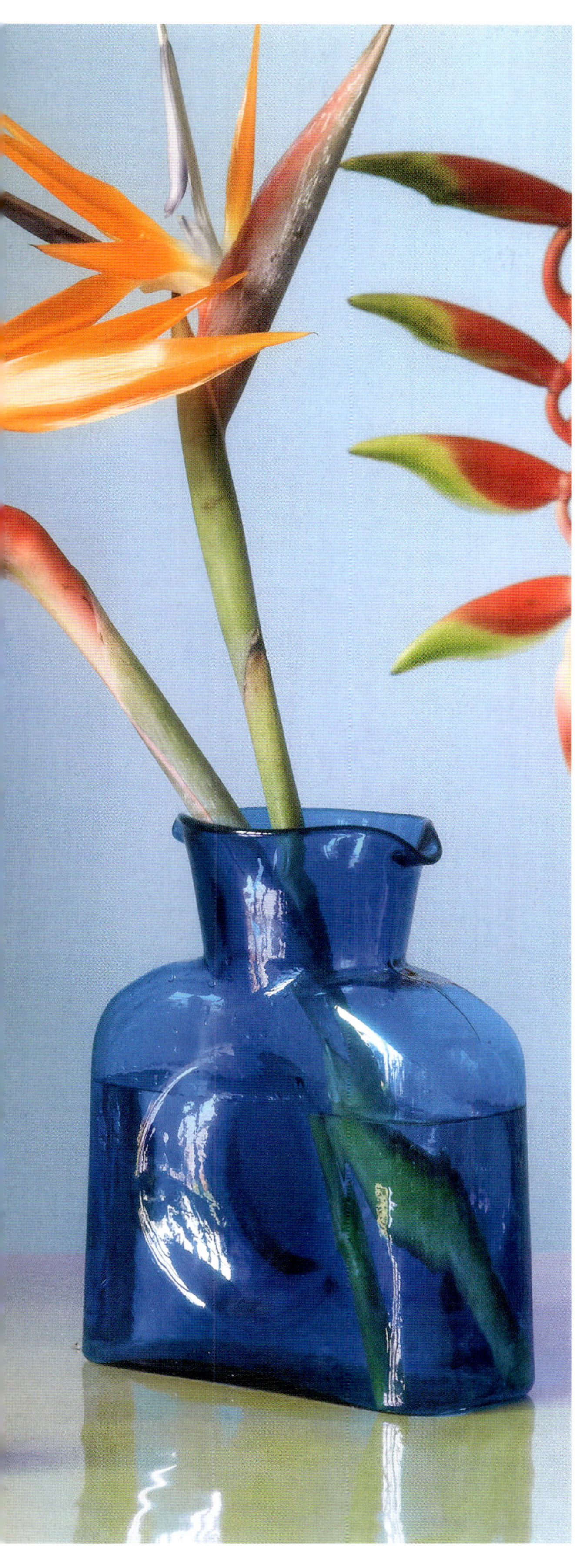

YOU CAN FIND ME RIGHT HERE

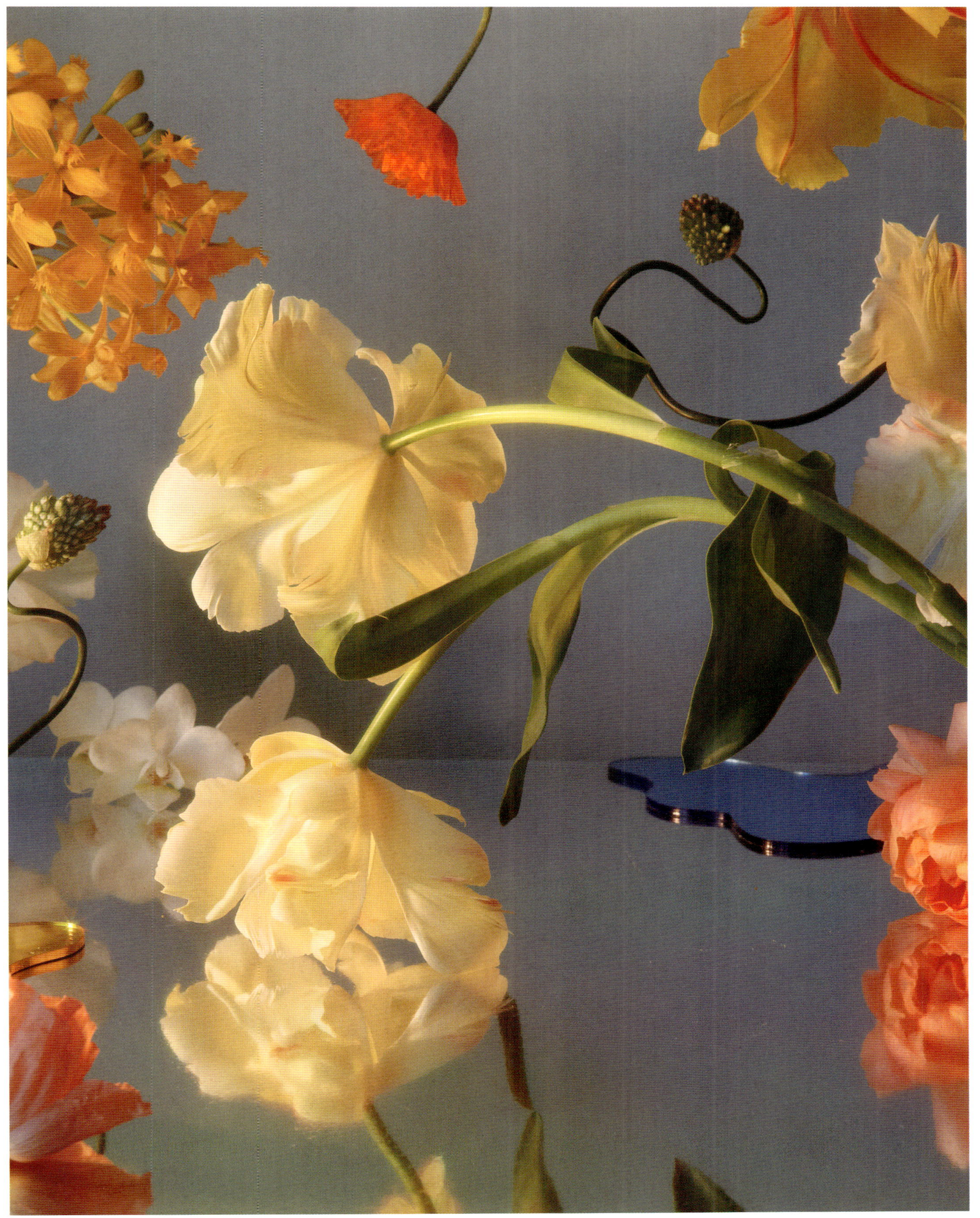

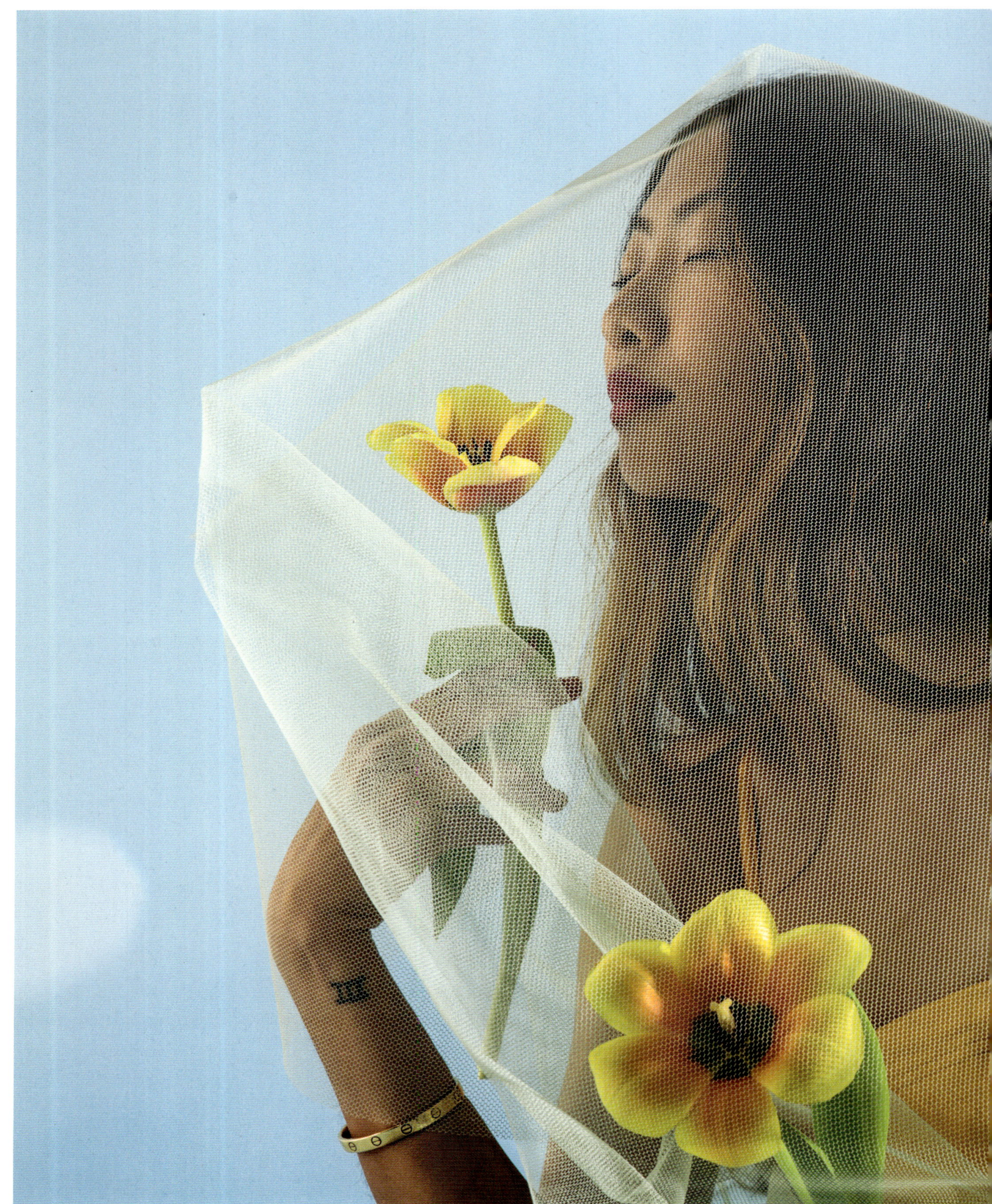

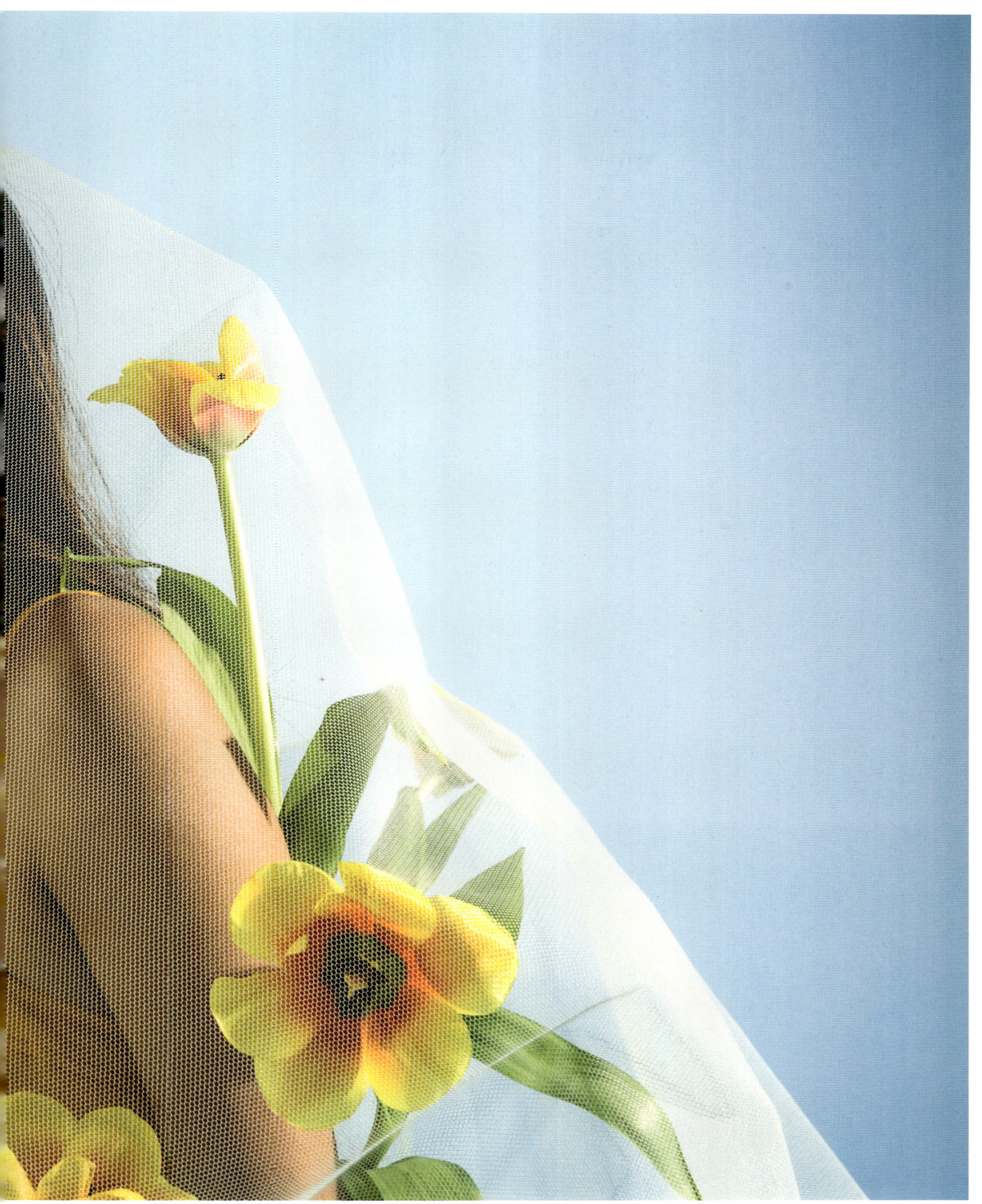

HERE

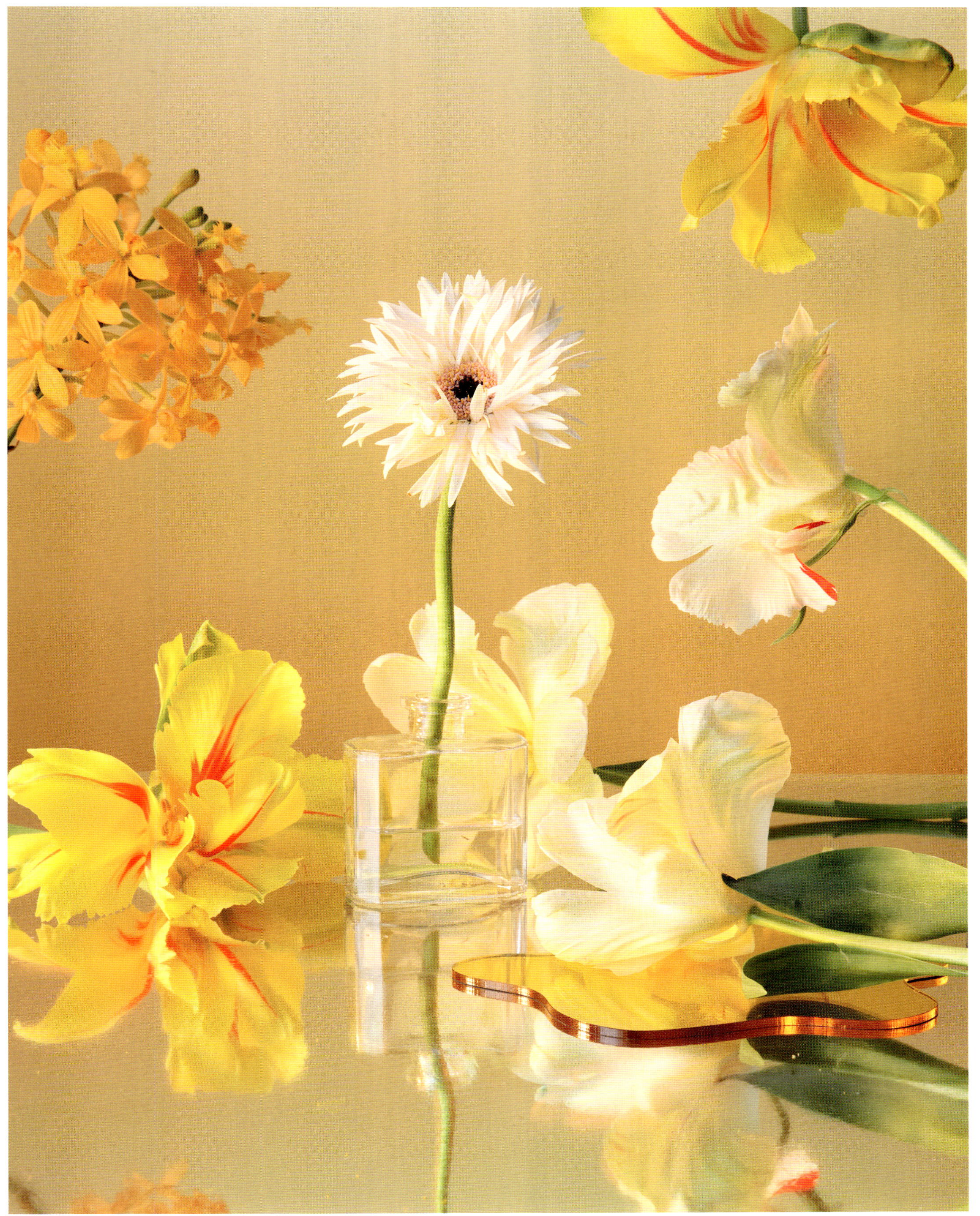

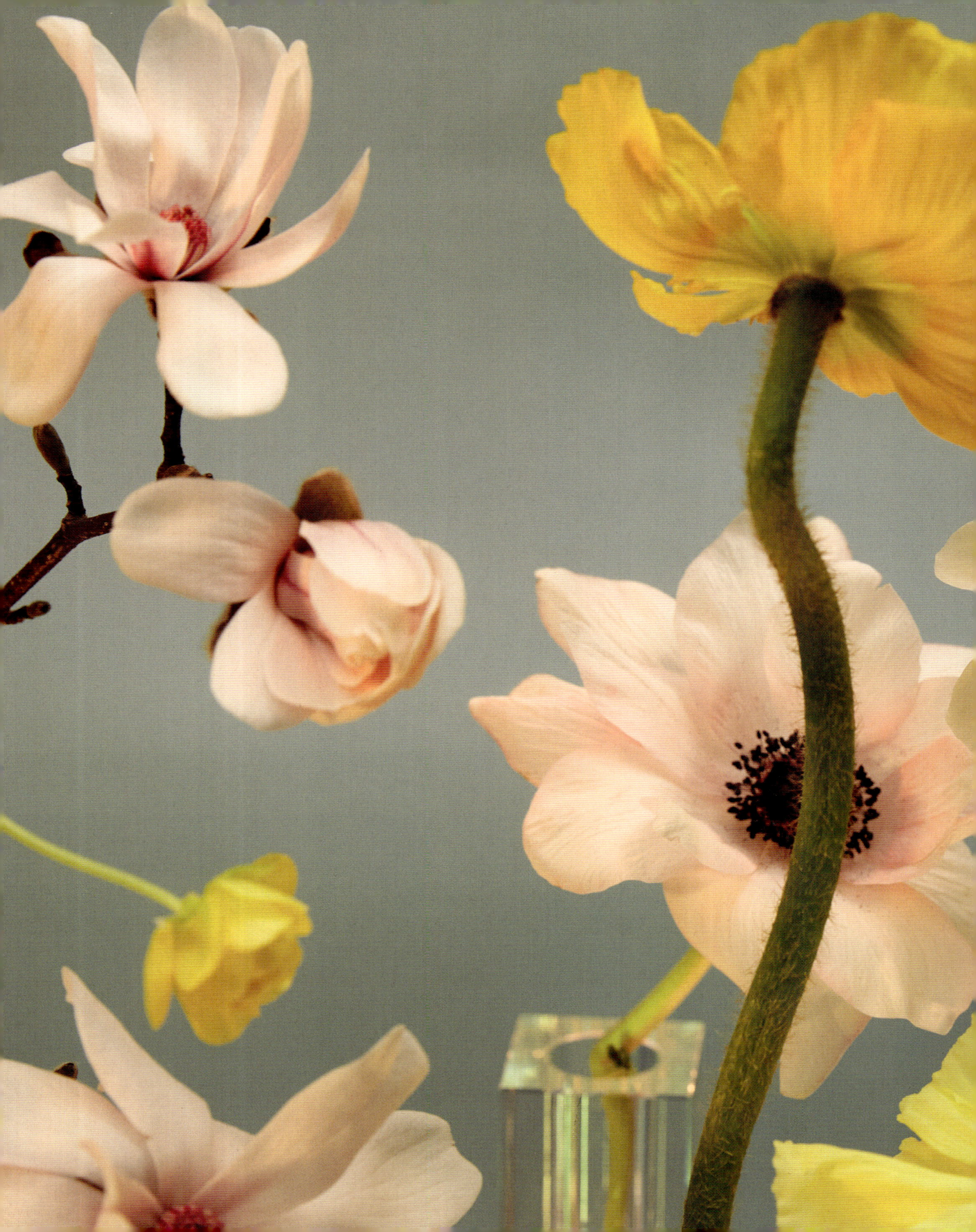

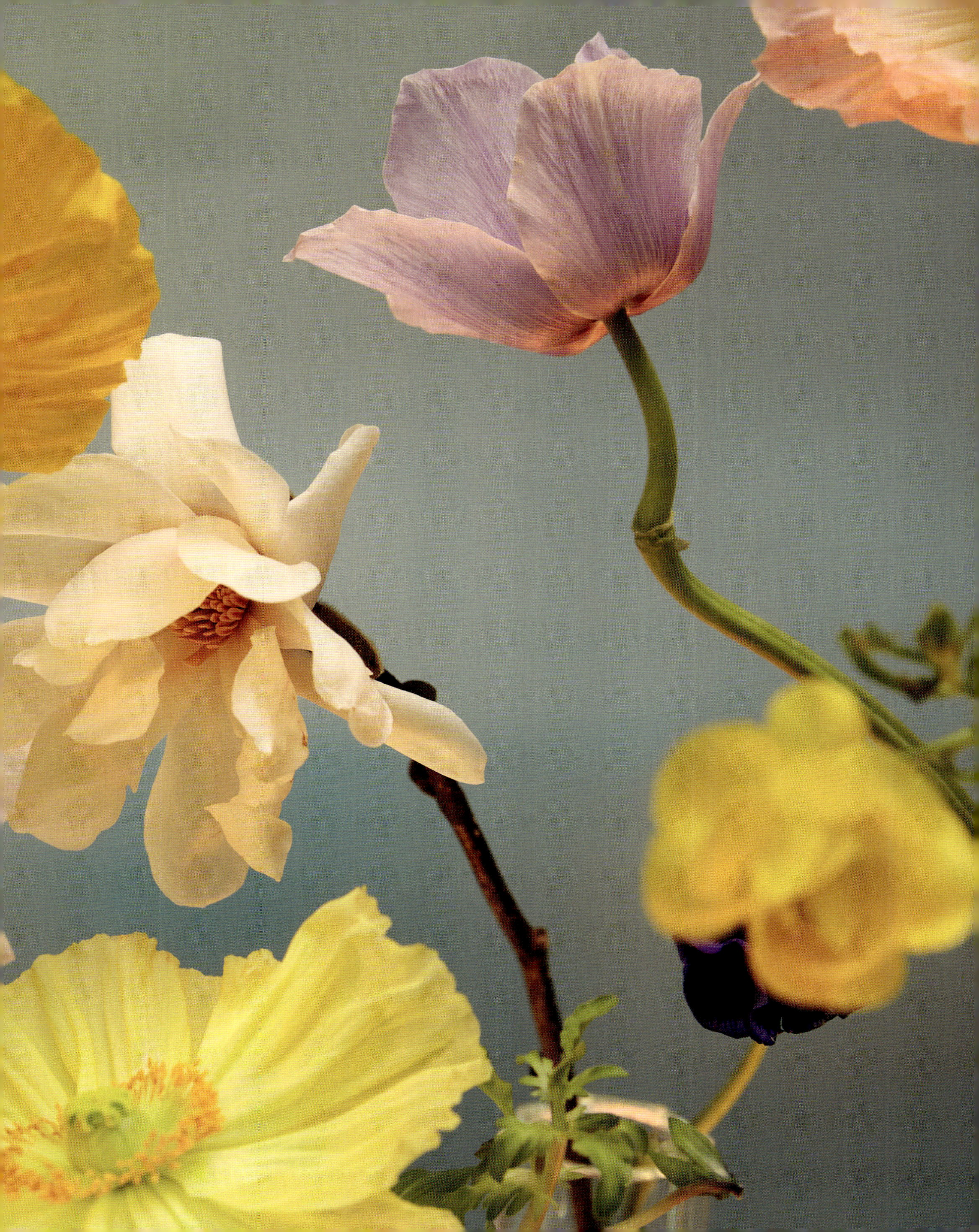

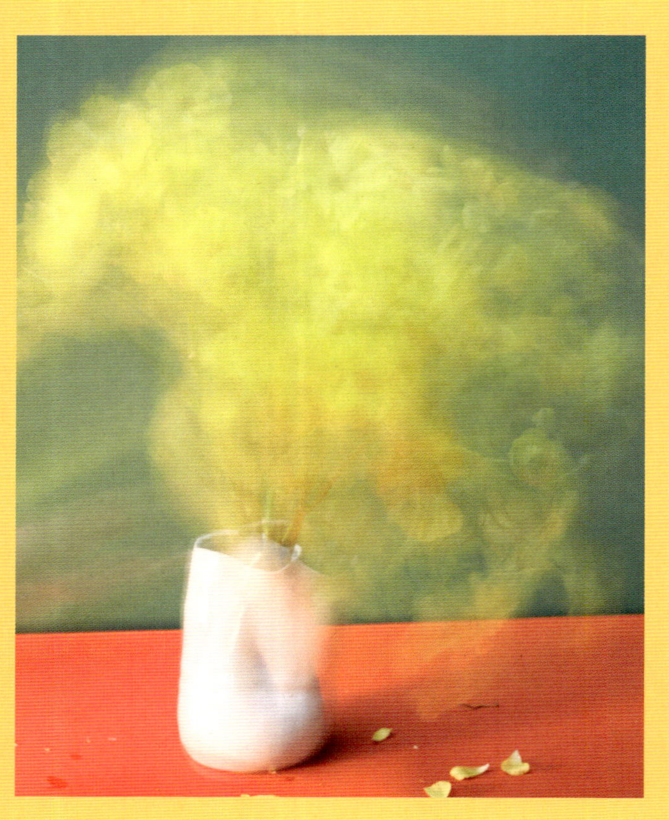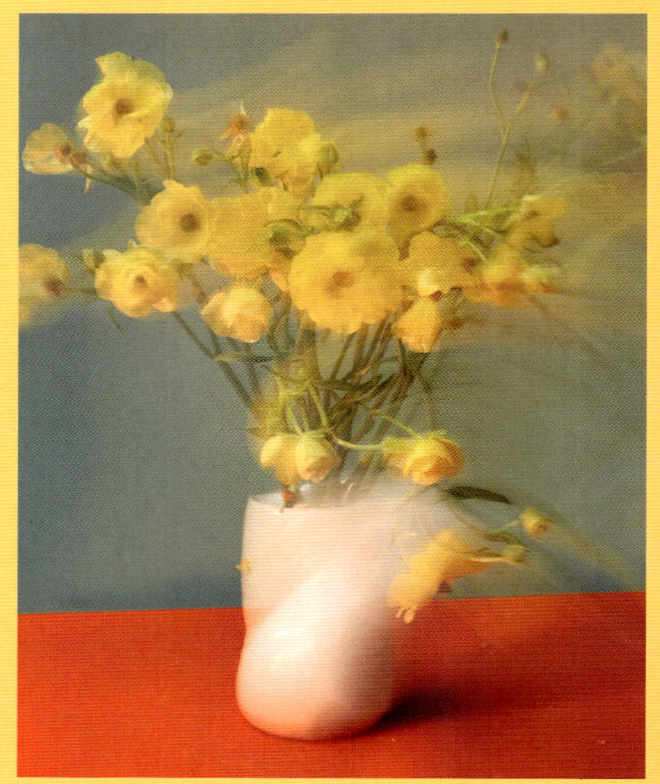

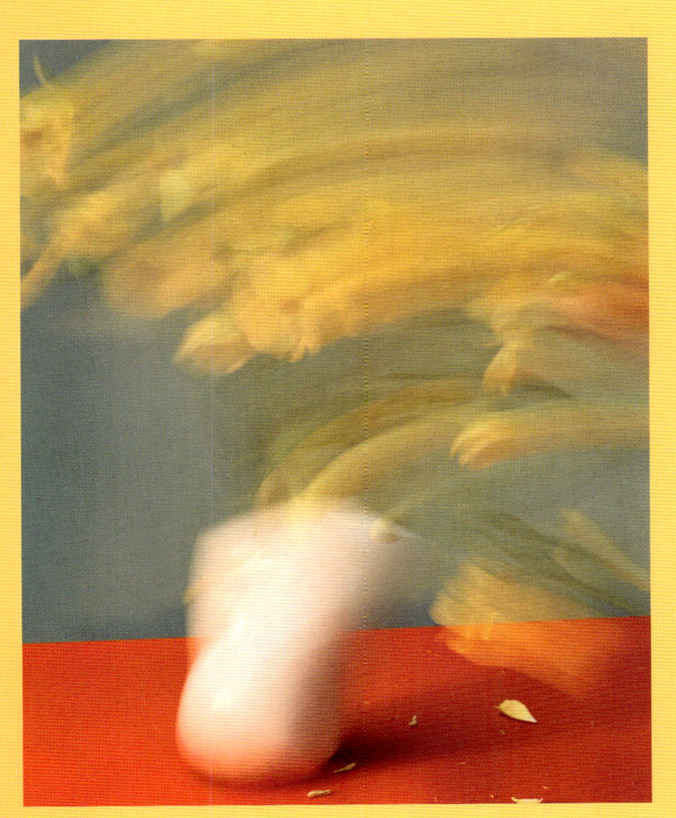

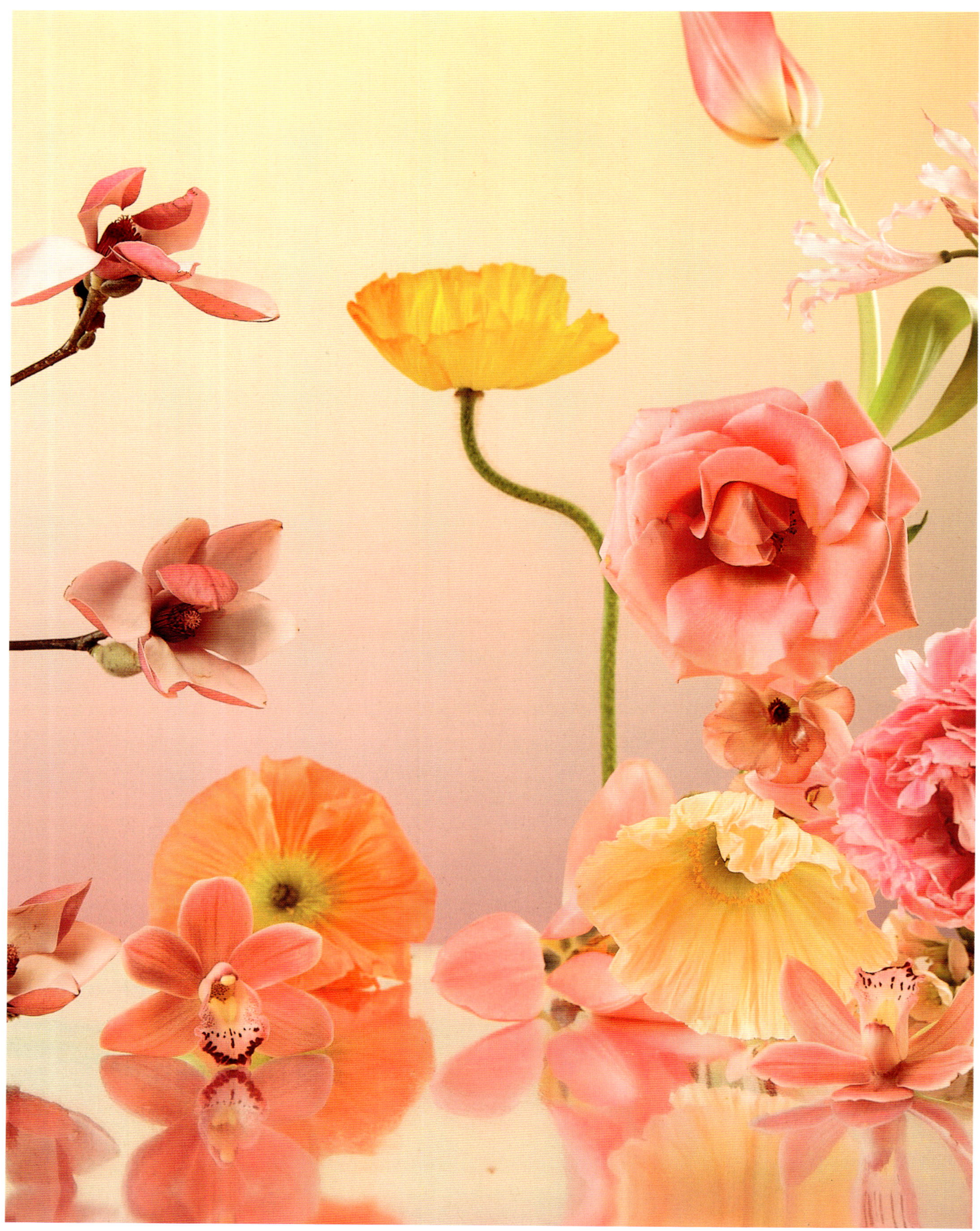

WALLFLOWERS

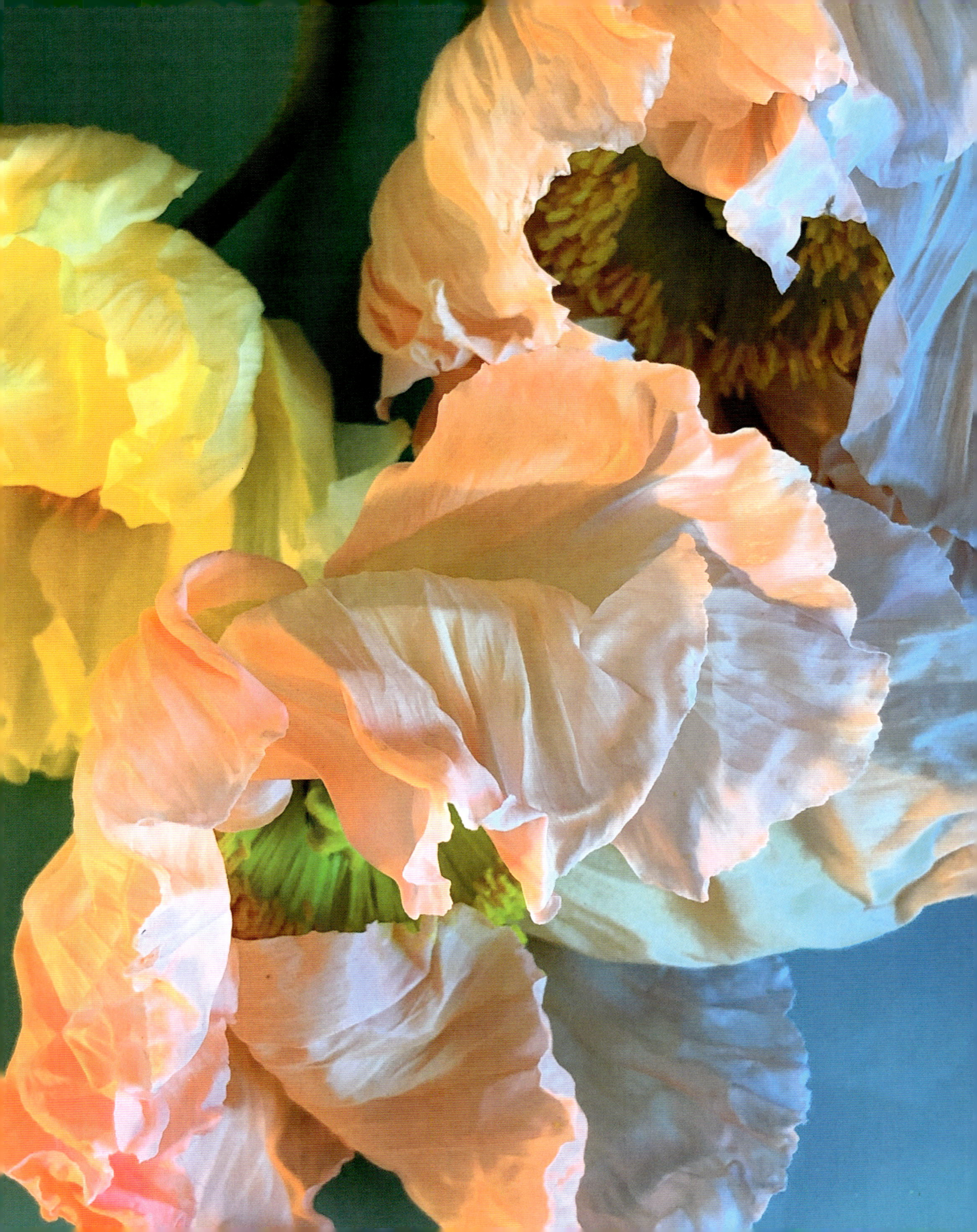

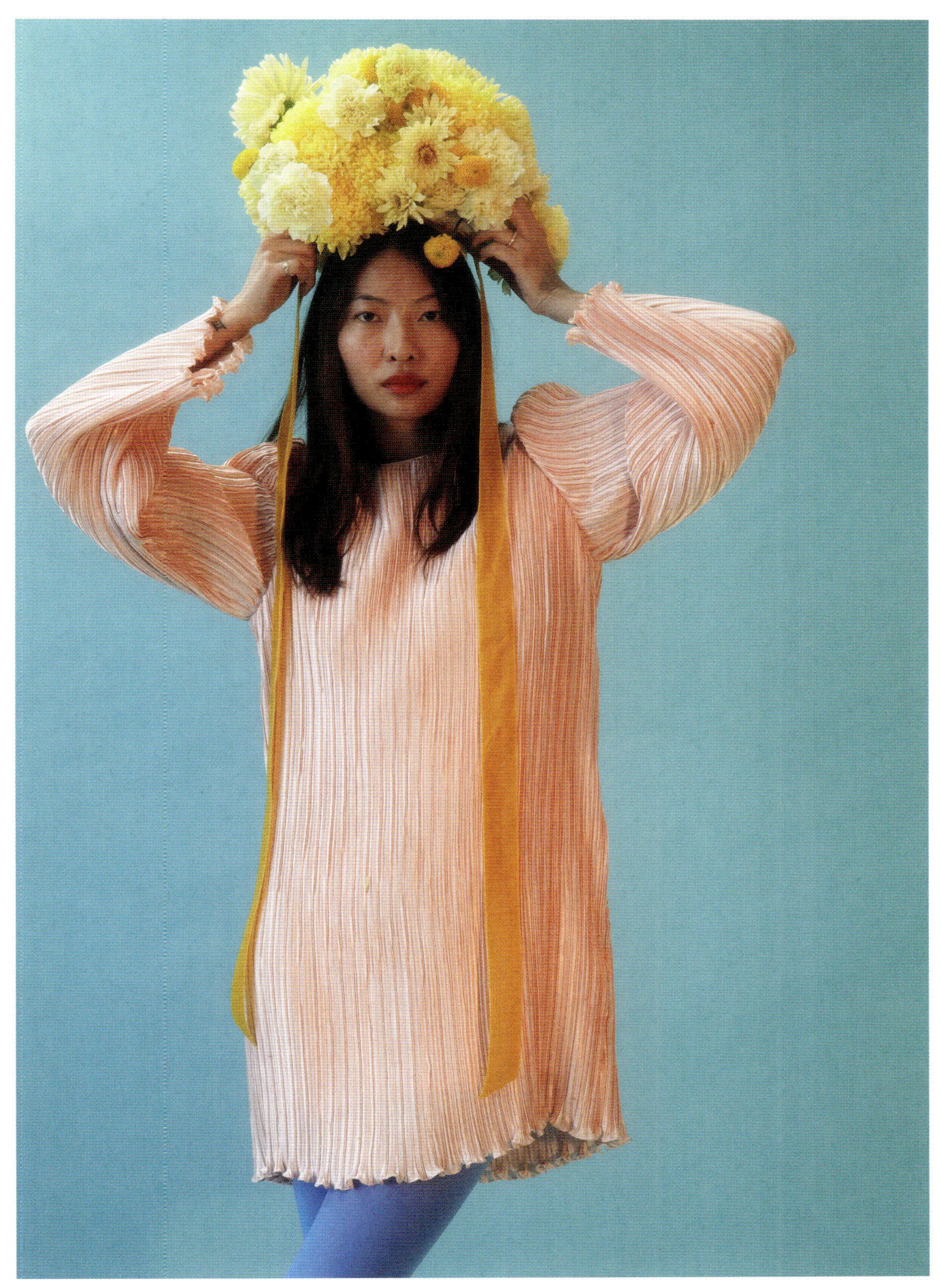

RELEASE THE DOVES!

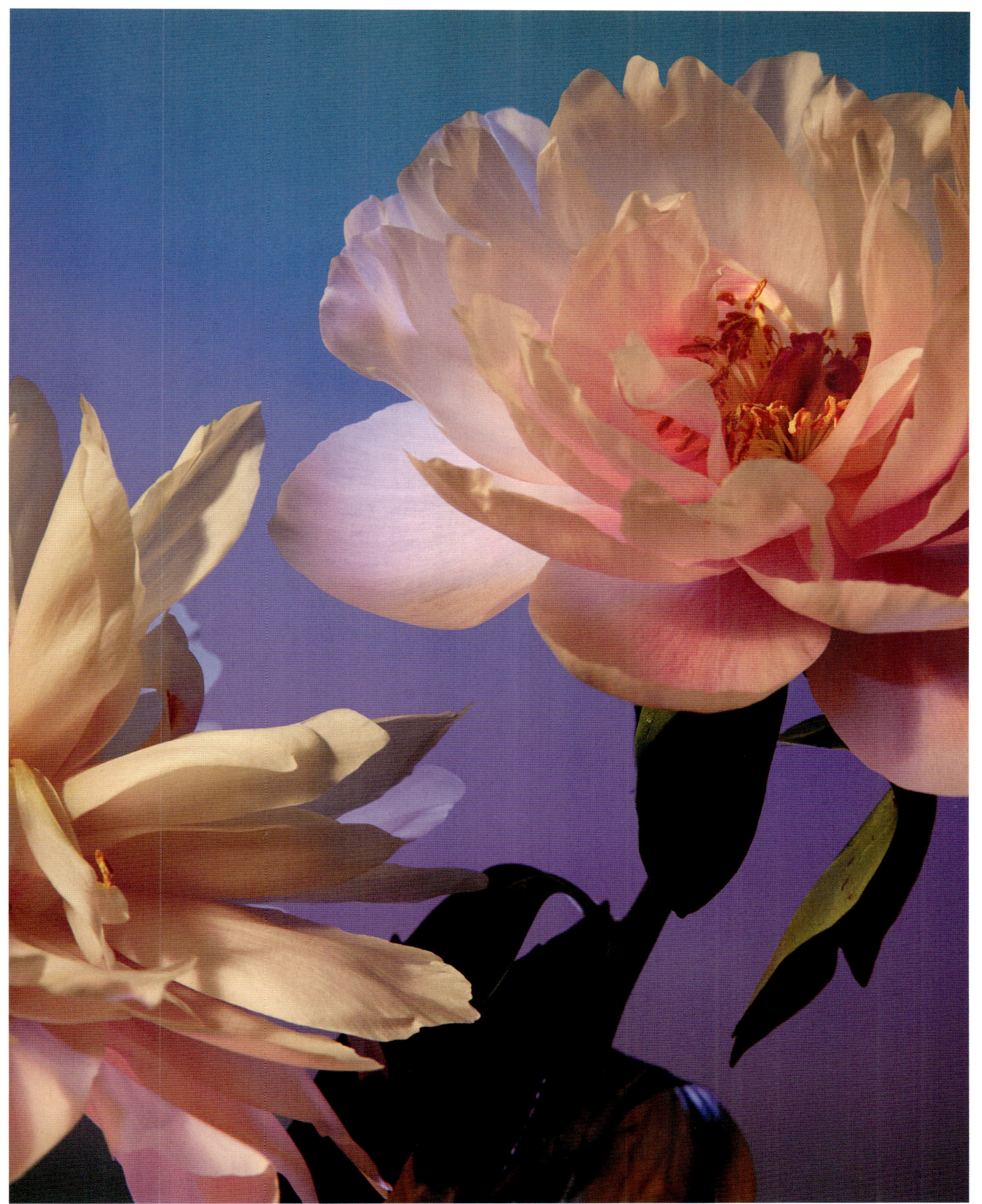

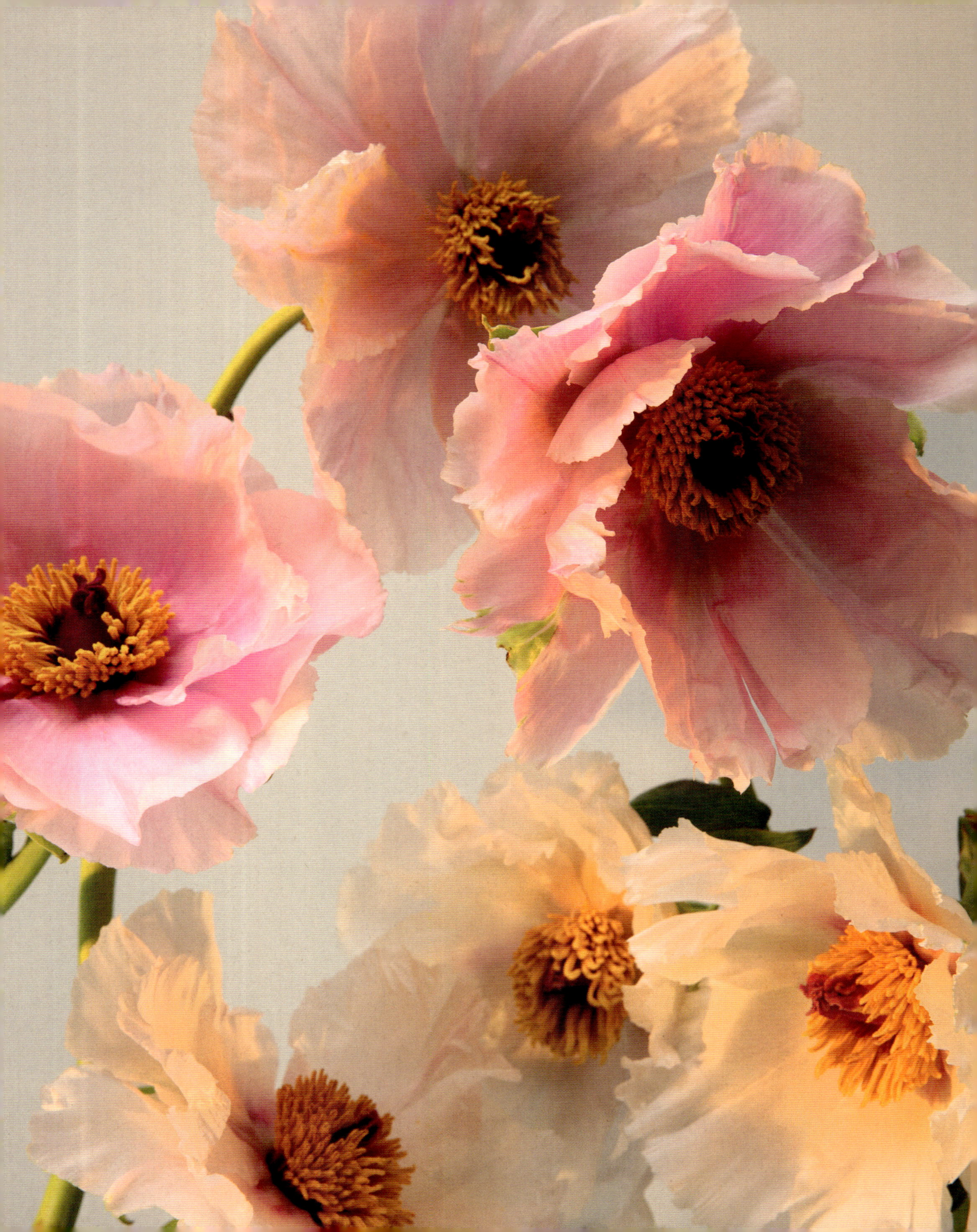

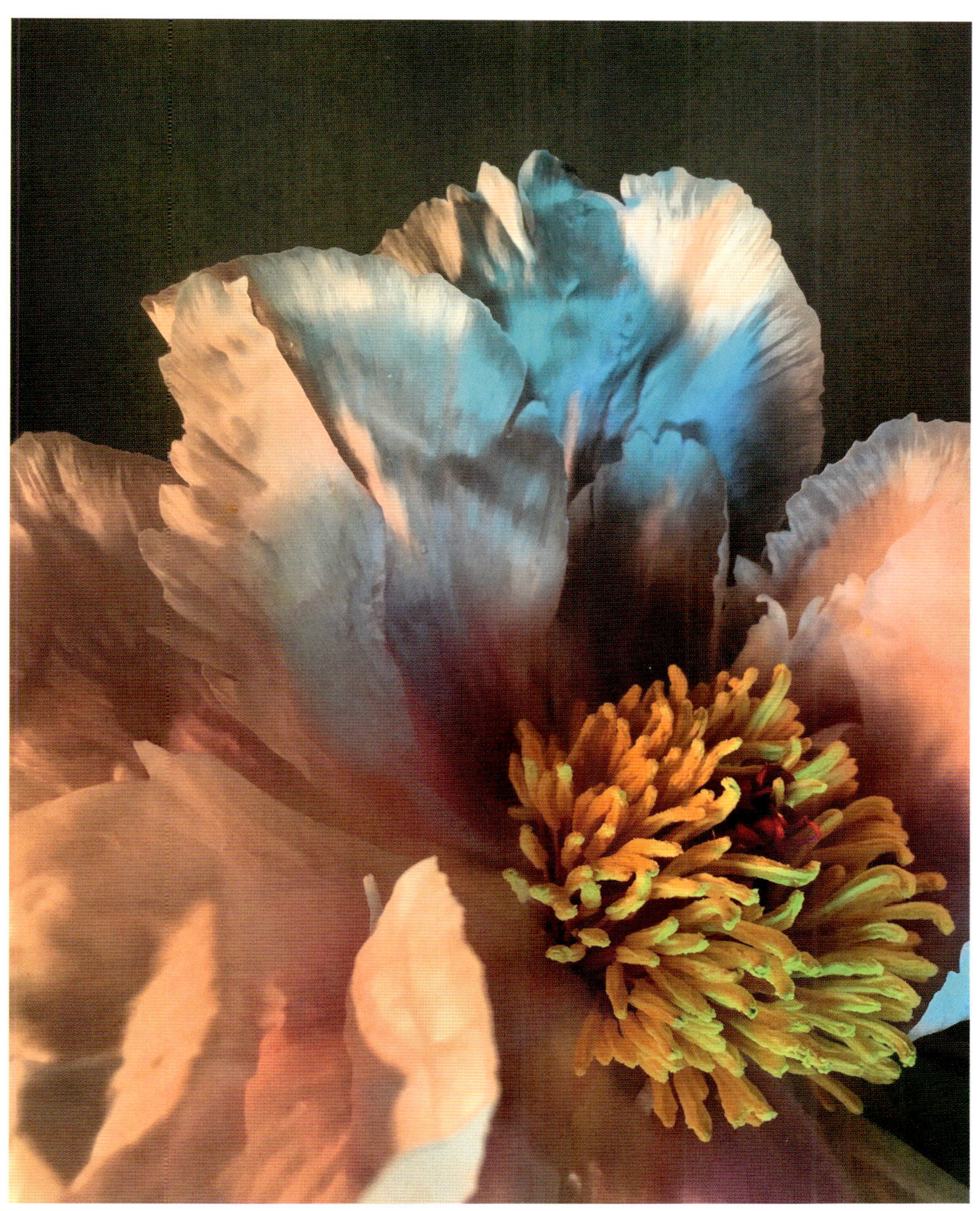

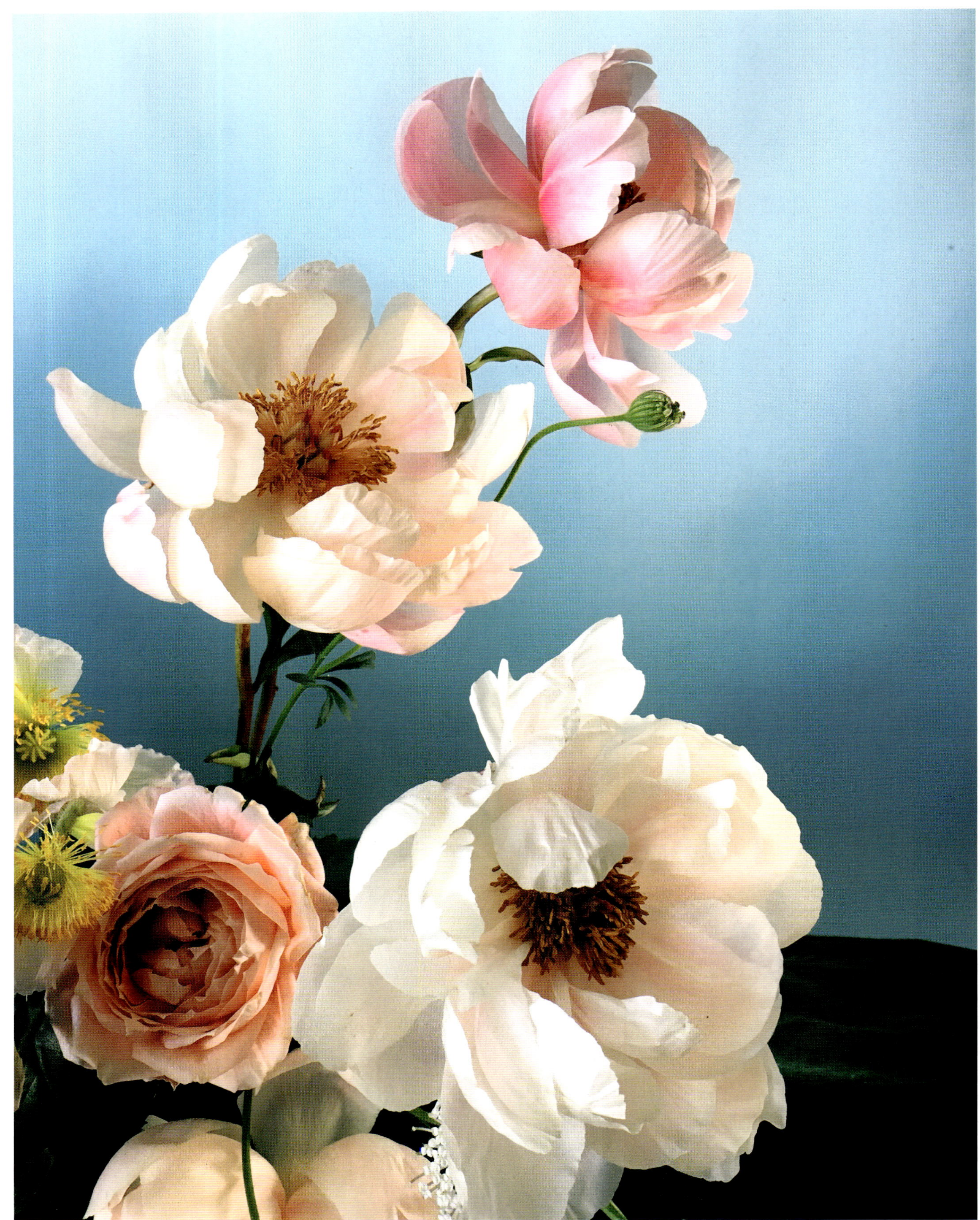

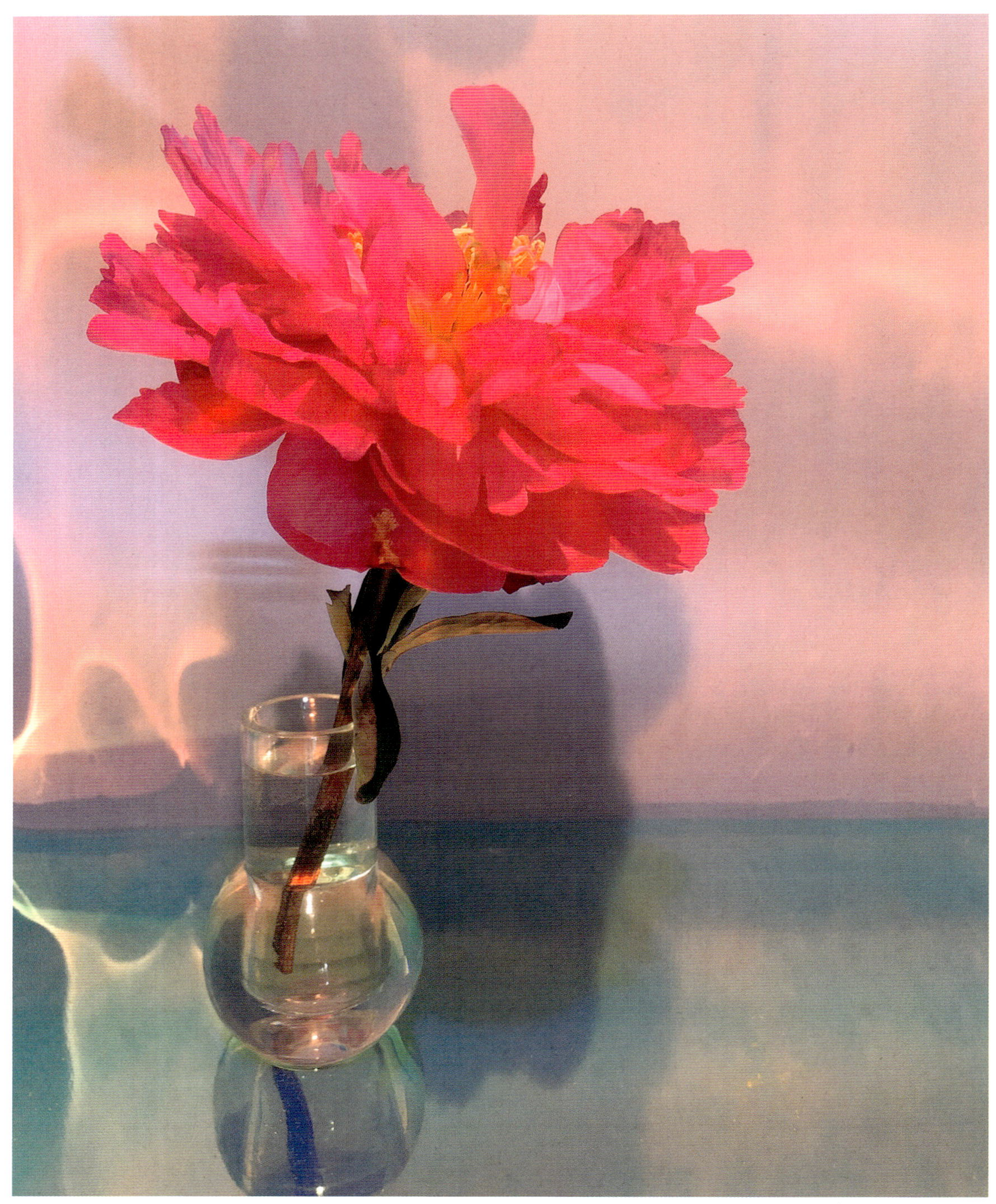

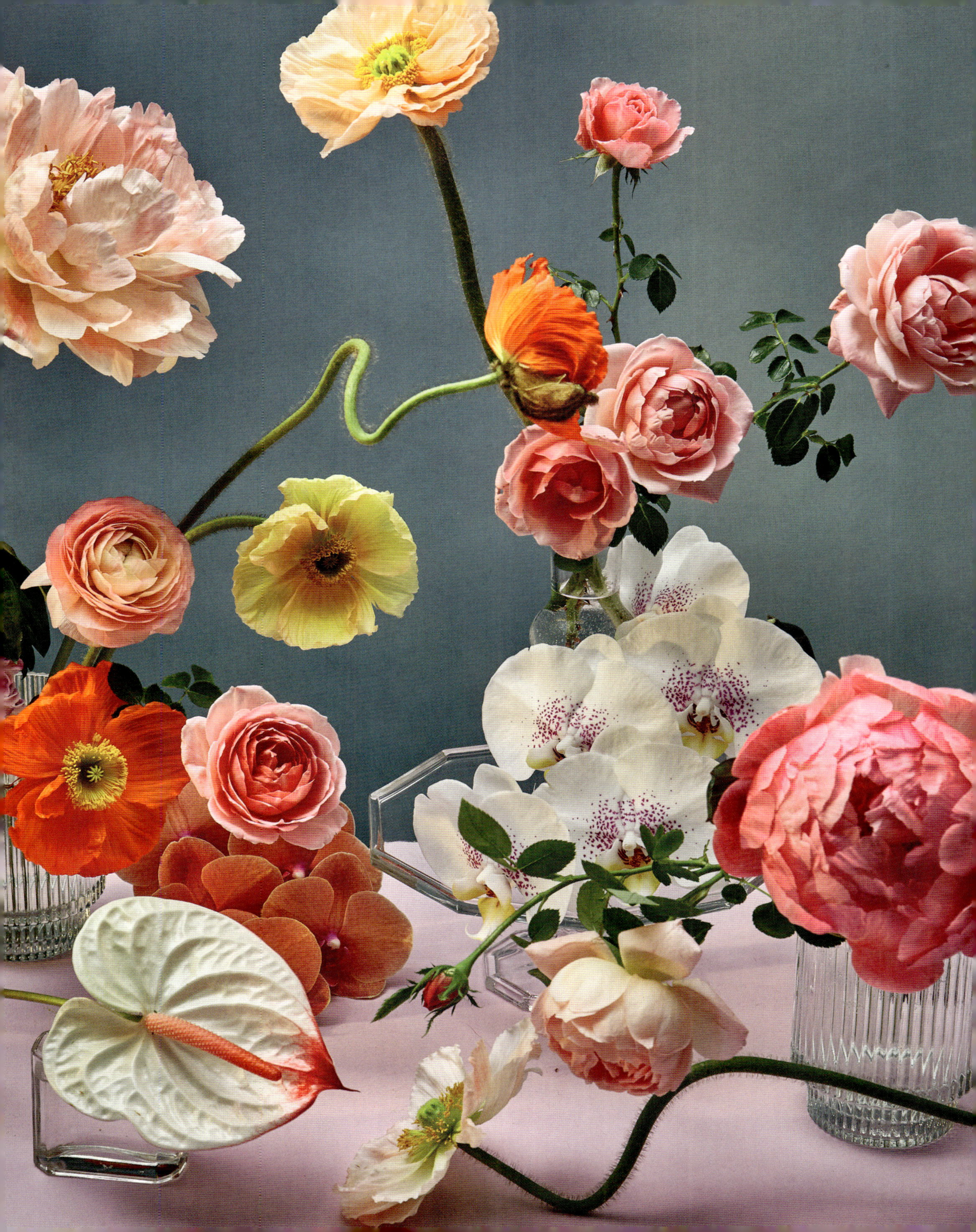

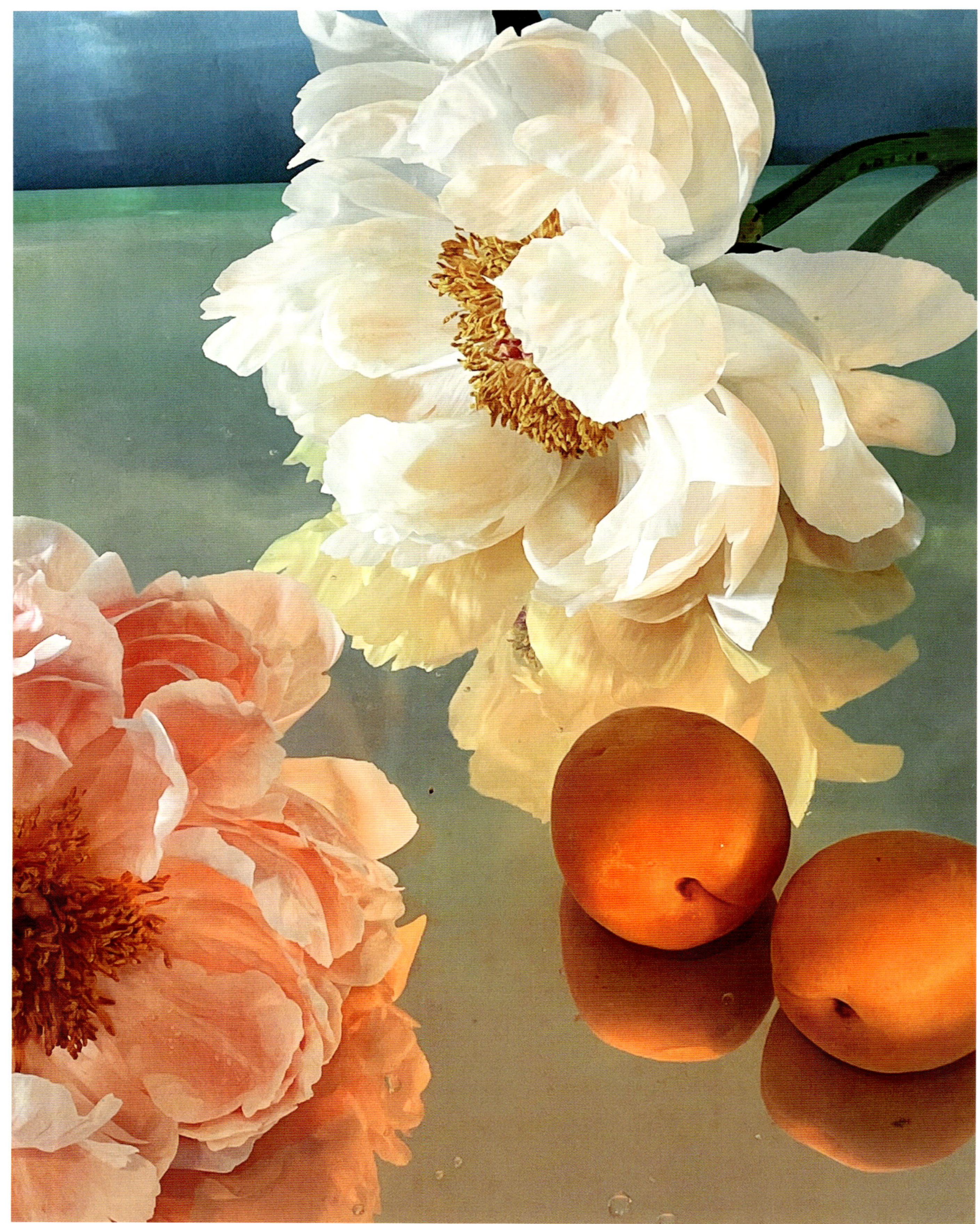

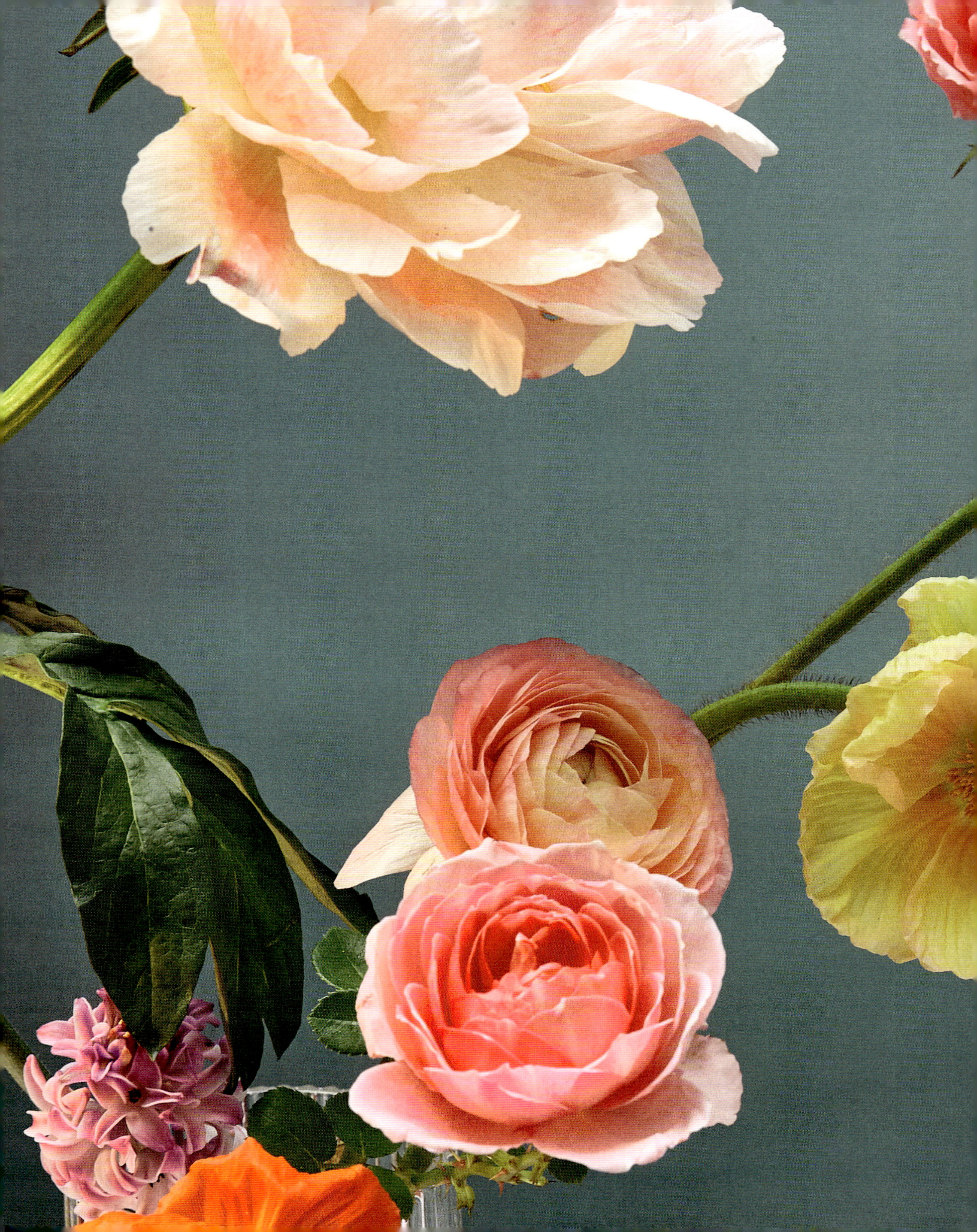

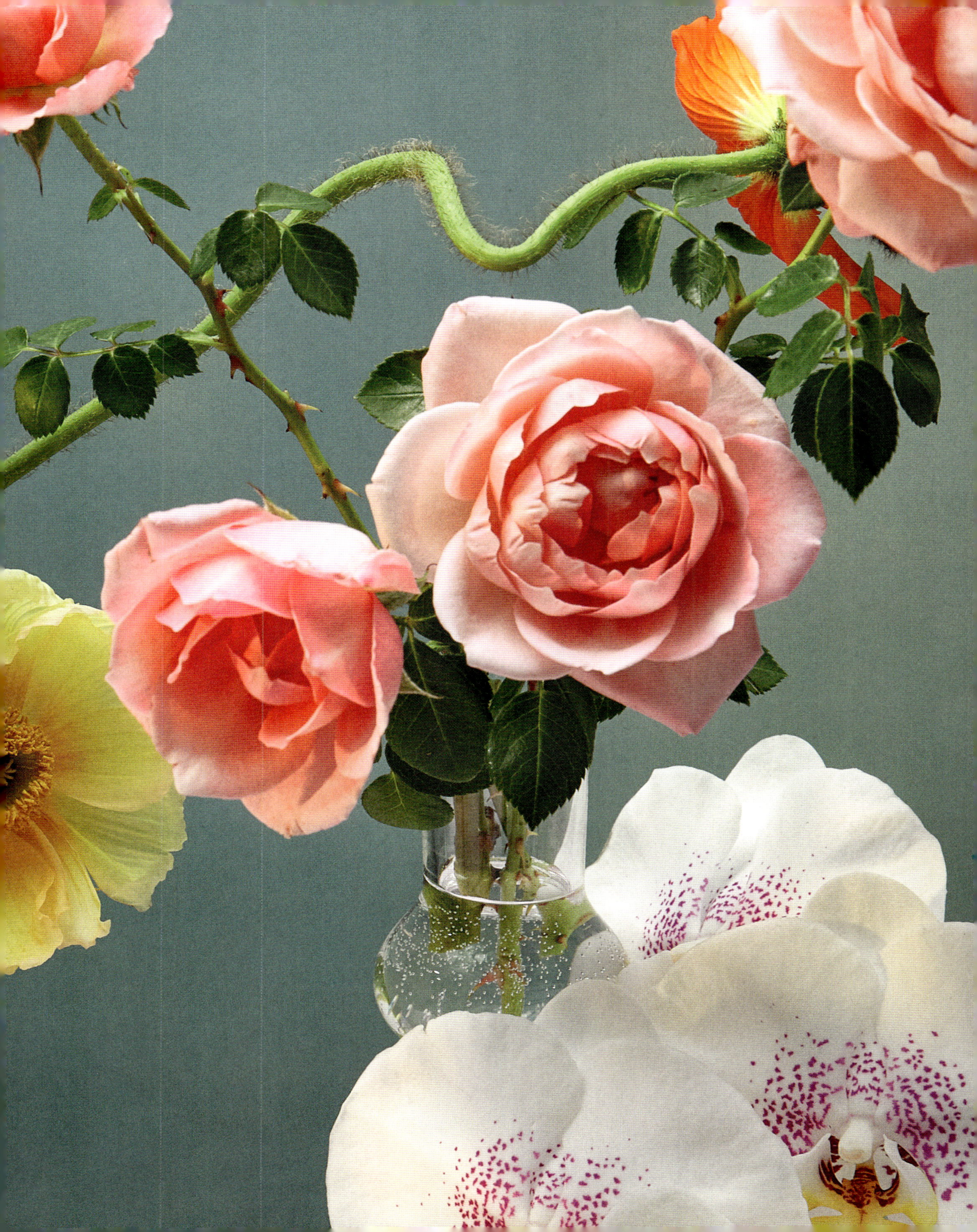

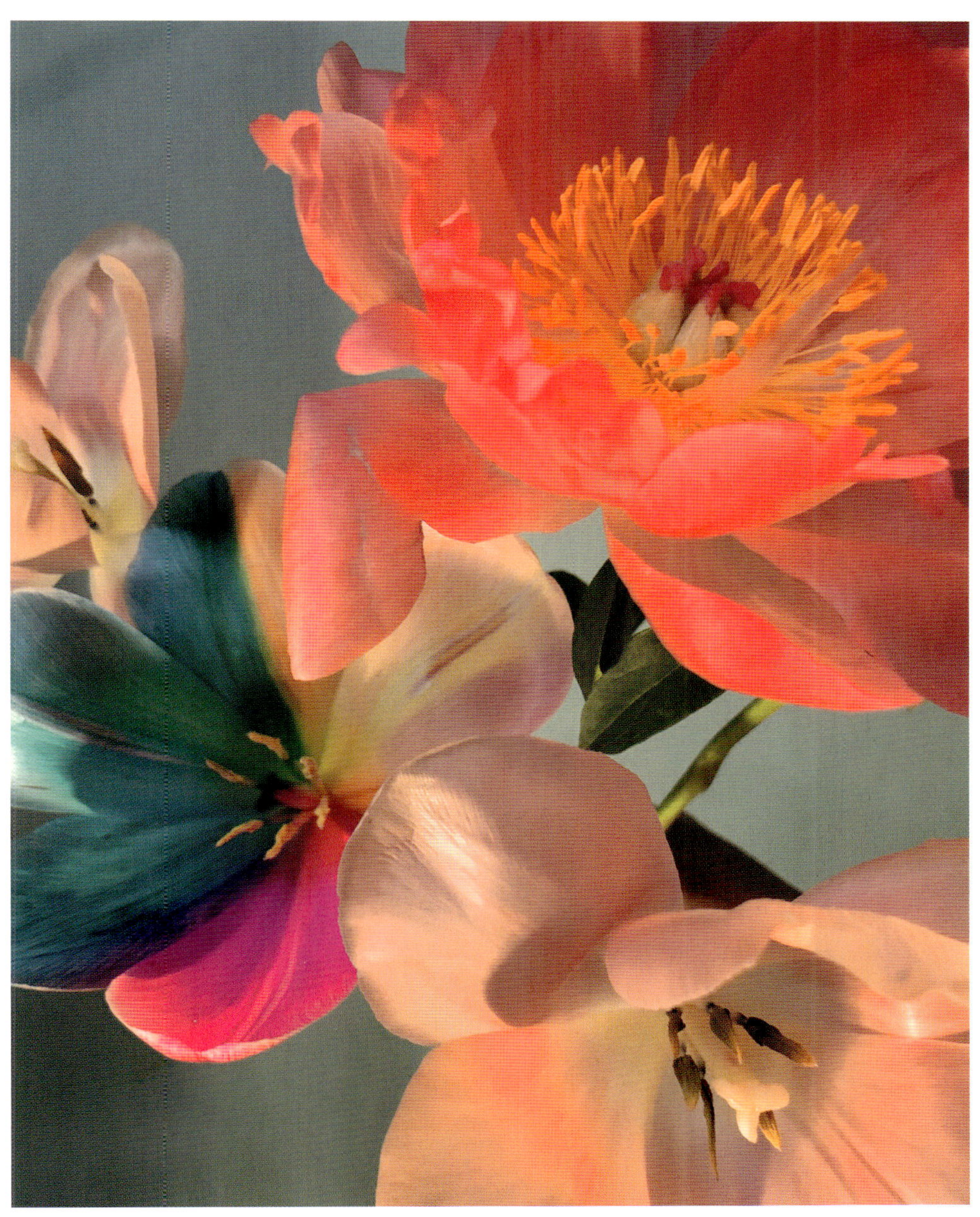

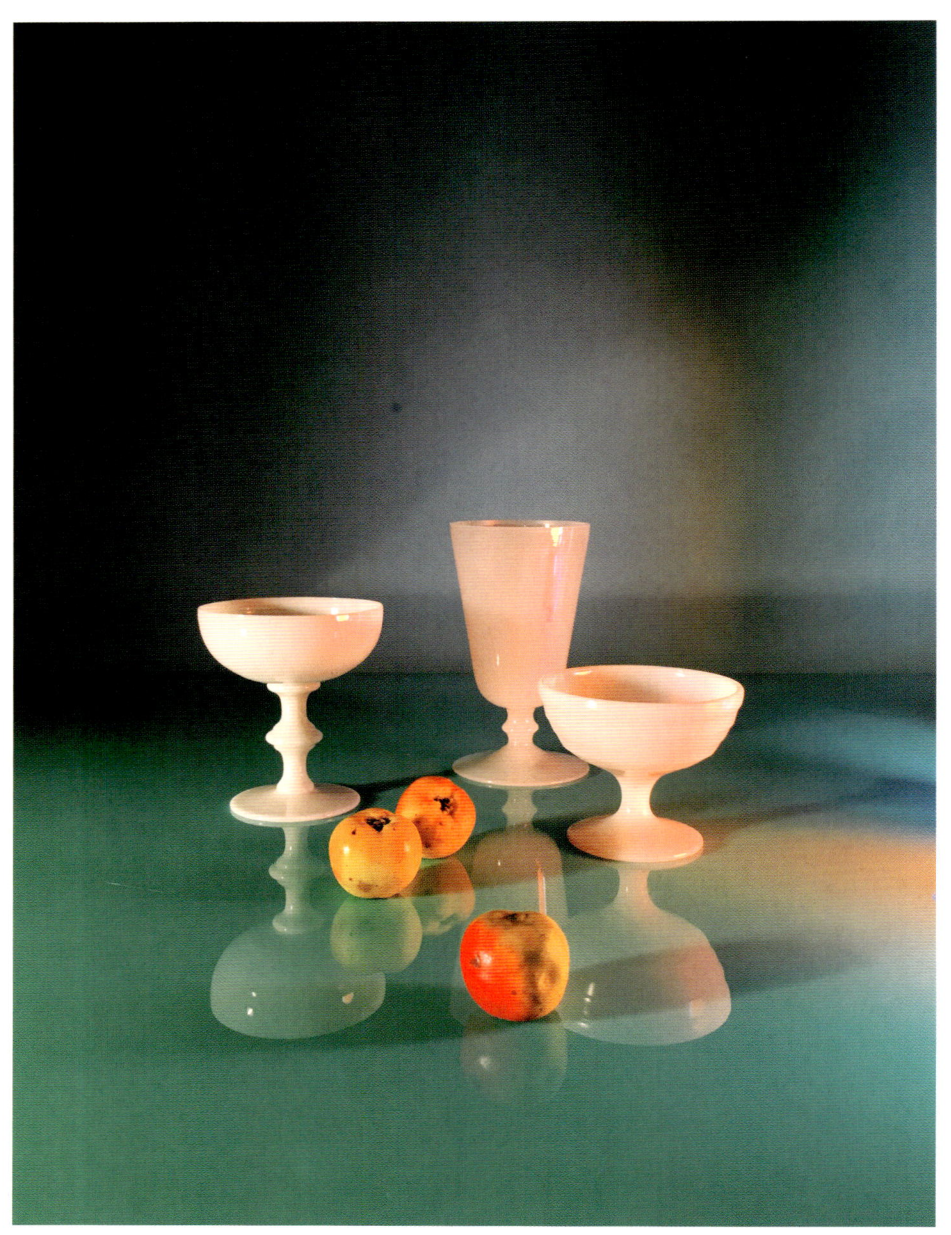

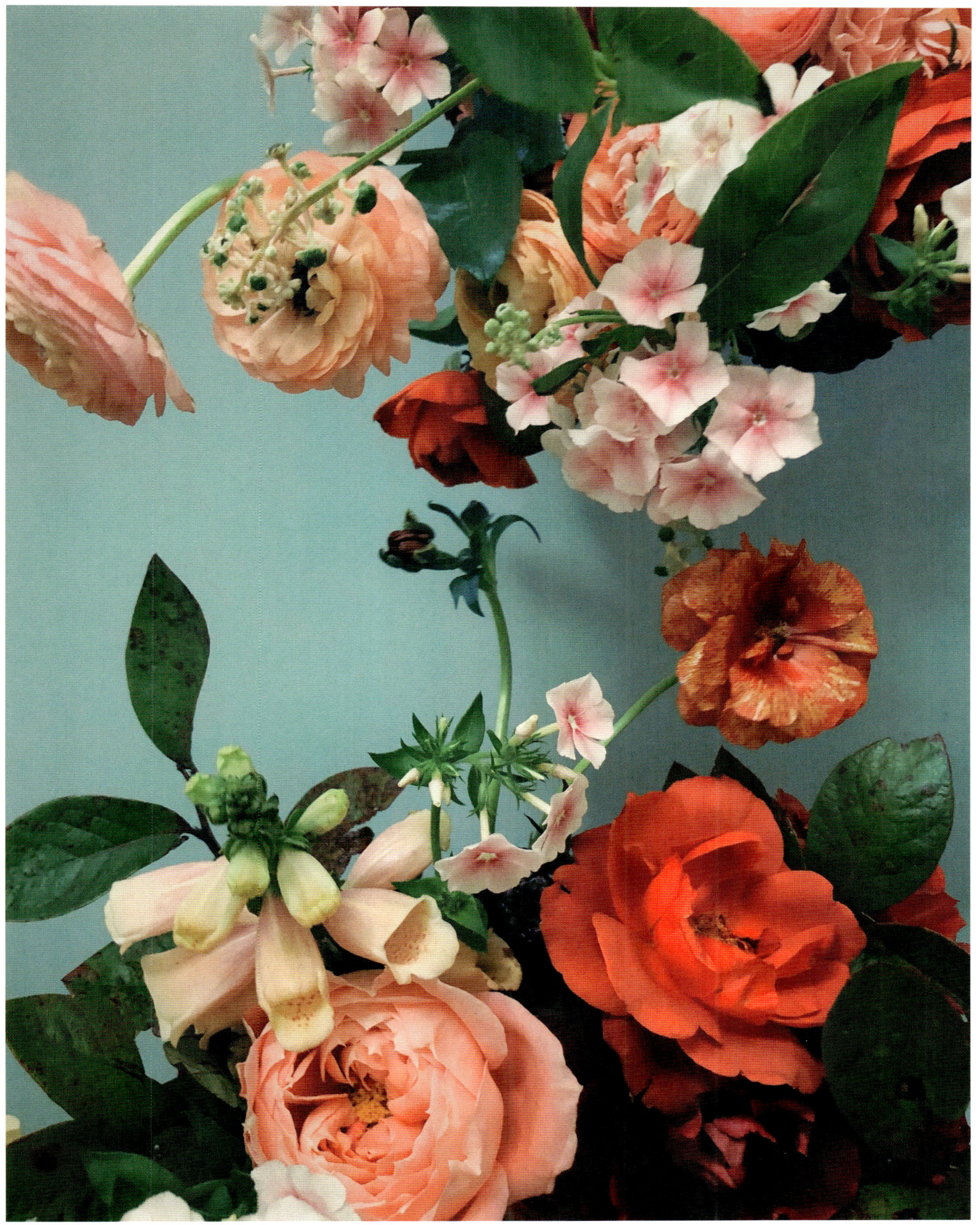

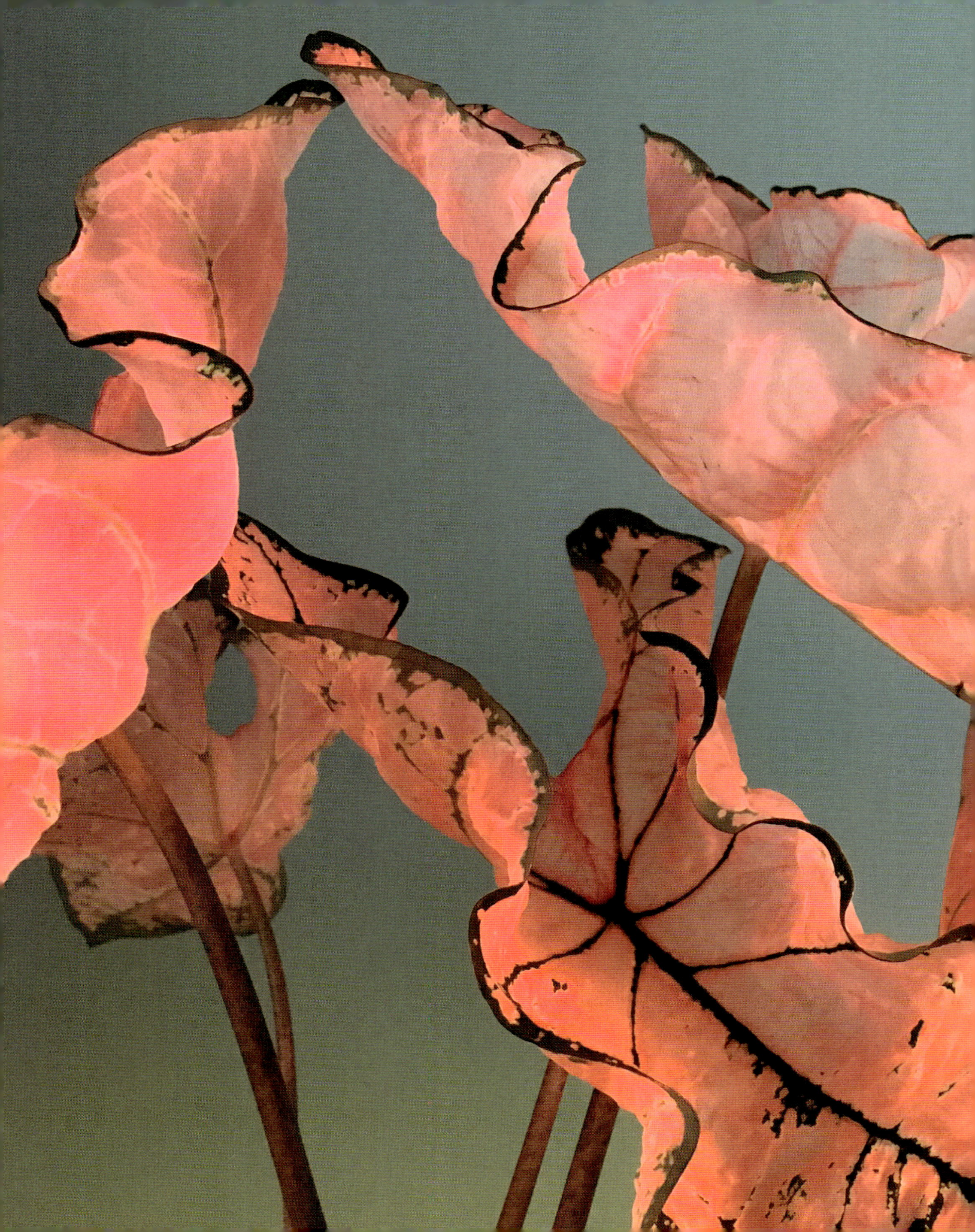

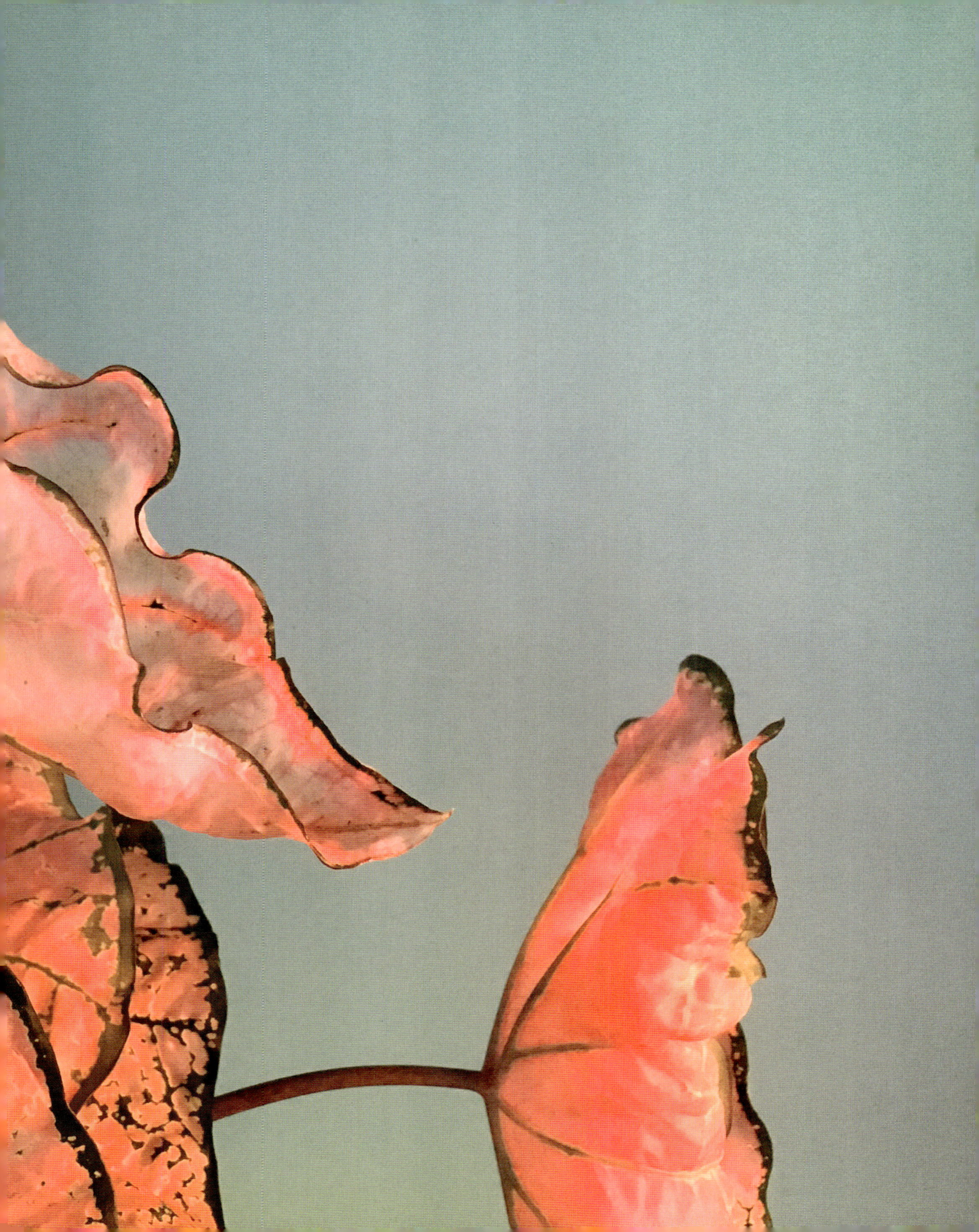

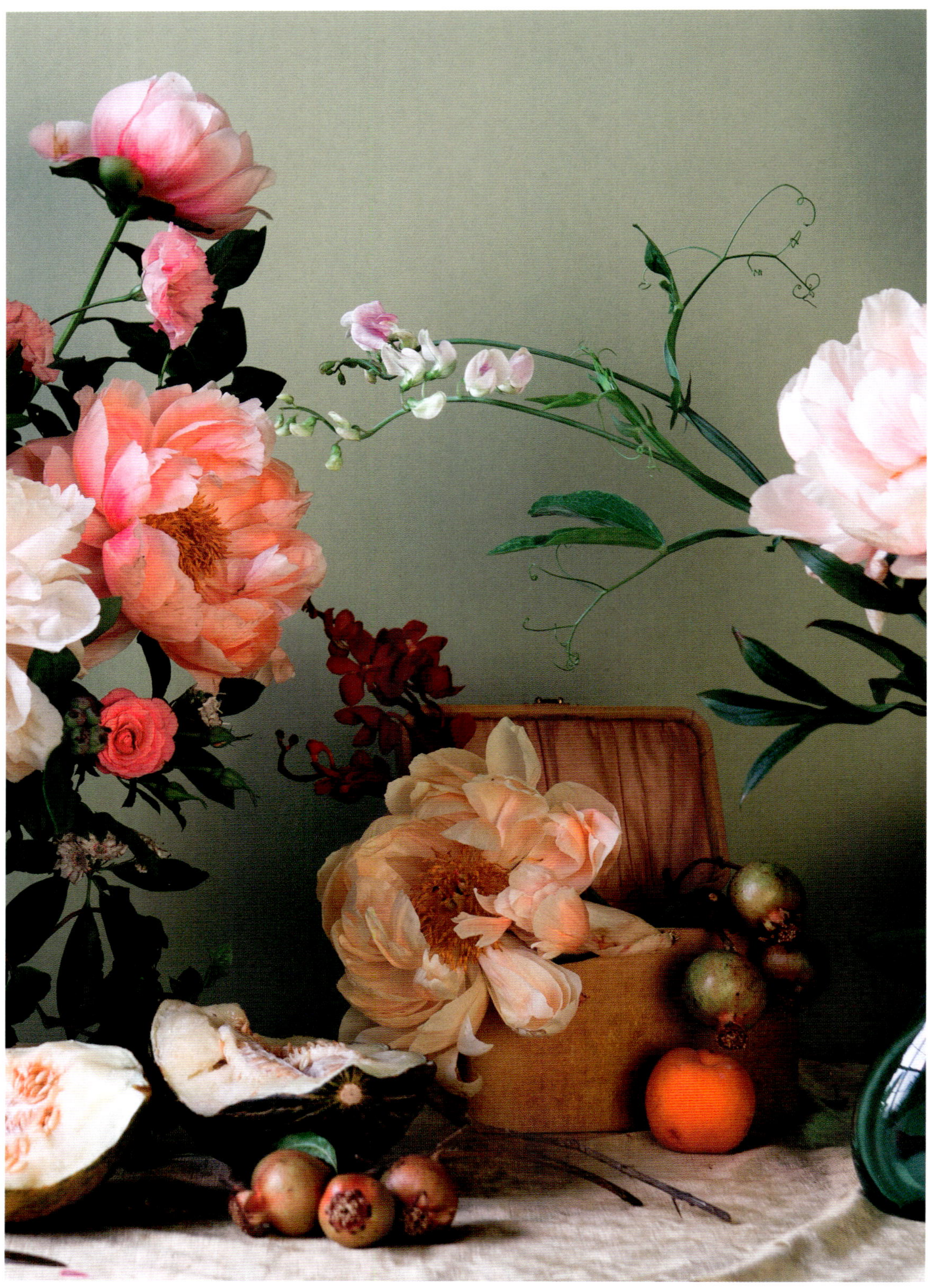

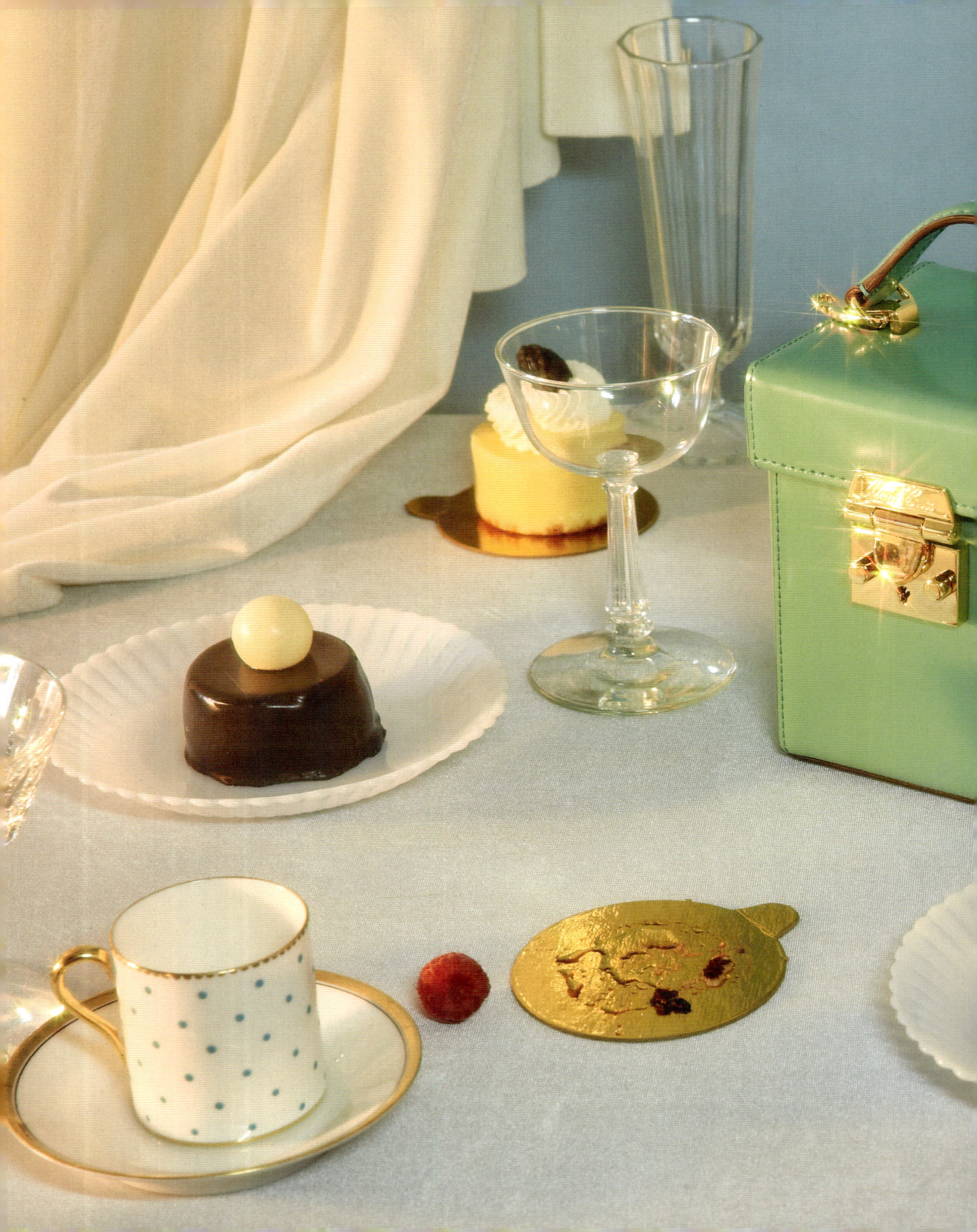

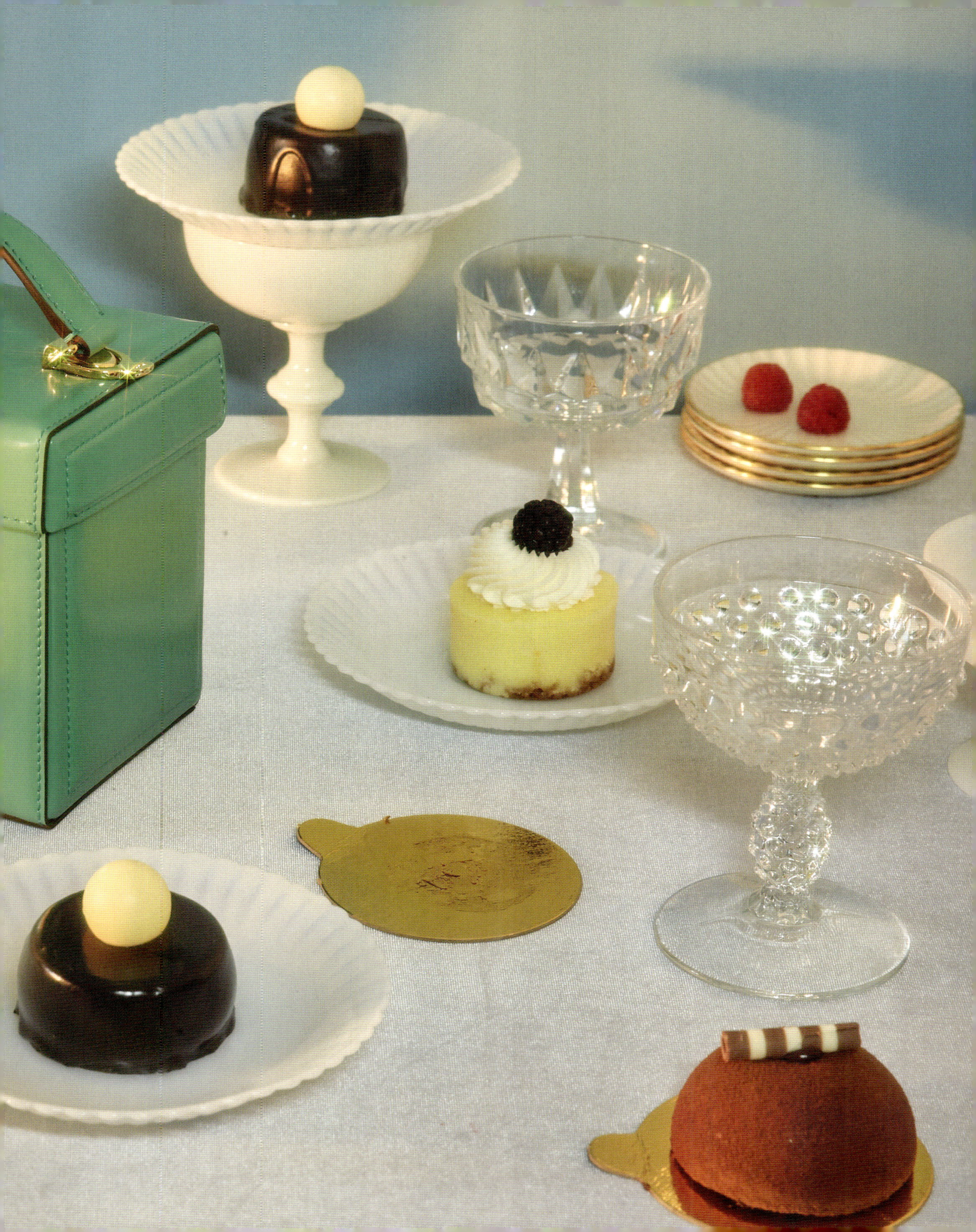

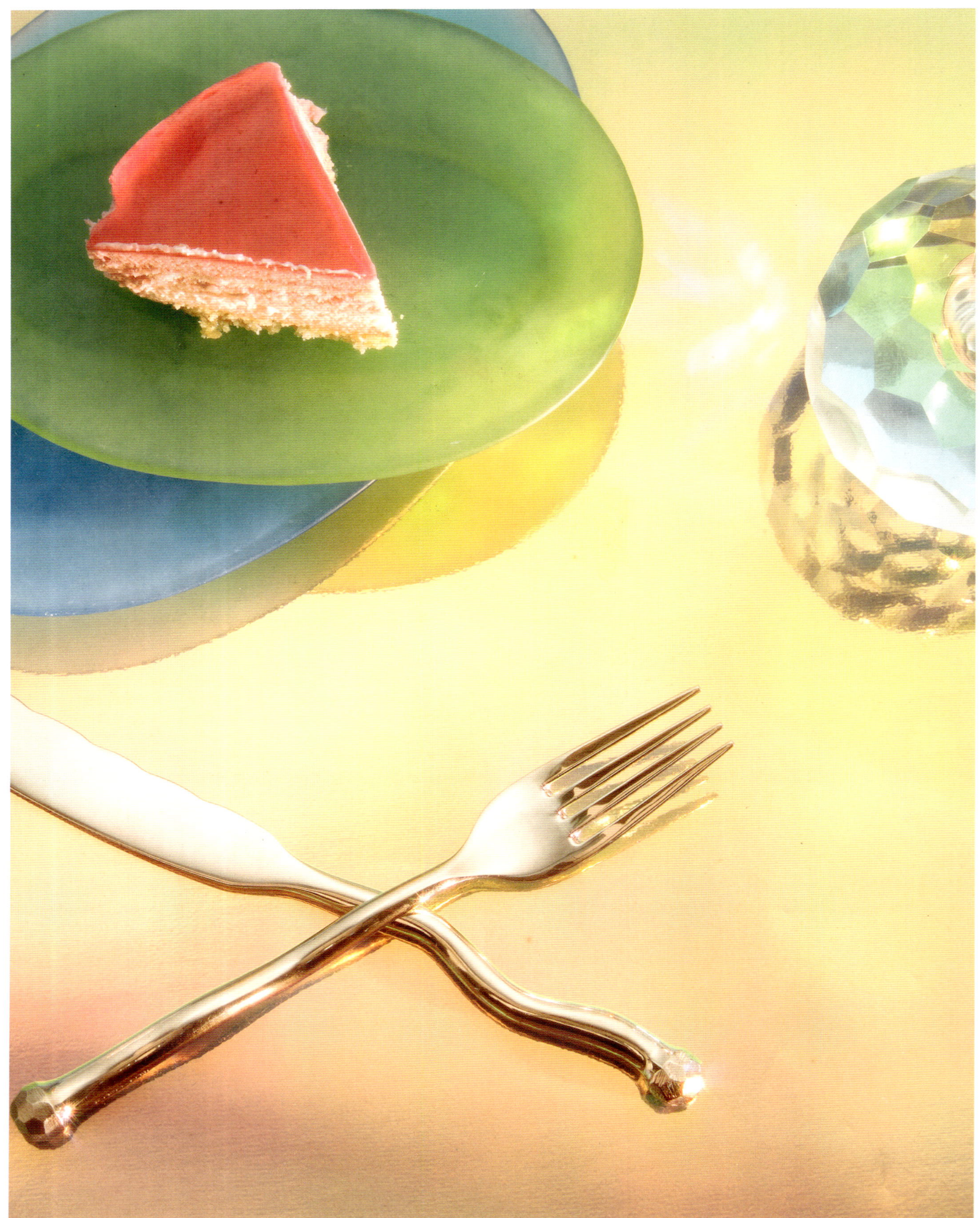

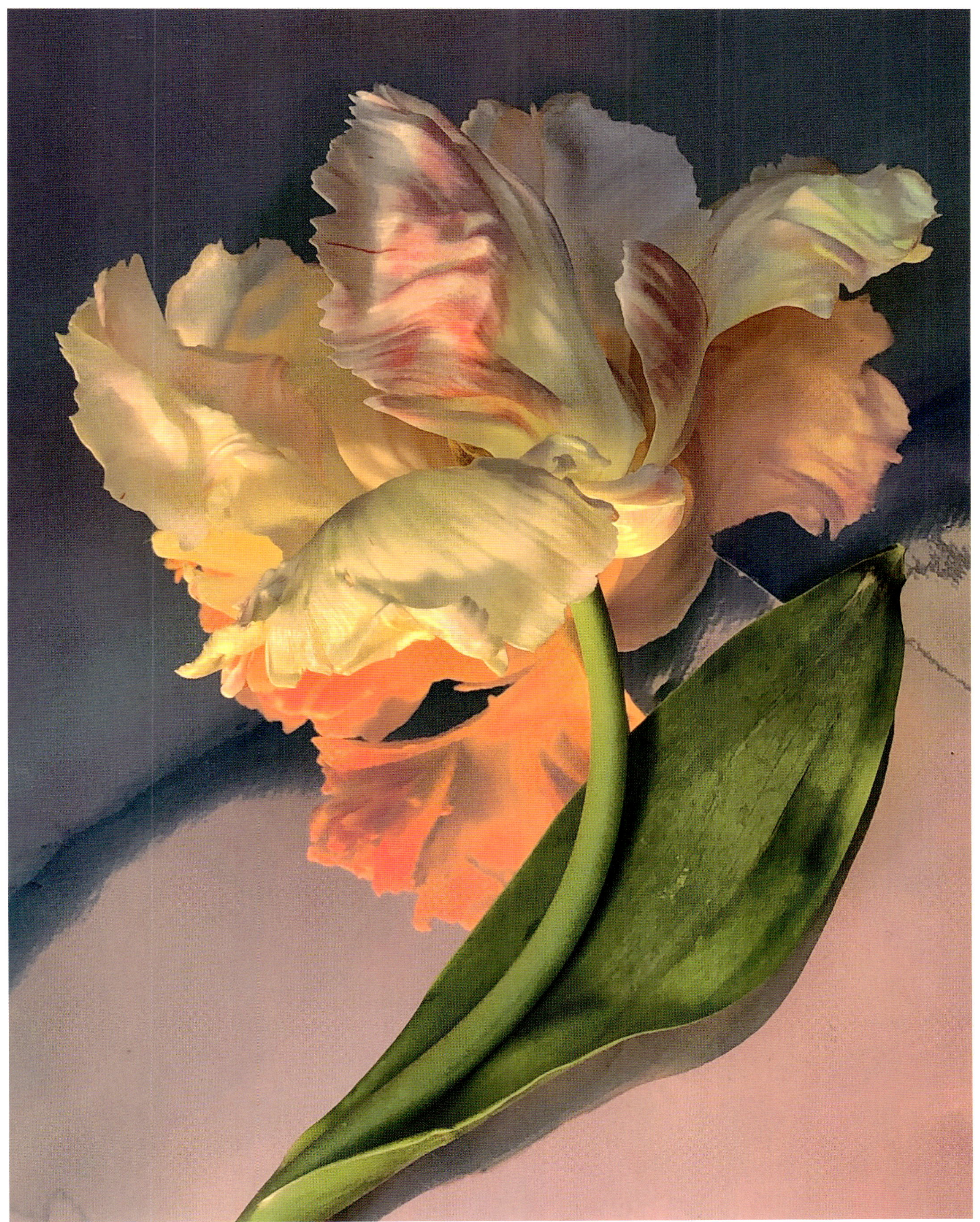

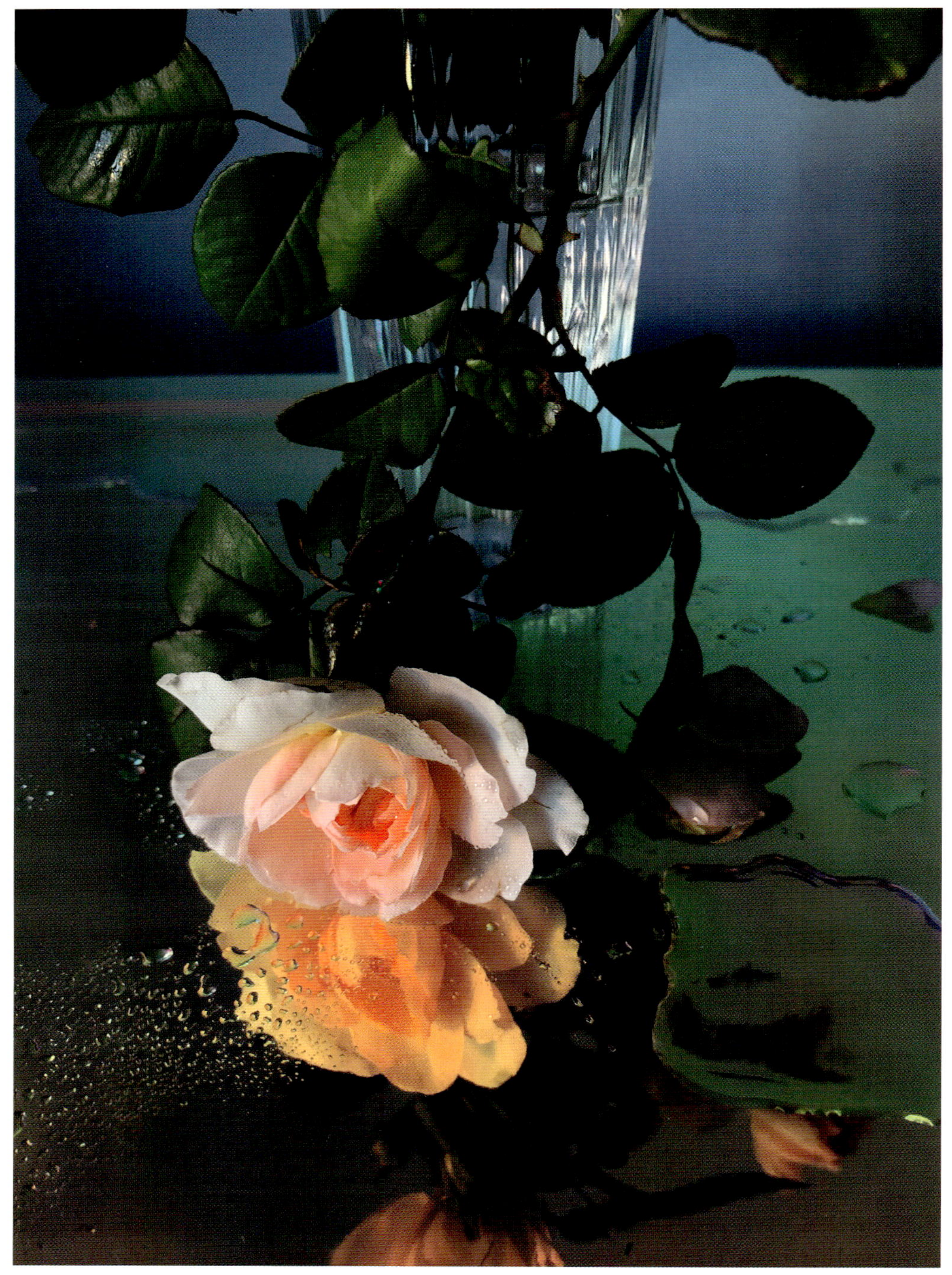

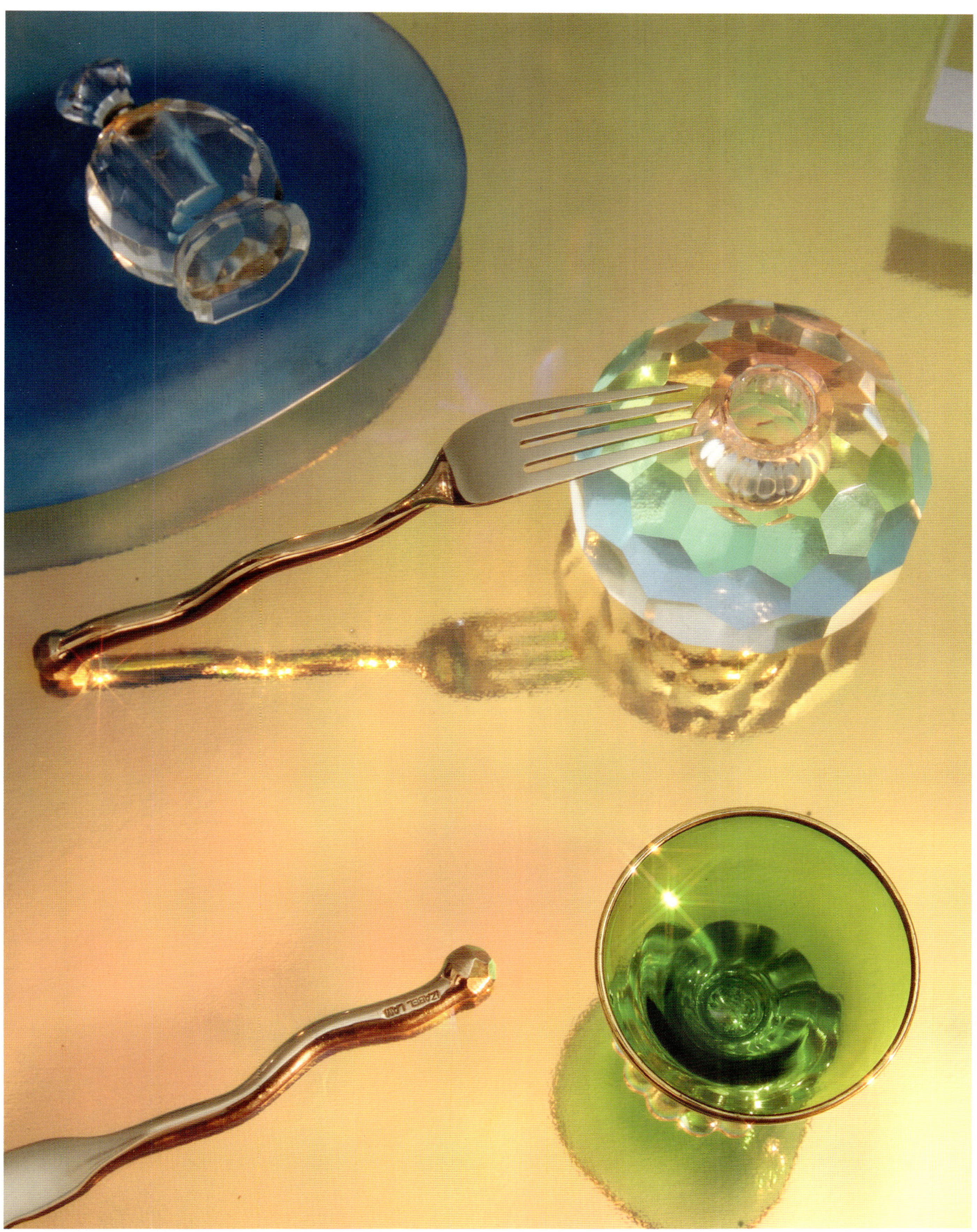

LUSH LIFE

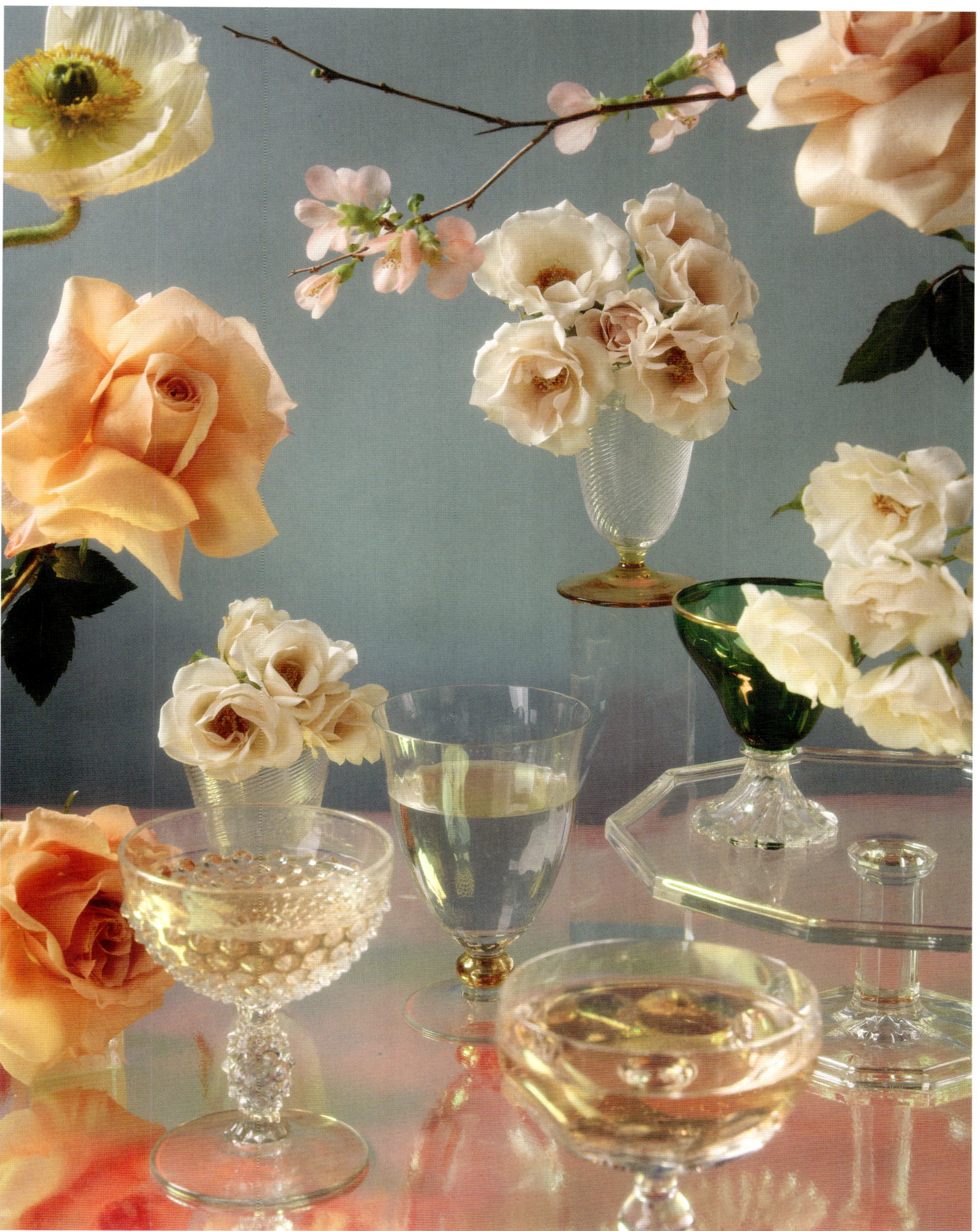

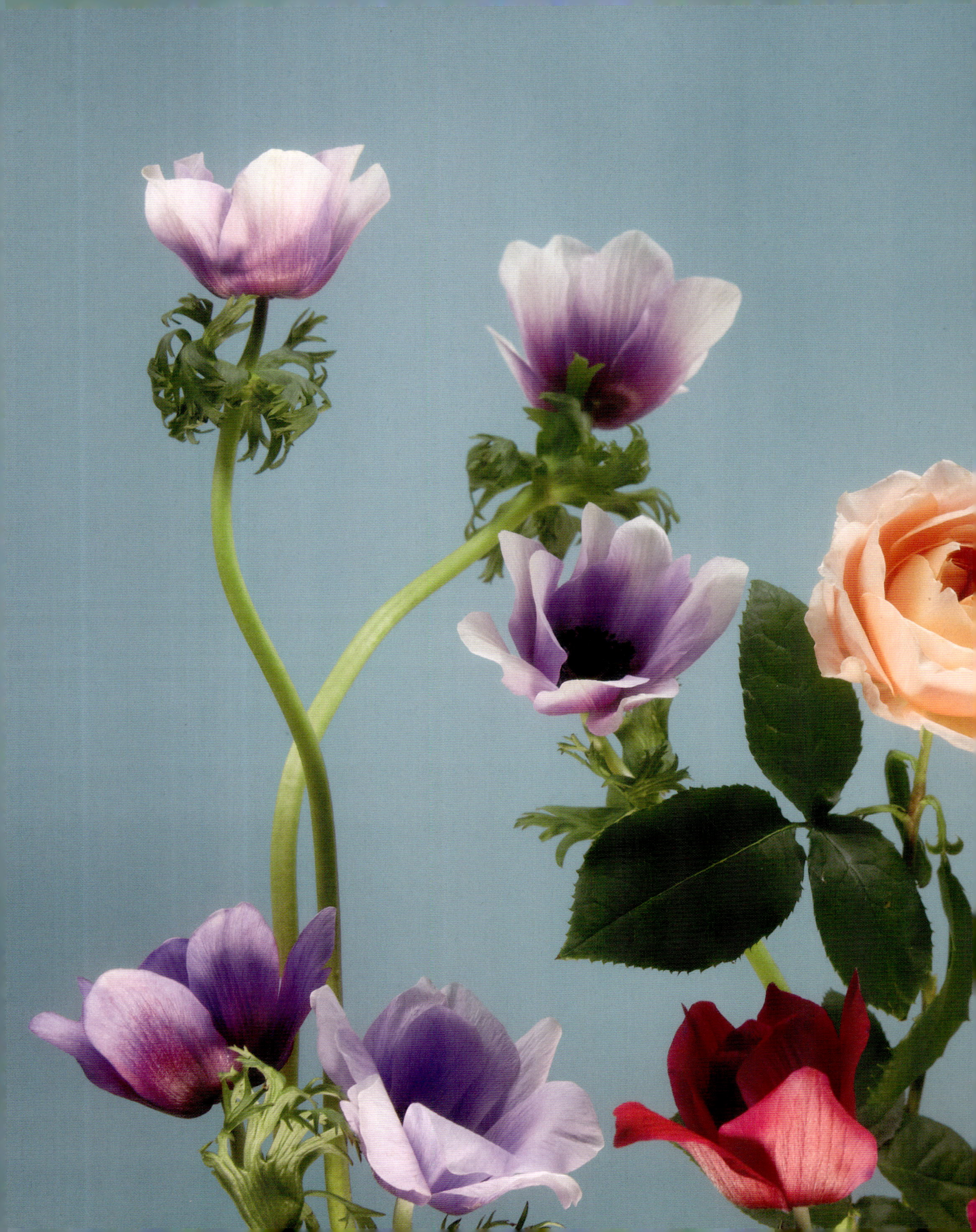

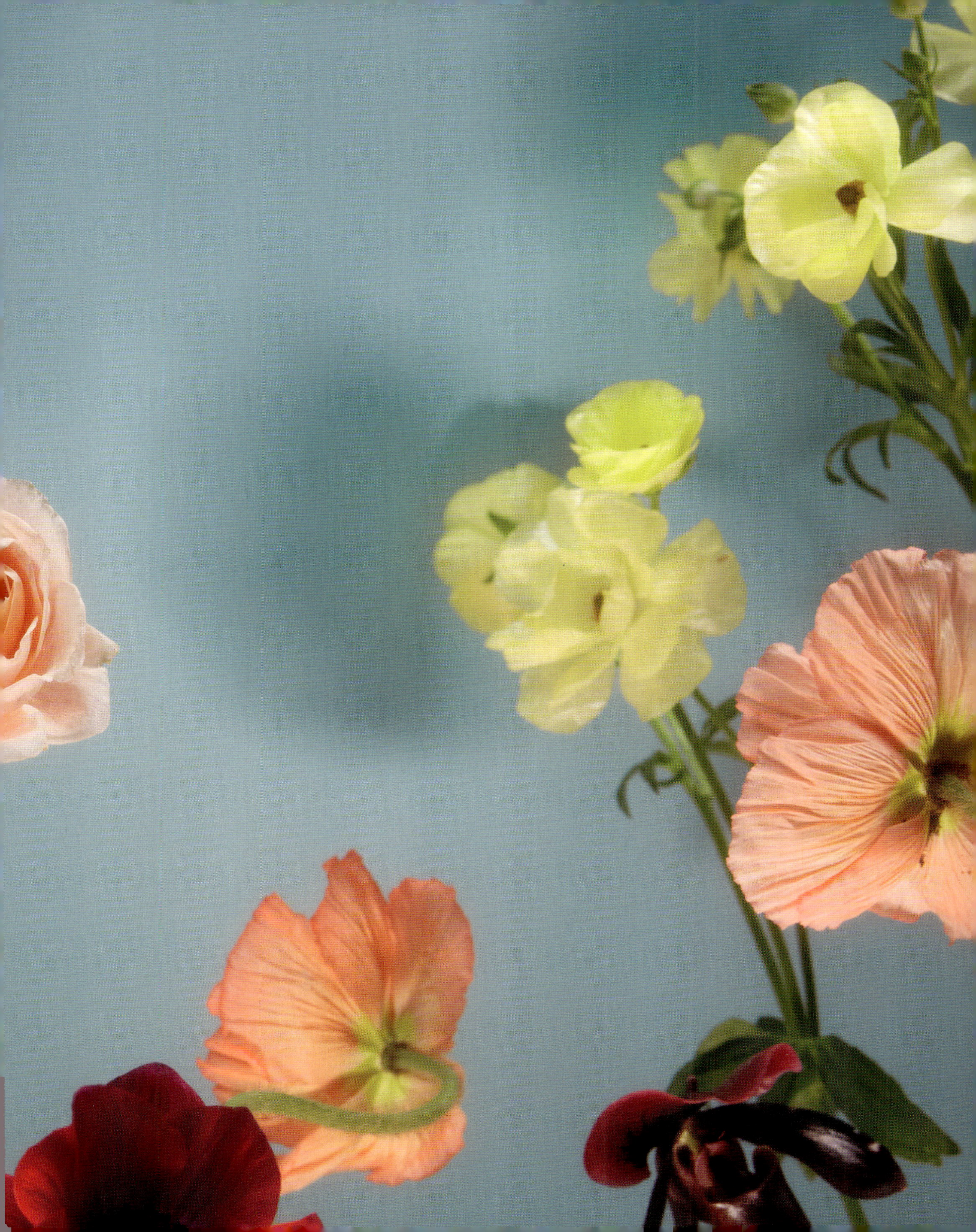

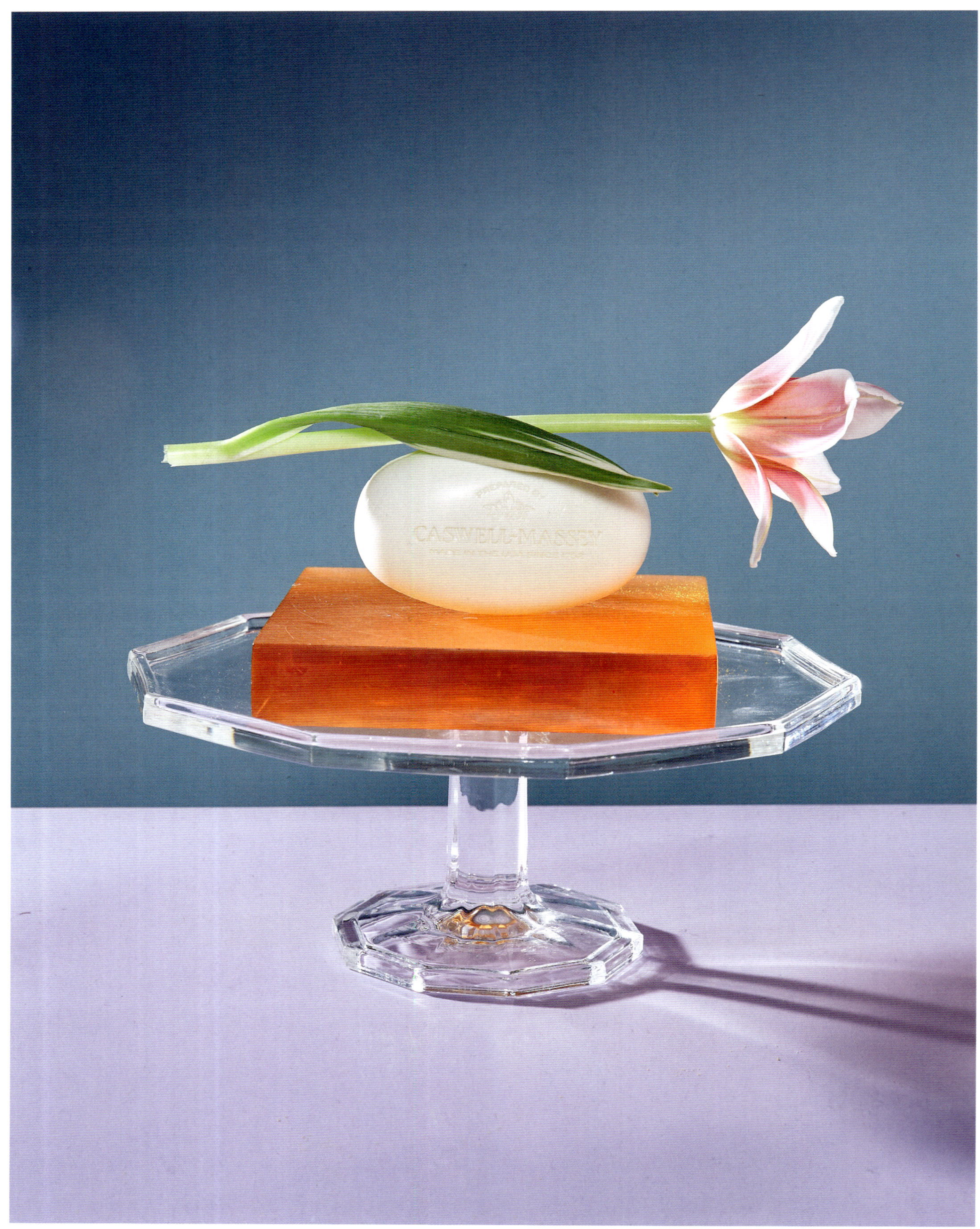
CASWELL-MASSEY

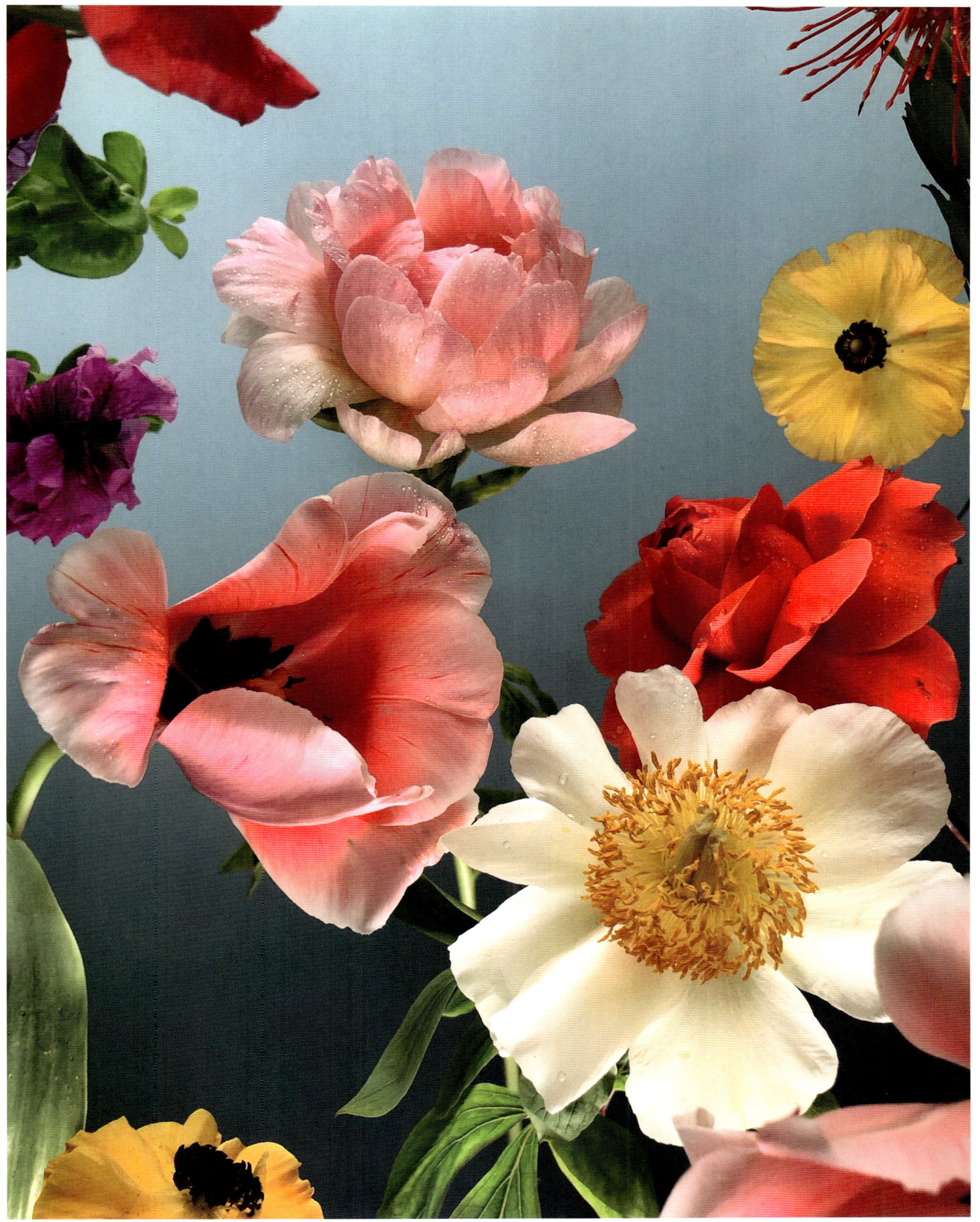

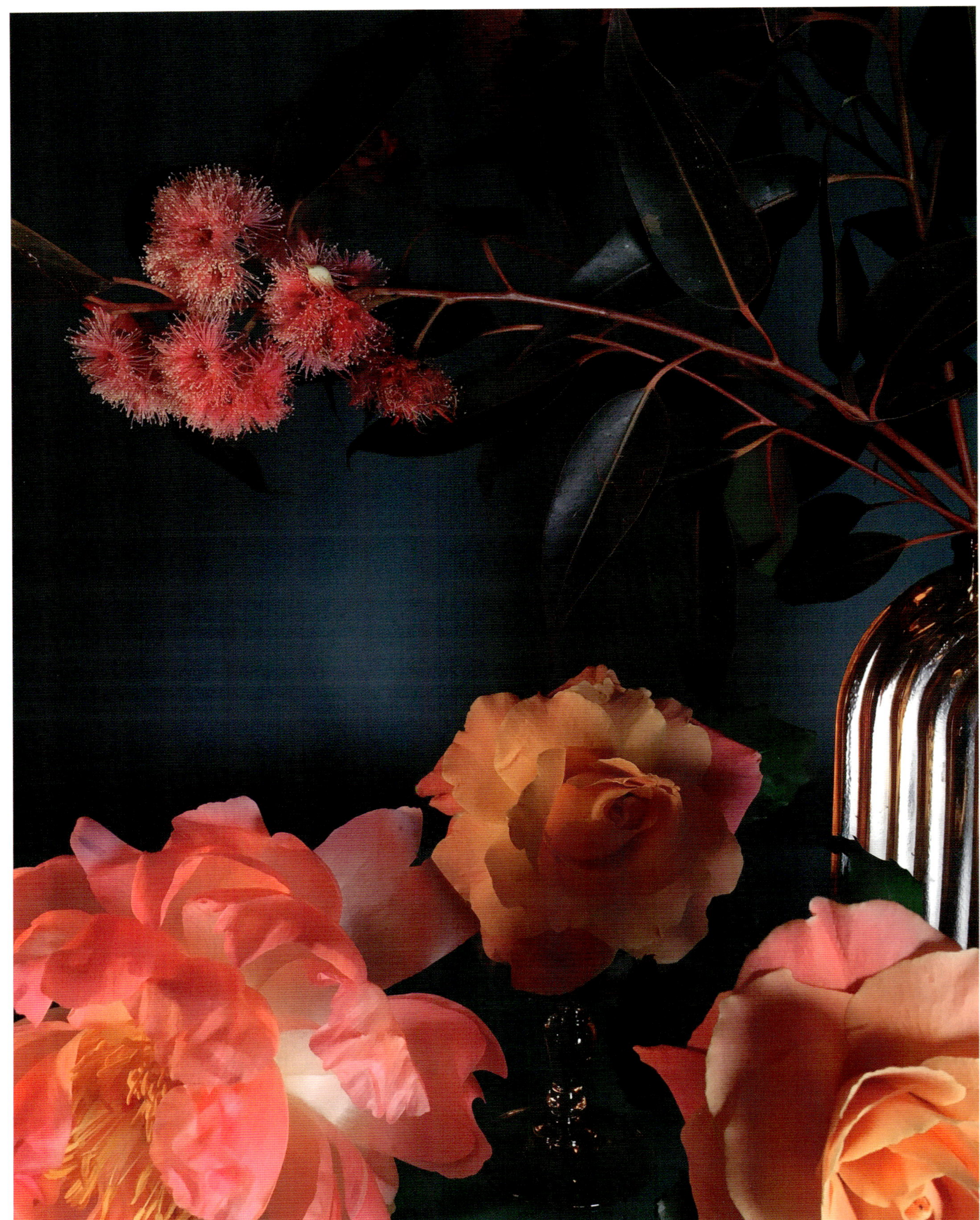

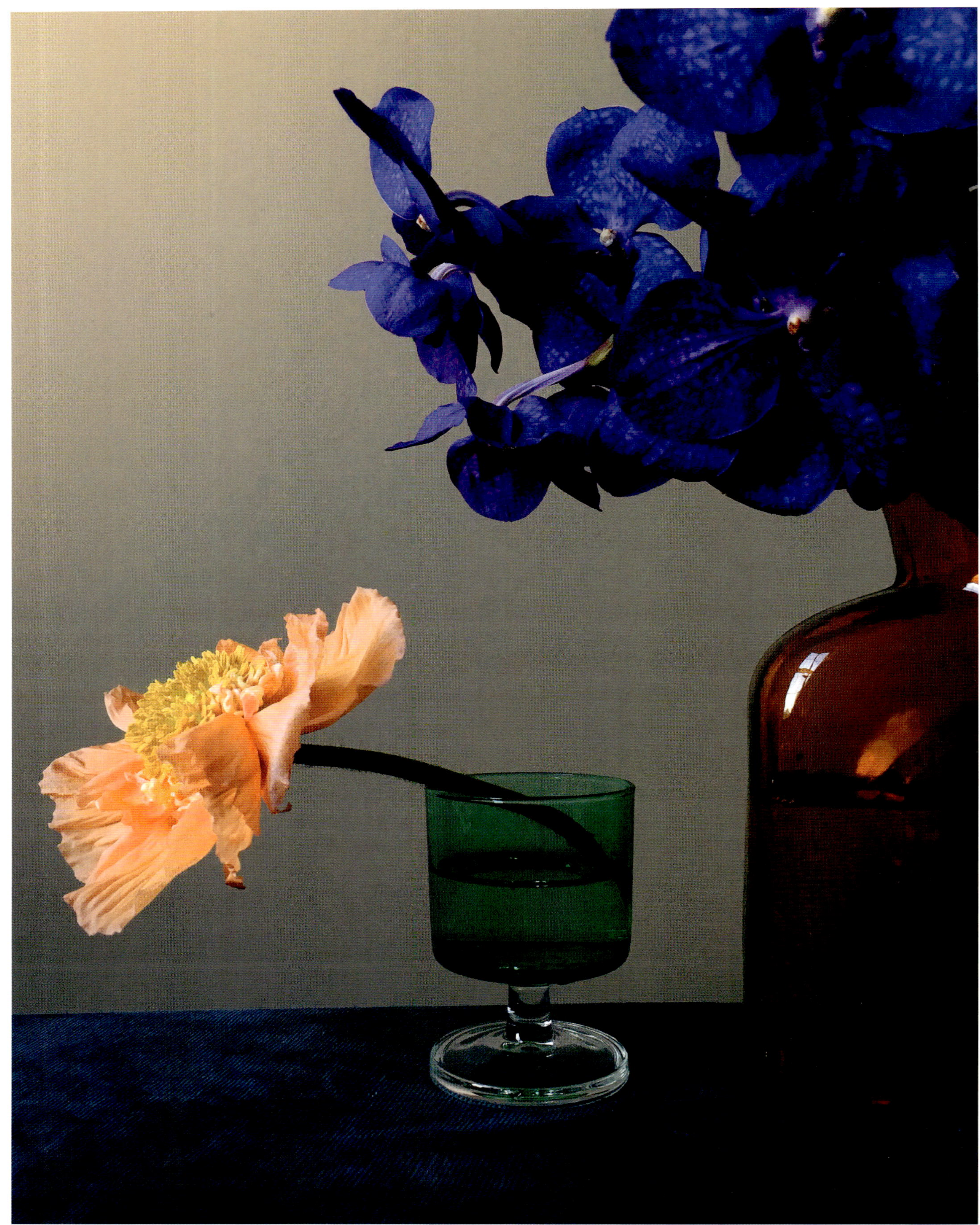

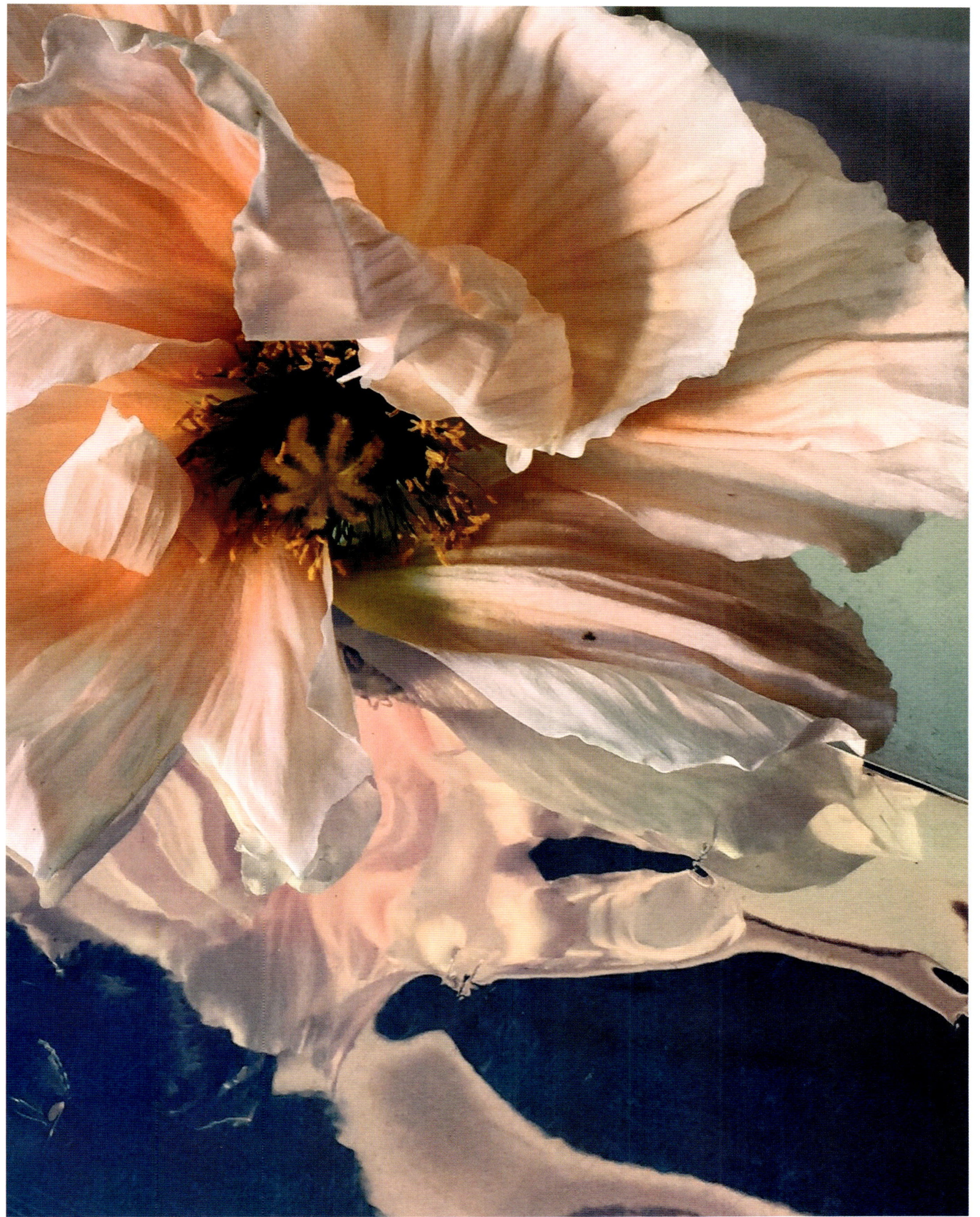

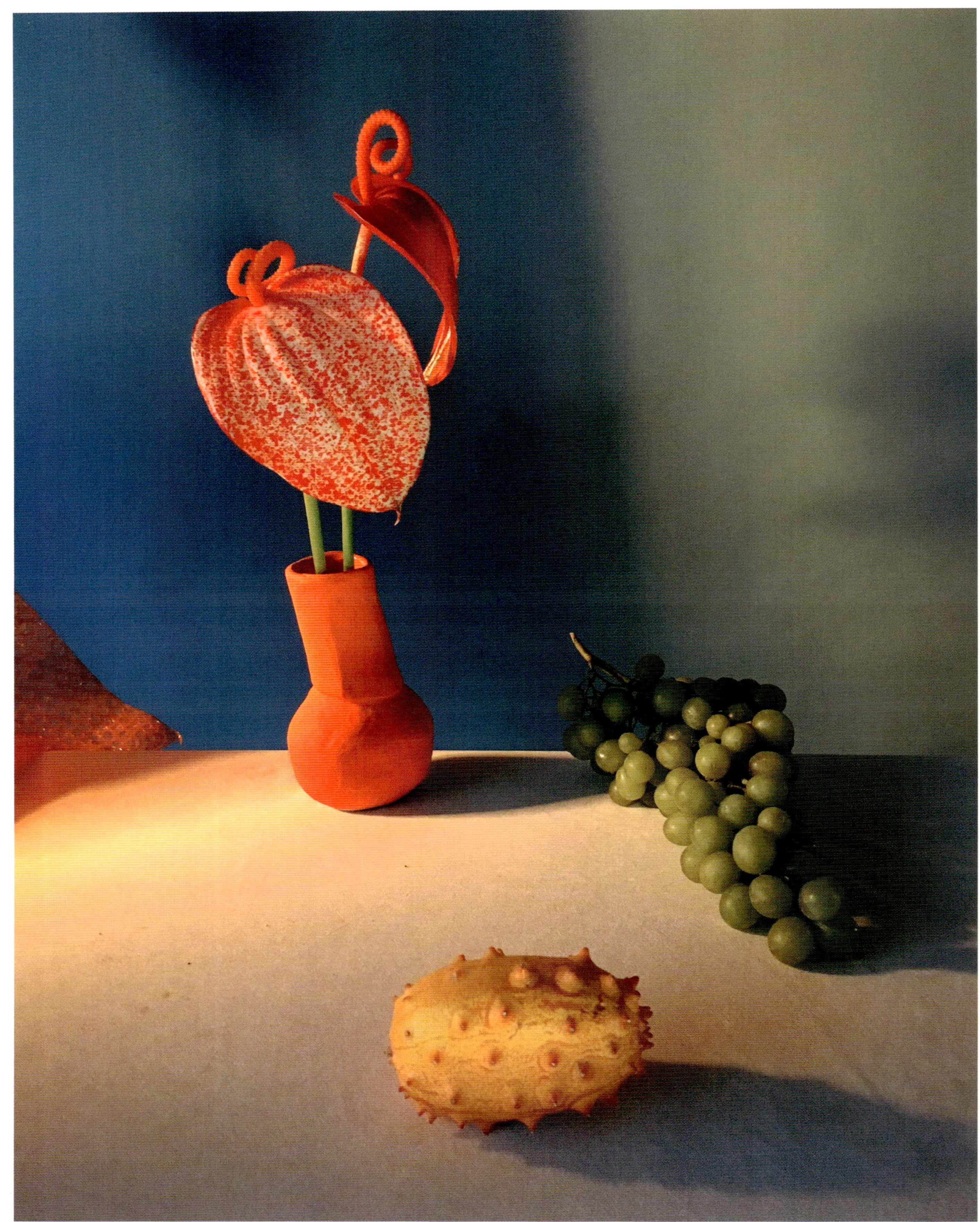

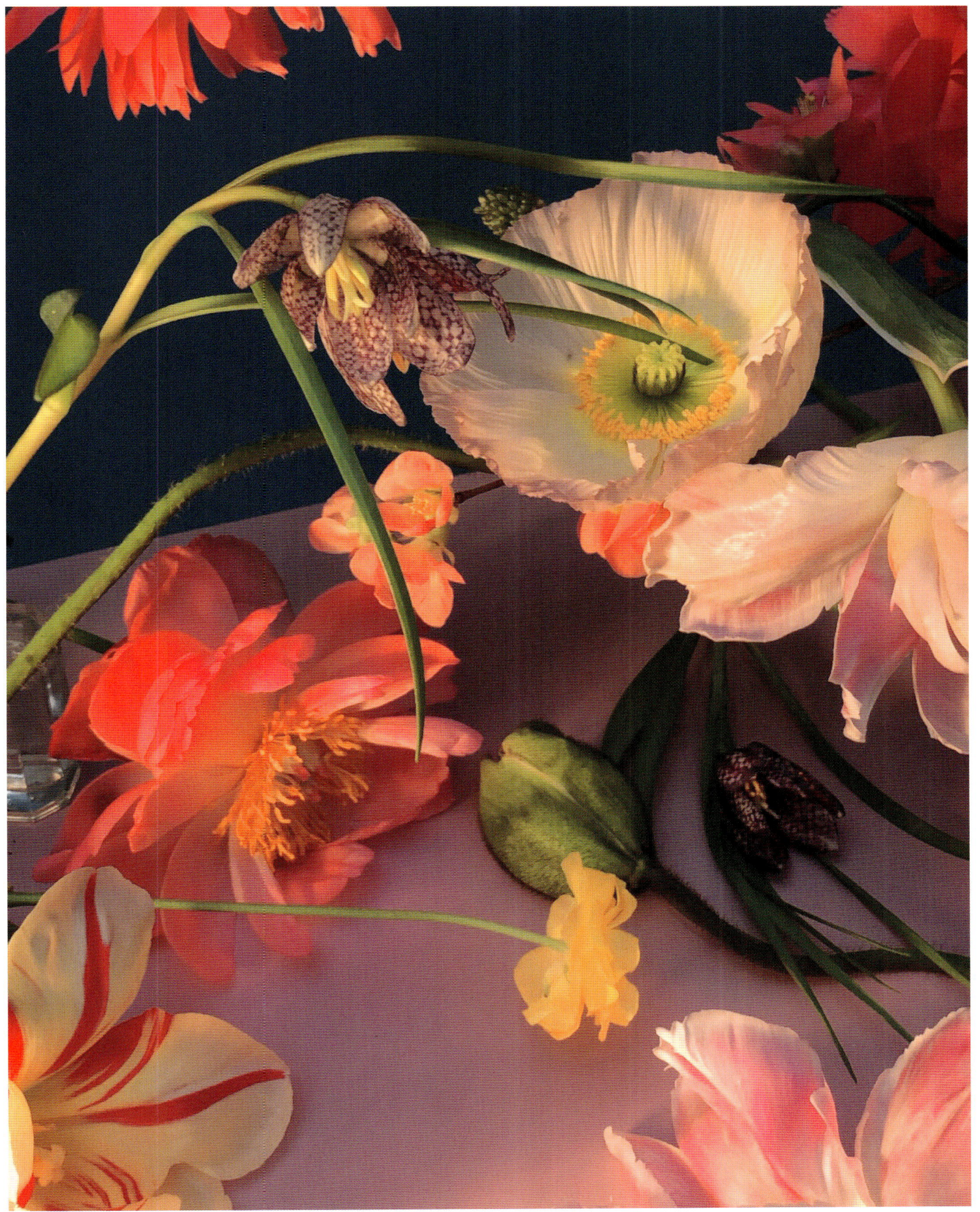

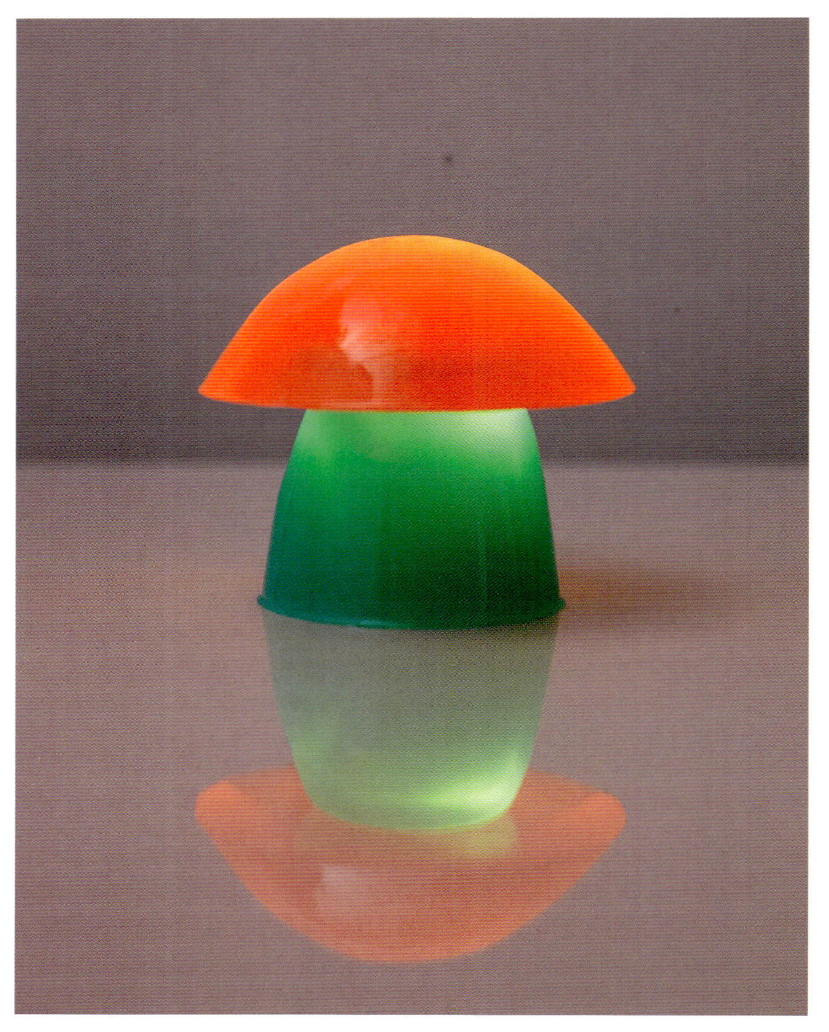

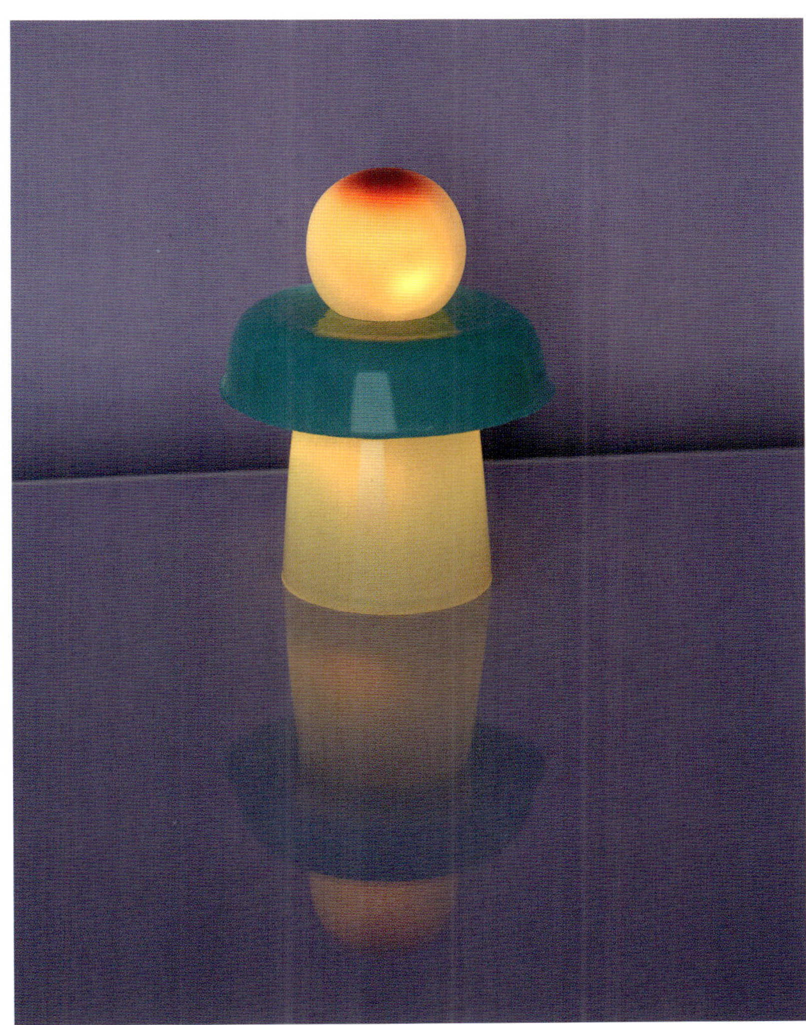

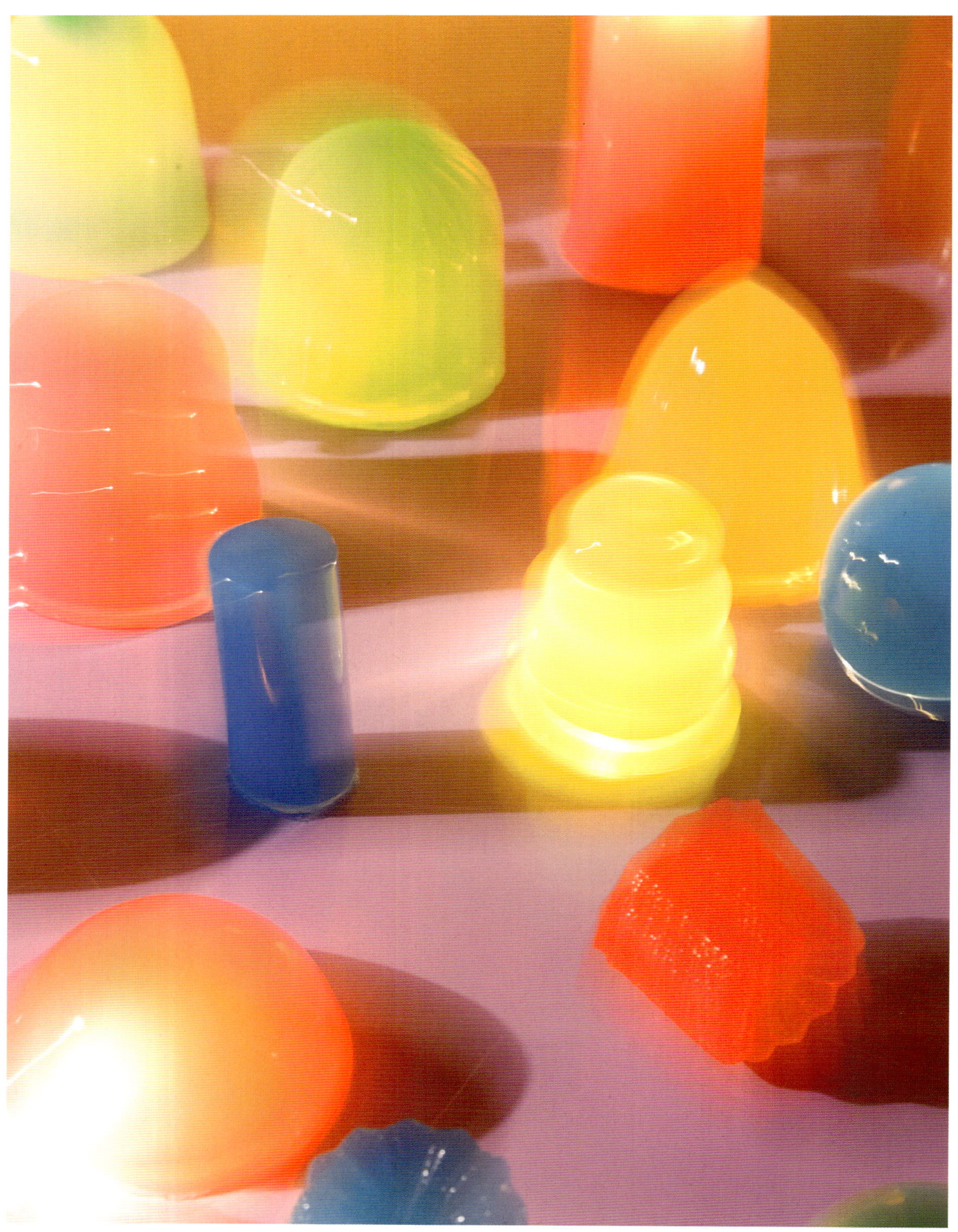

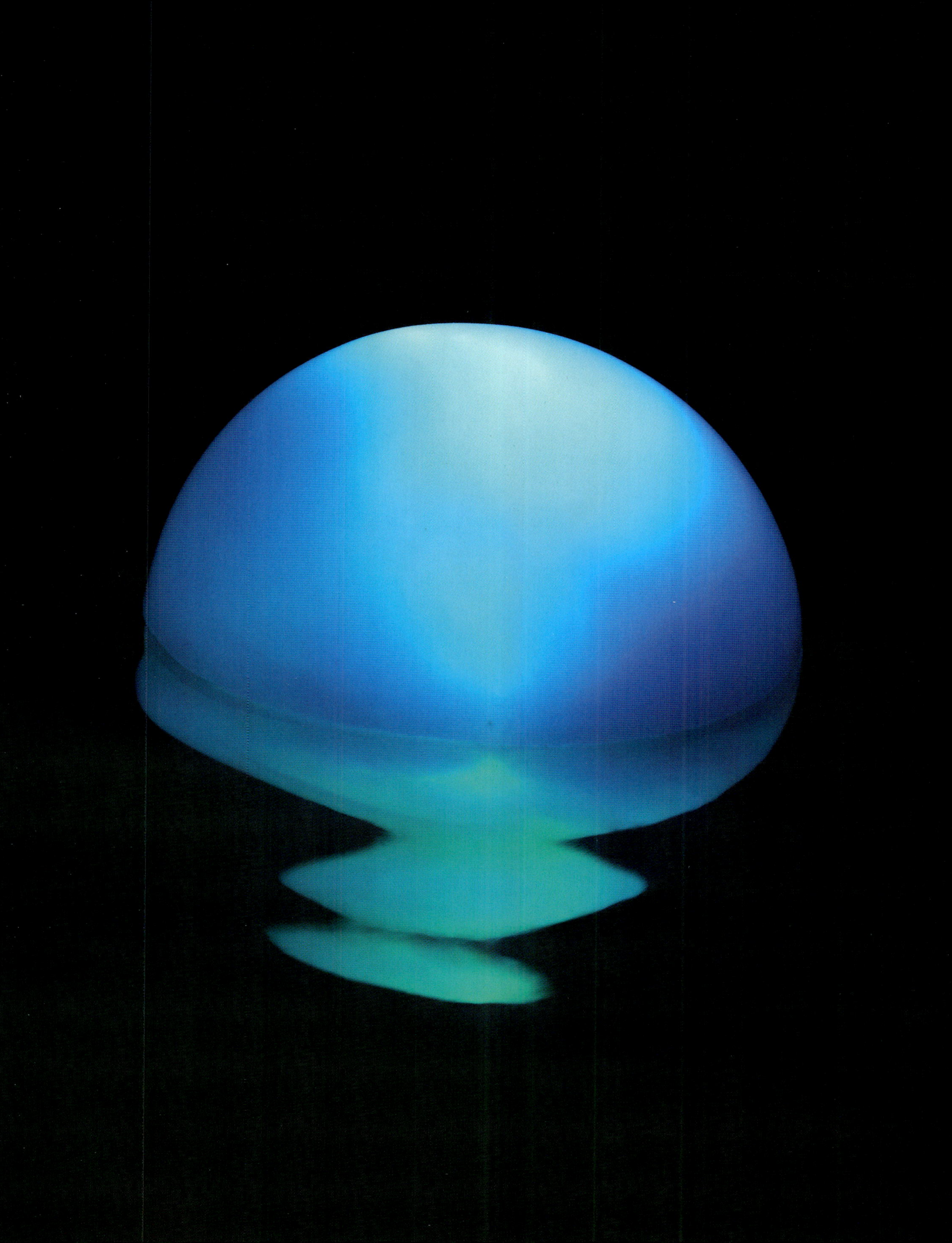

OLD FLAME

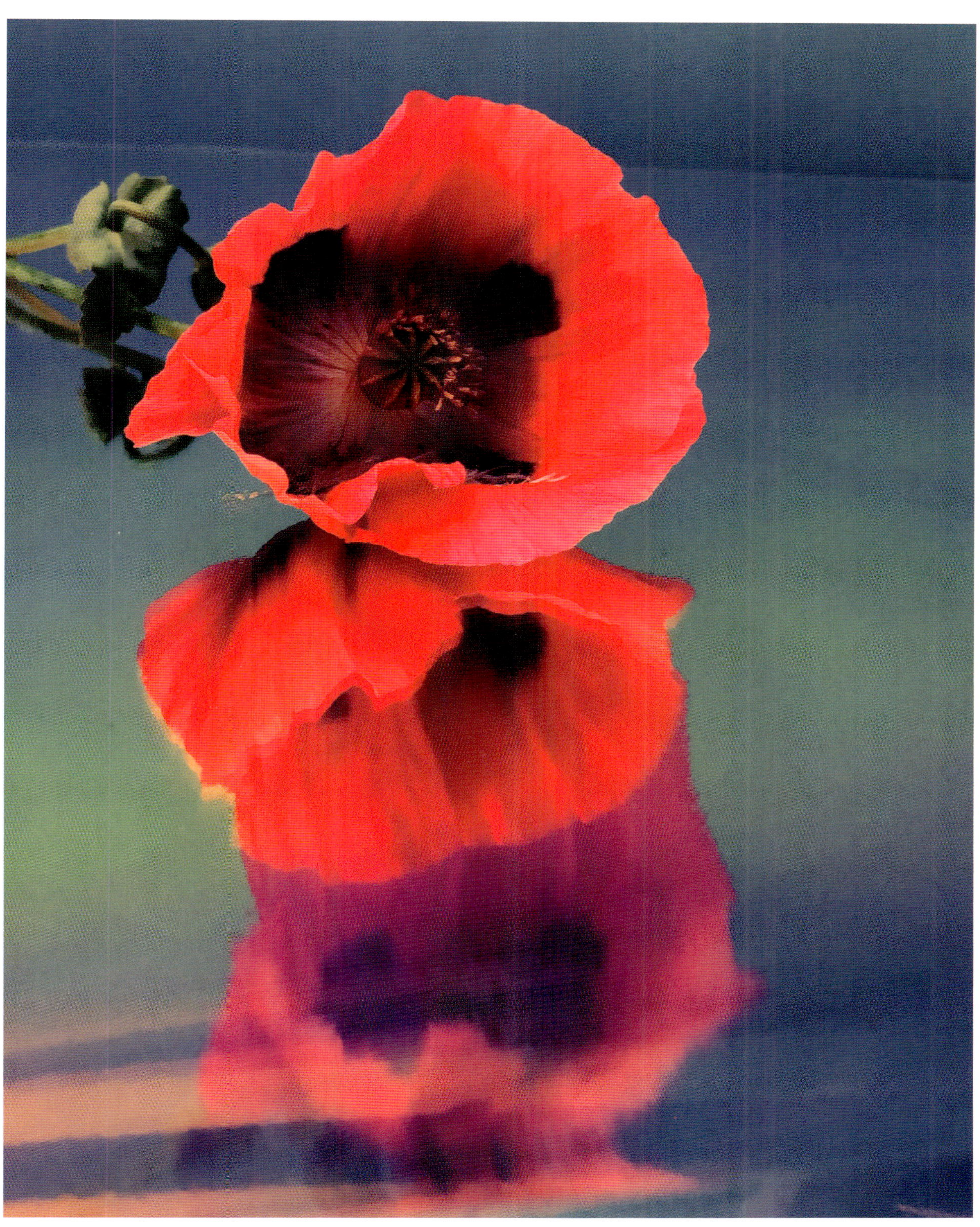

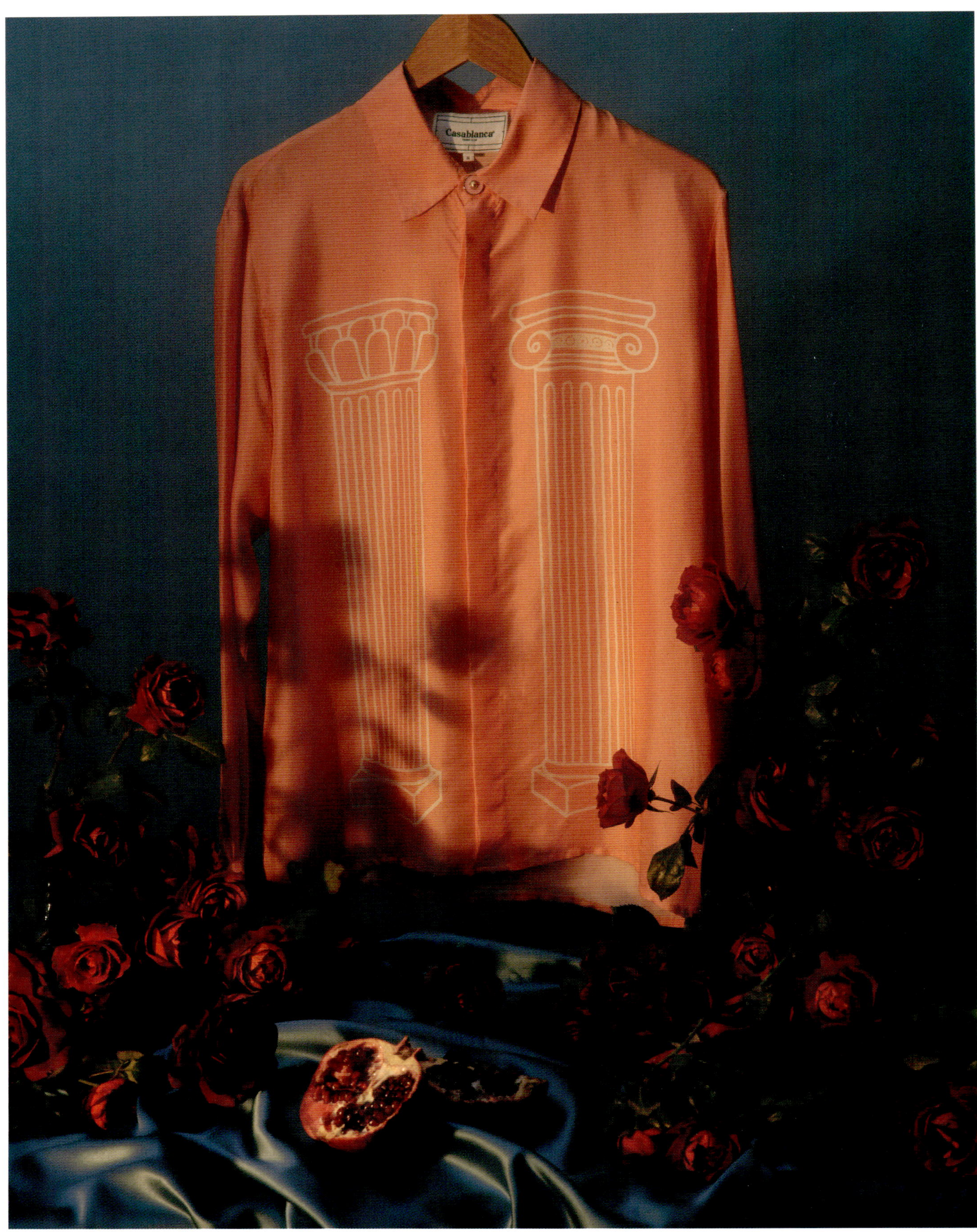

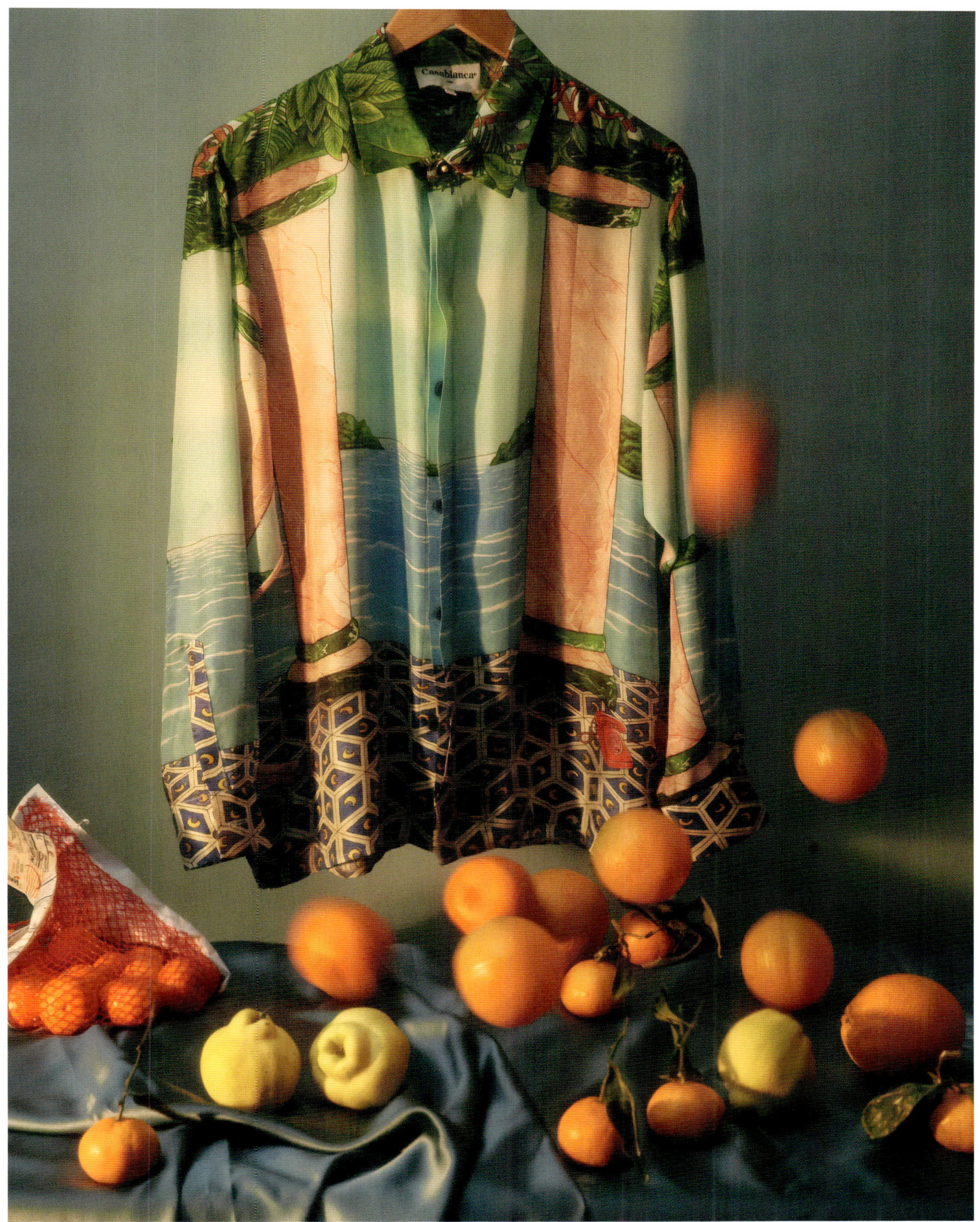
Casablanca

JUNGLE

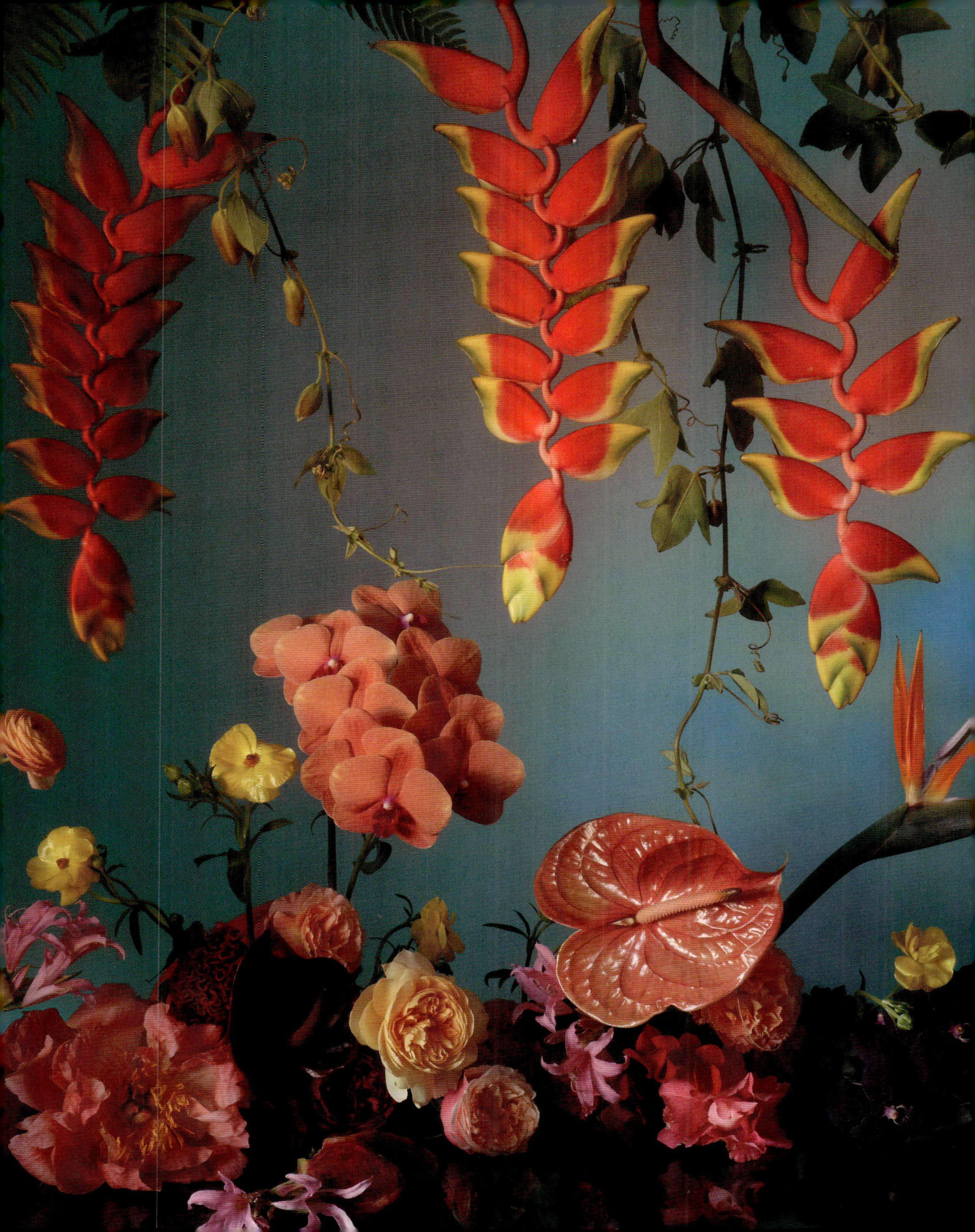

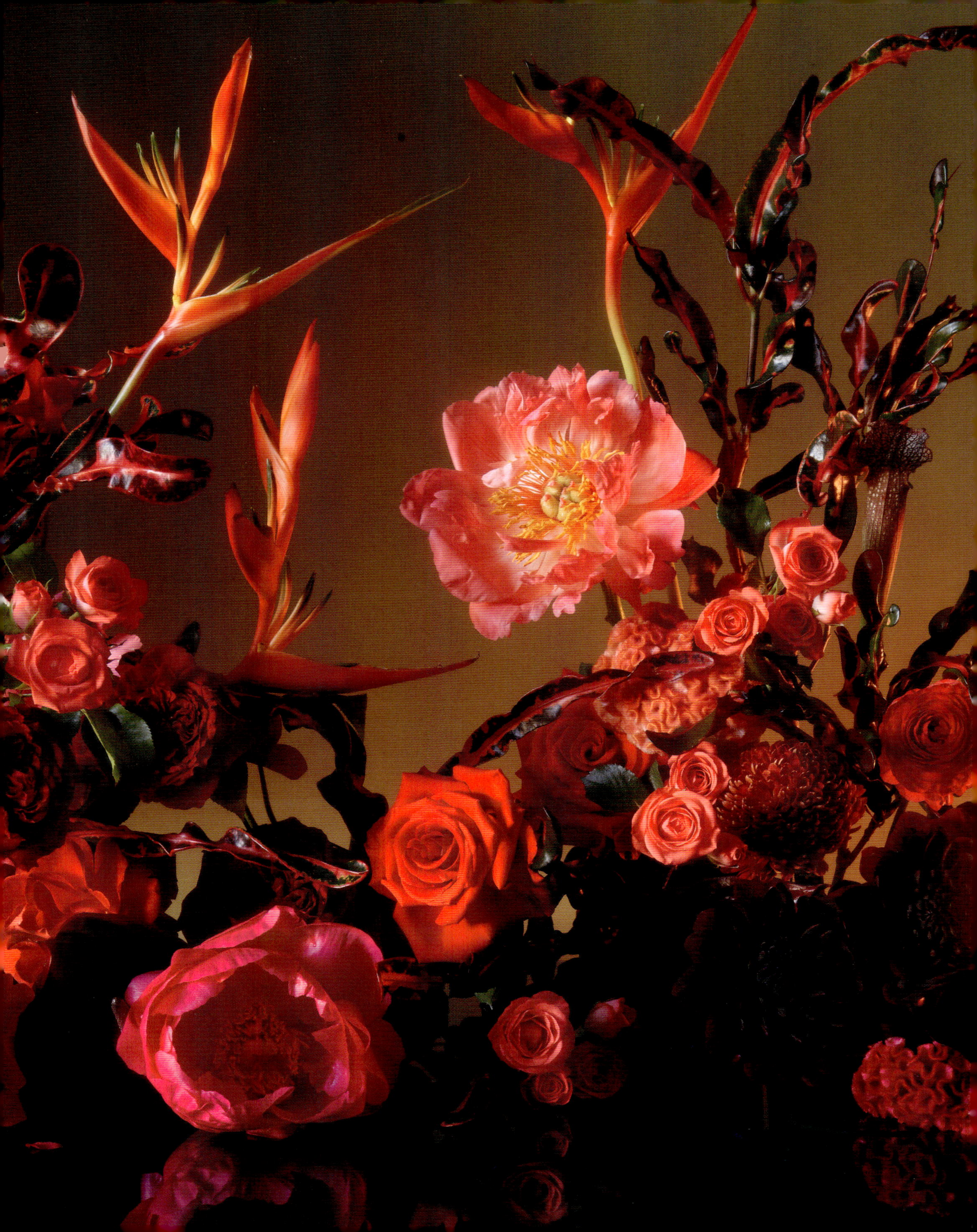

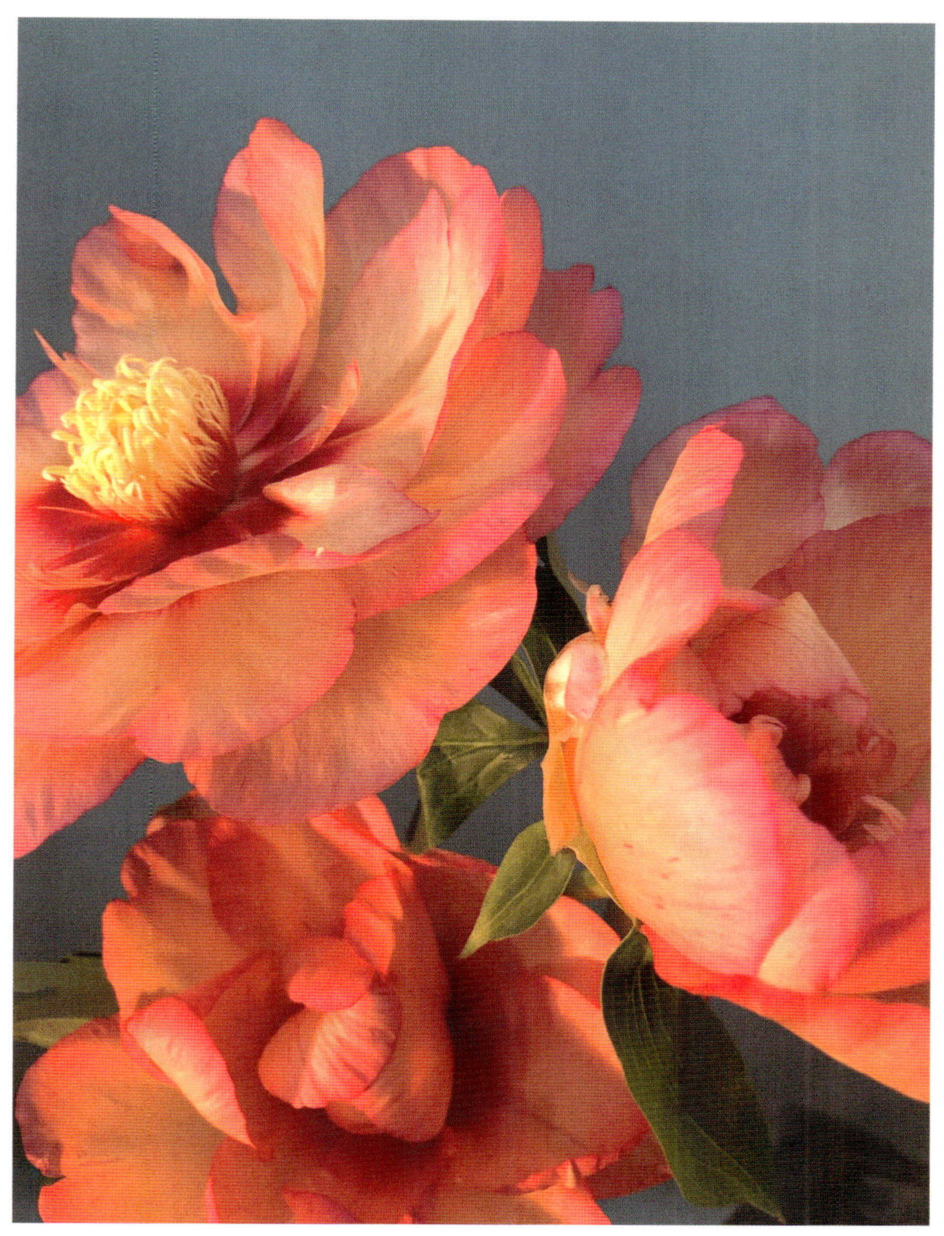

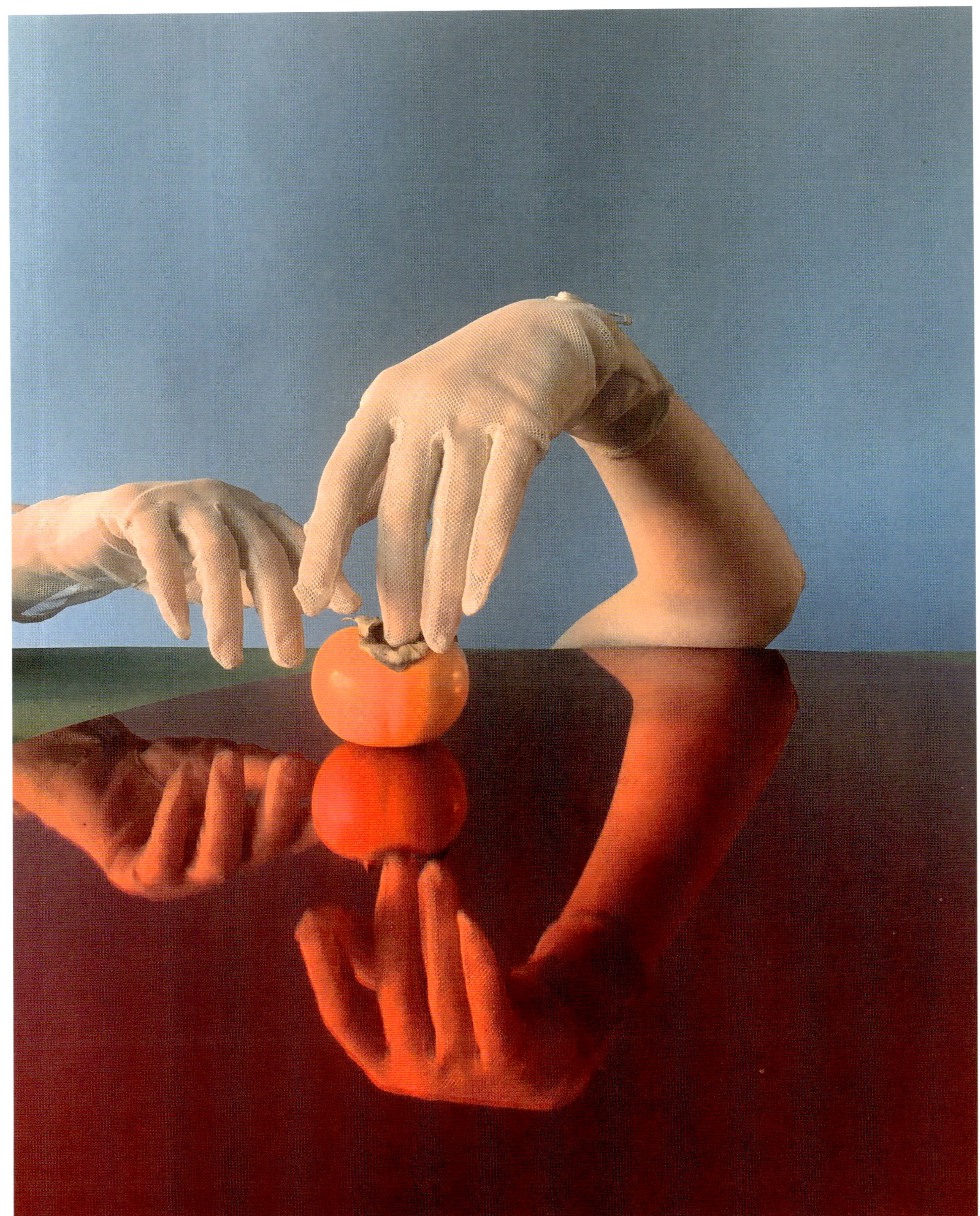

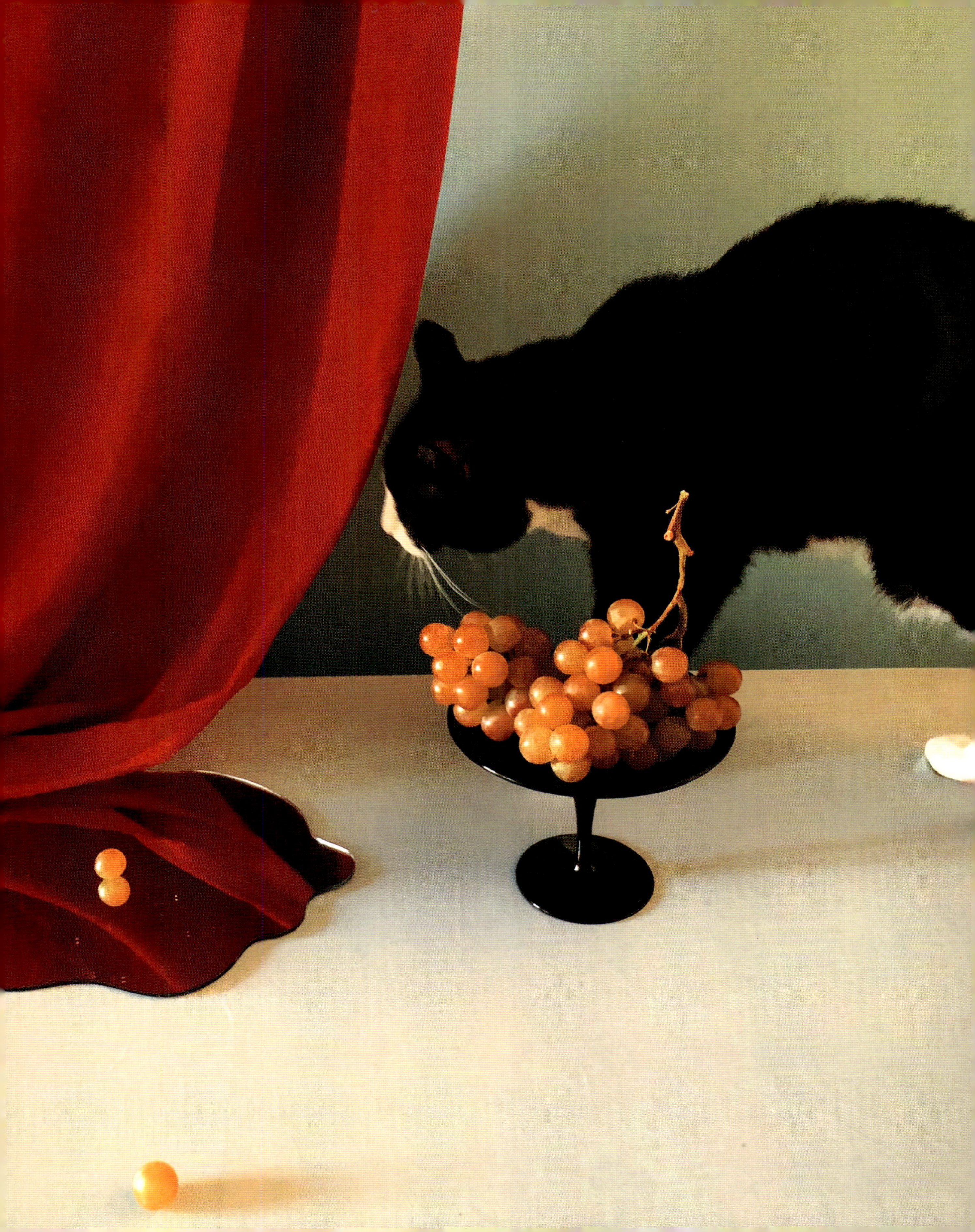

COME TO MY FEAST

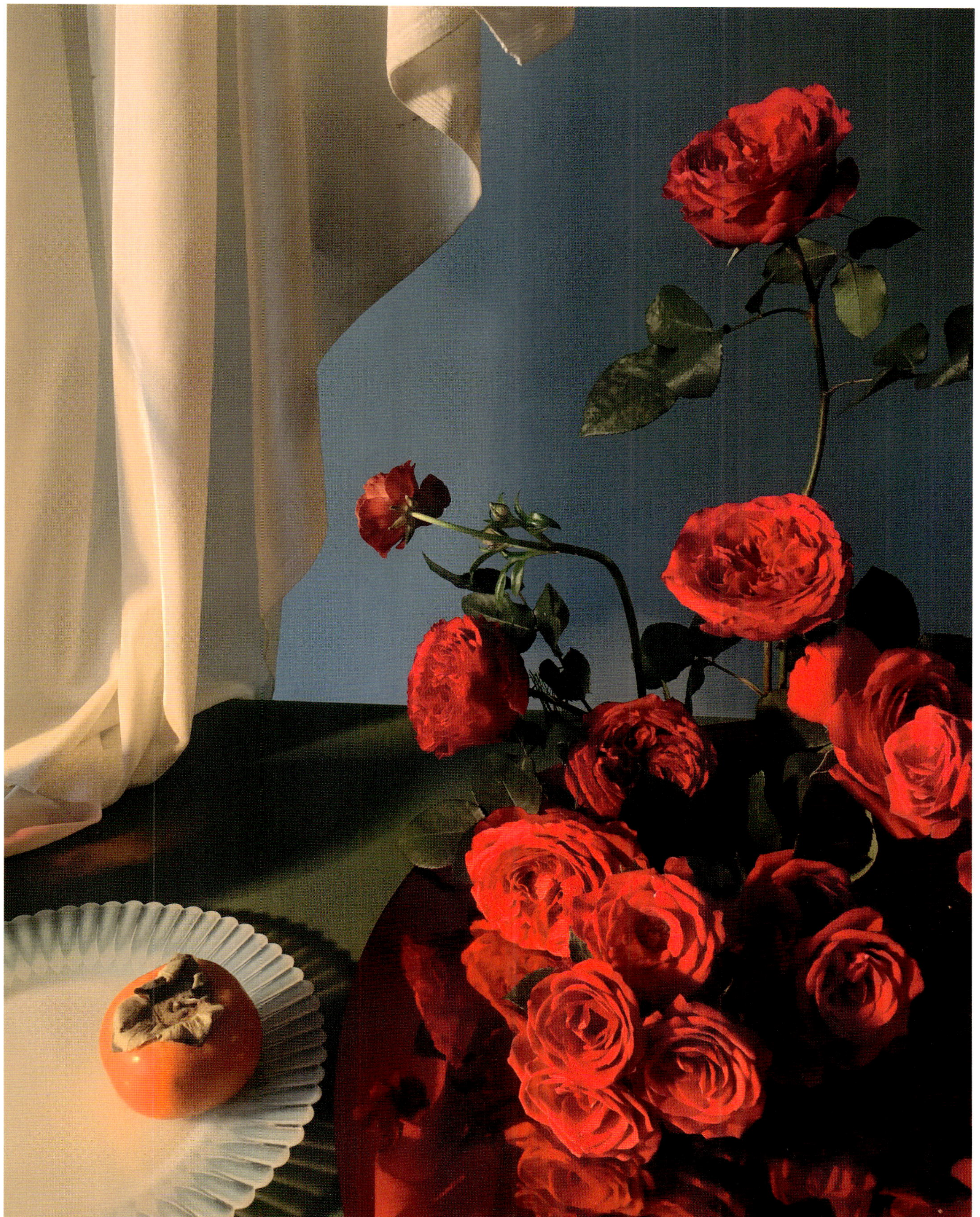

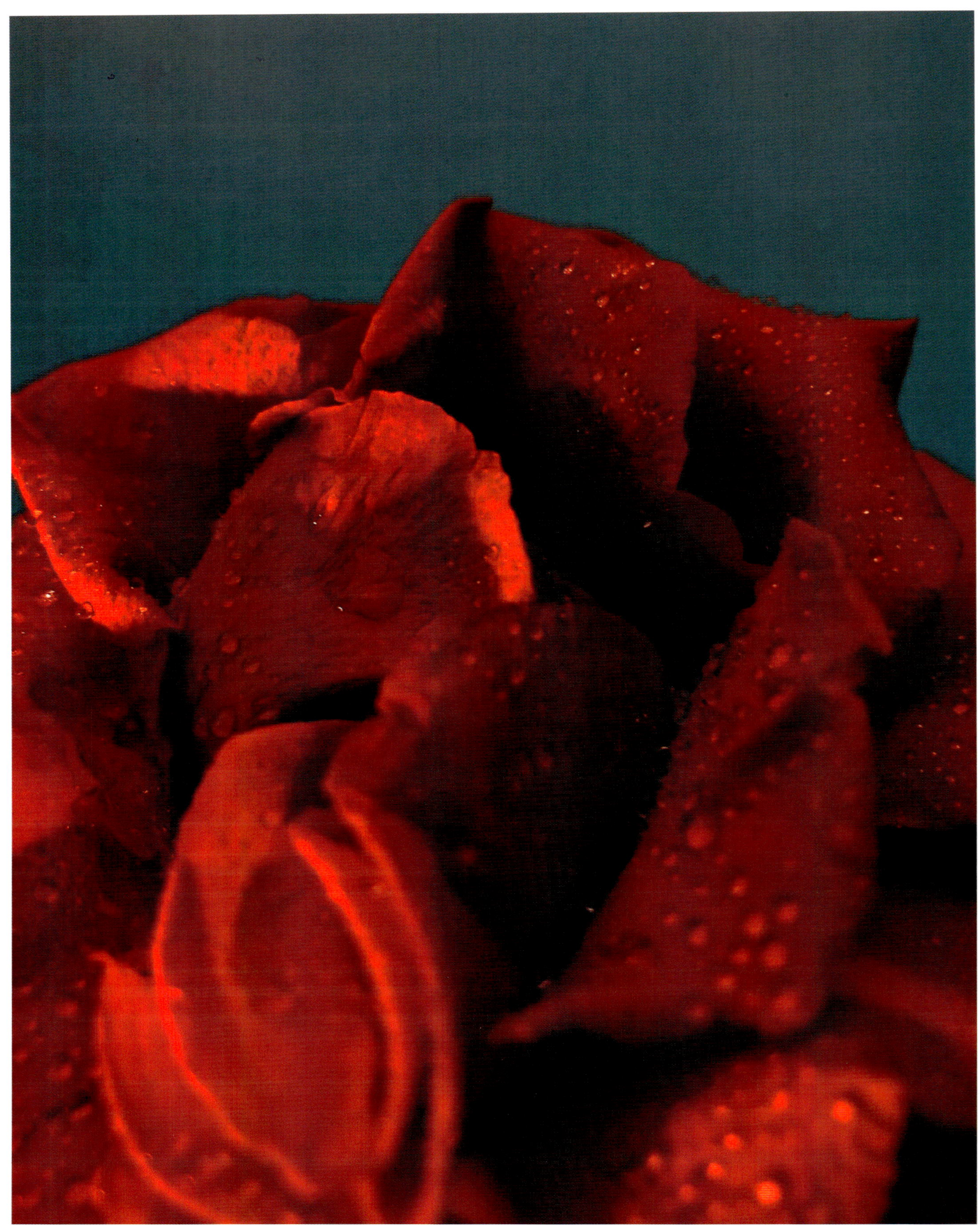

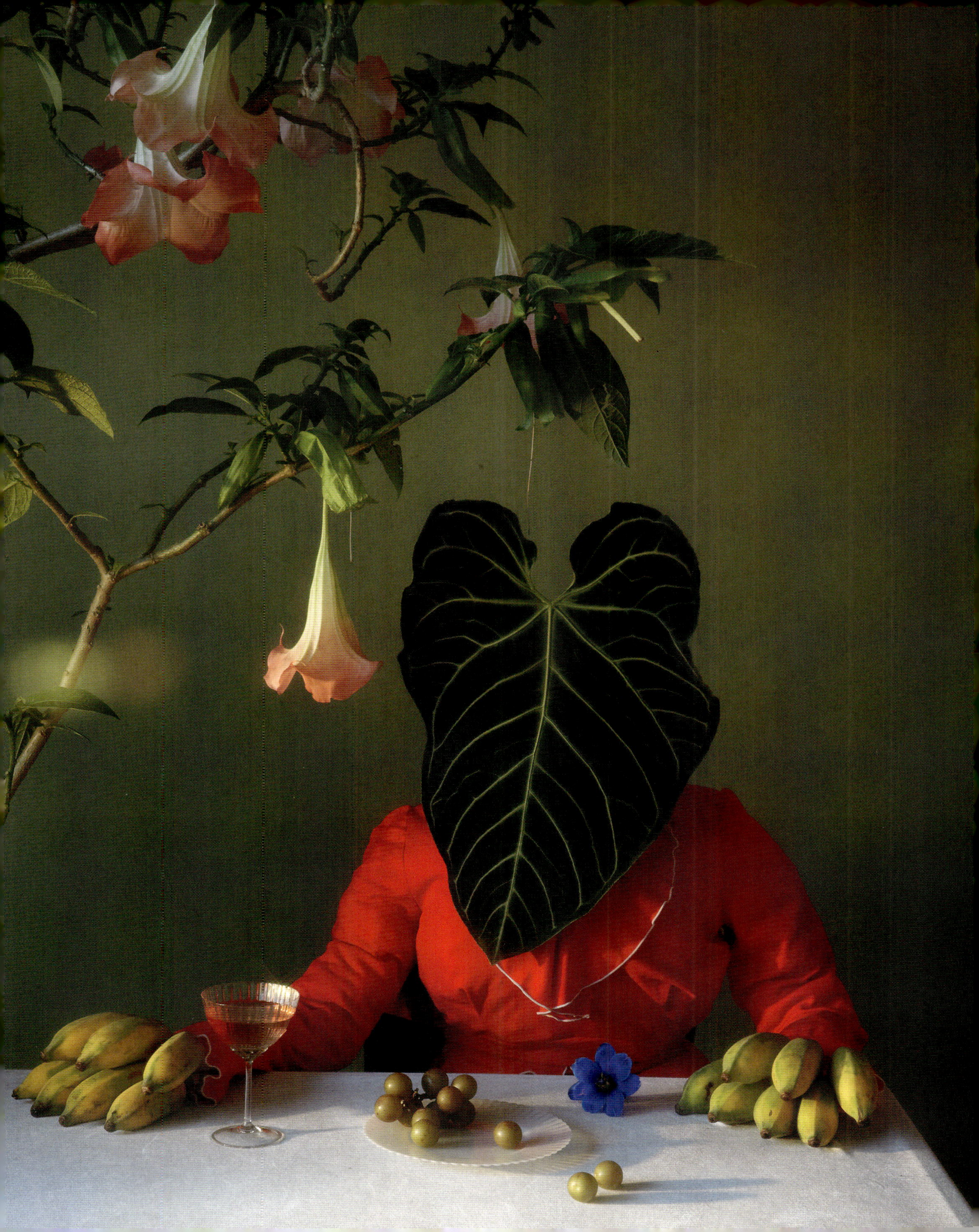

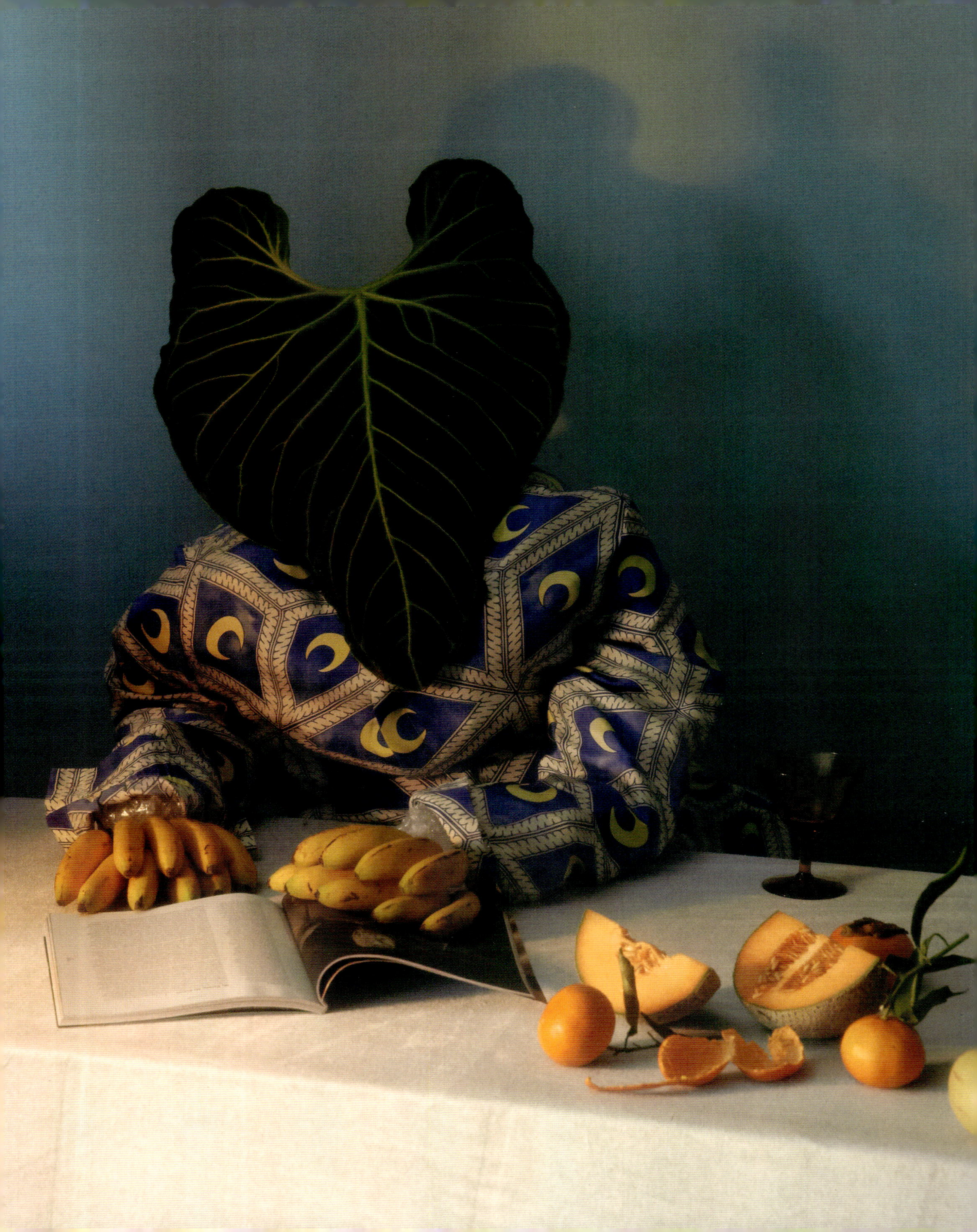

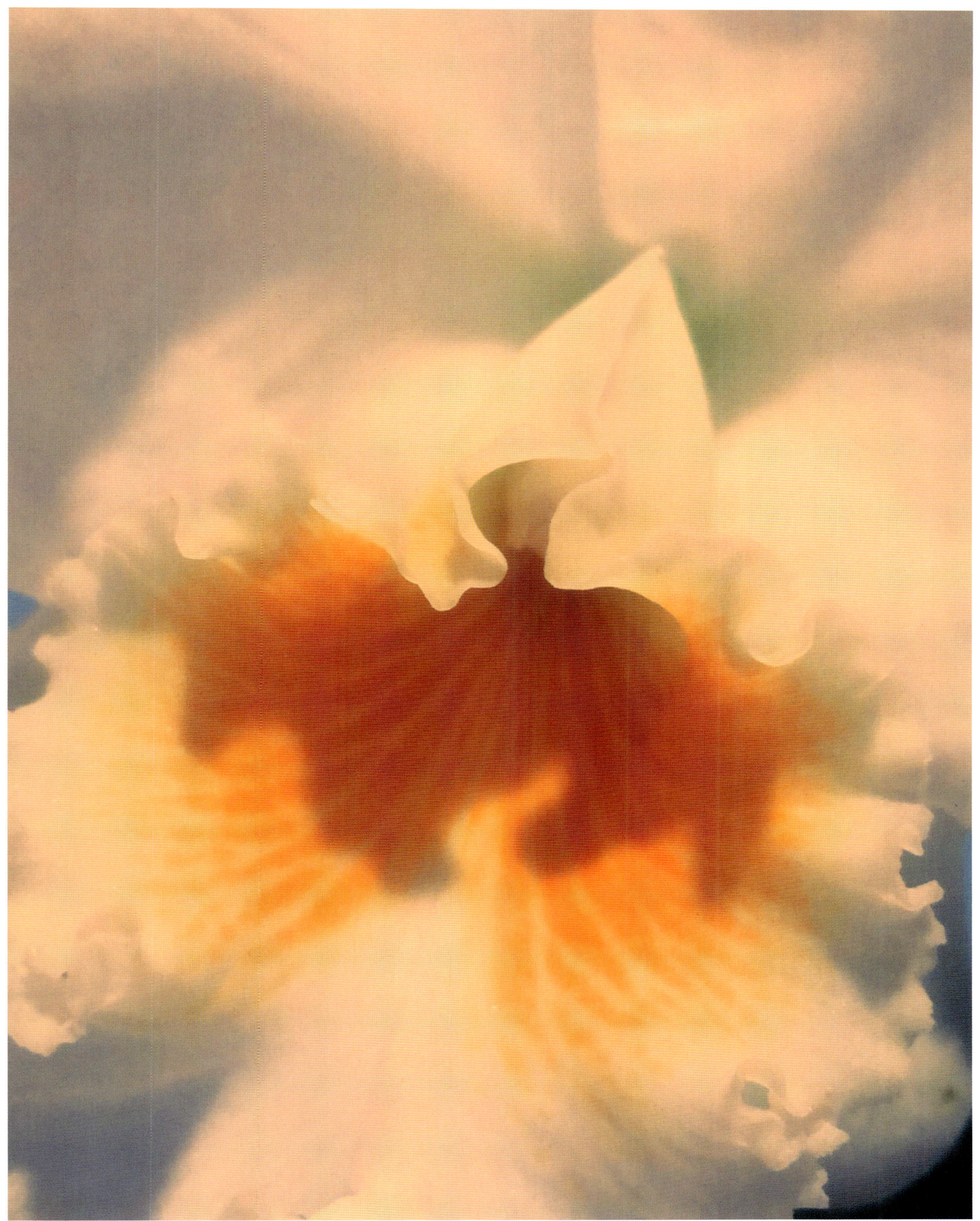

FLOWER POWER

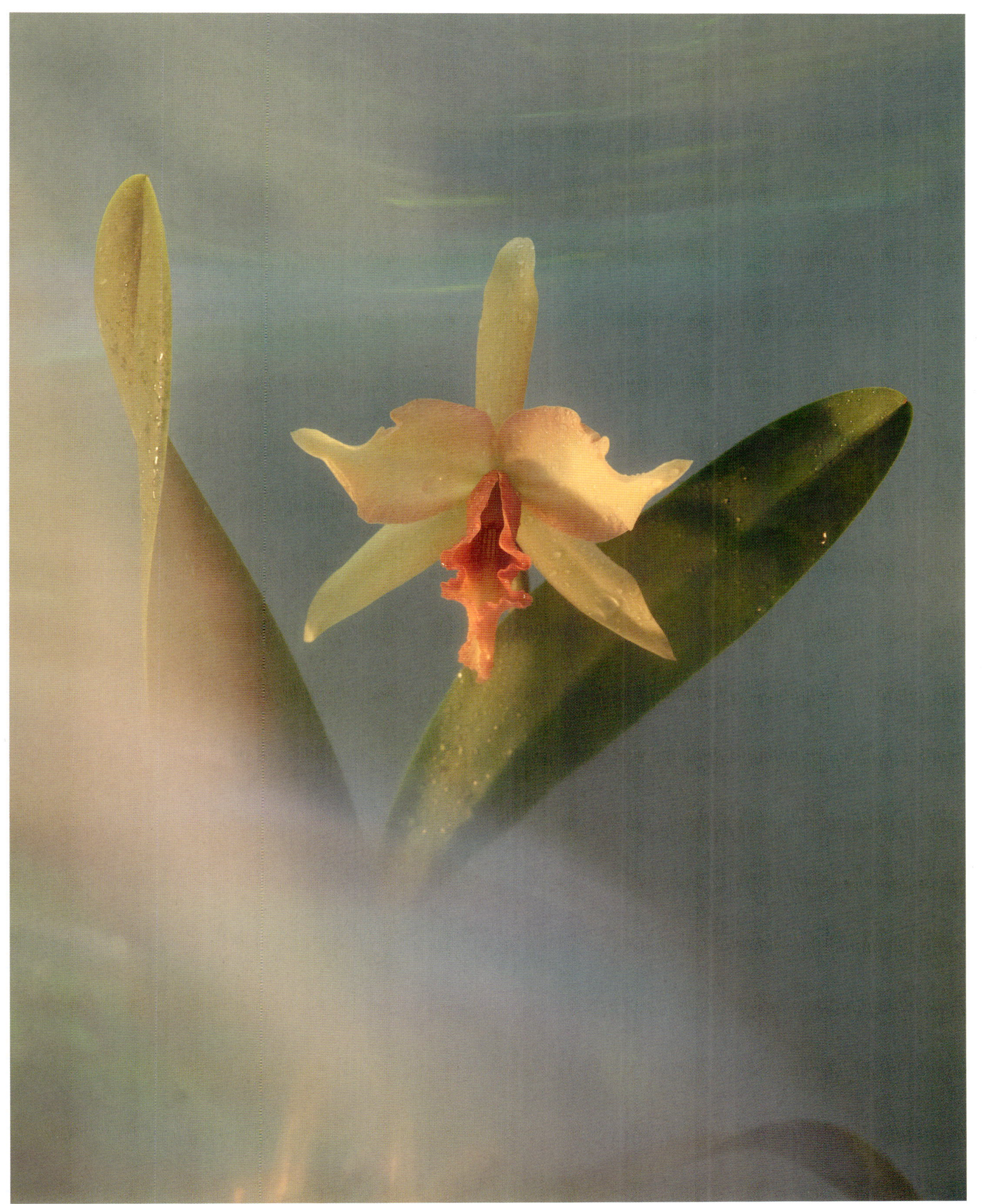

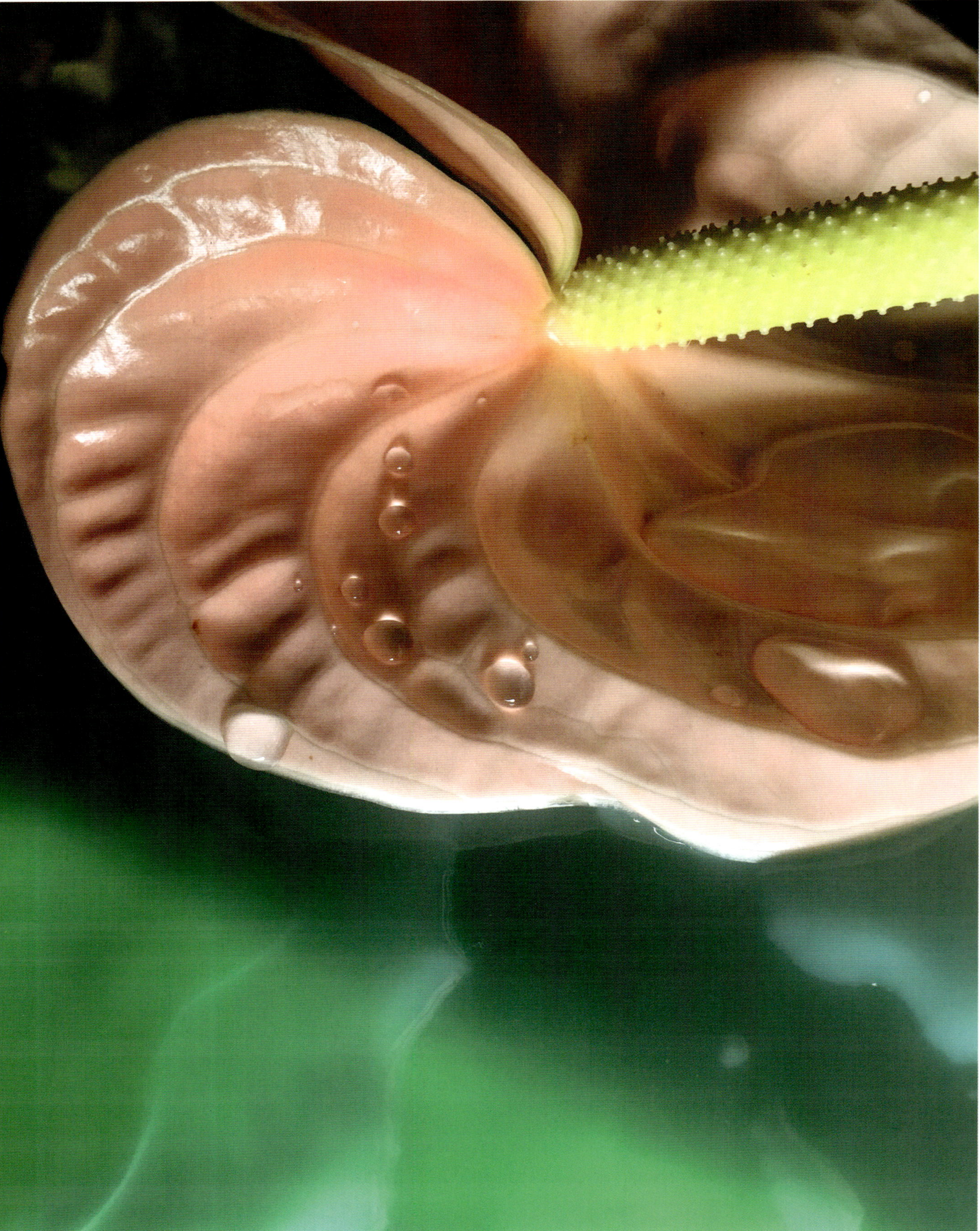

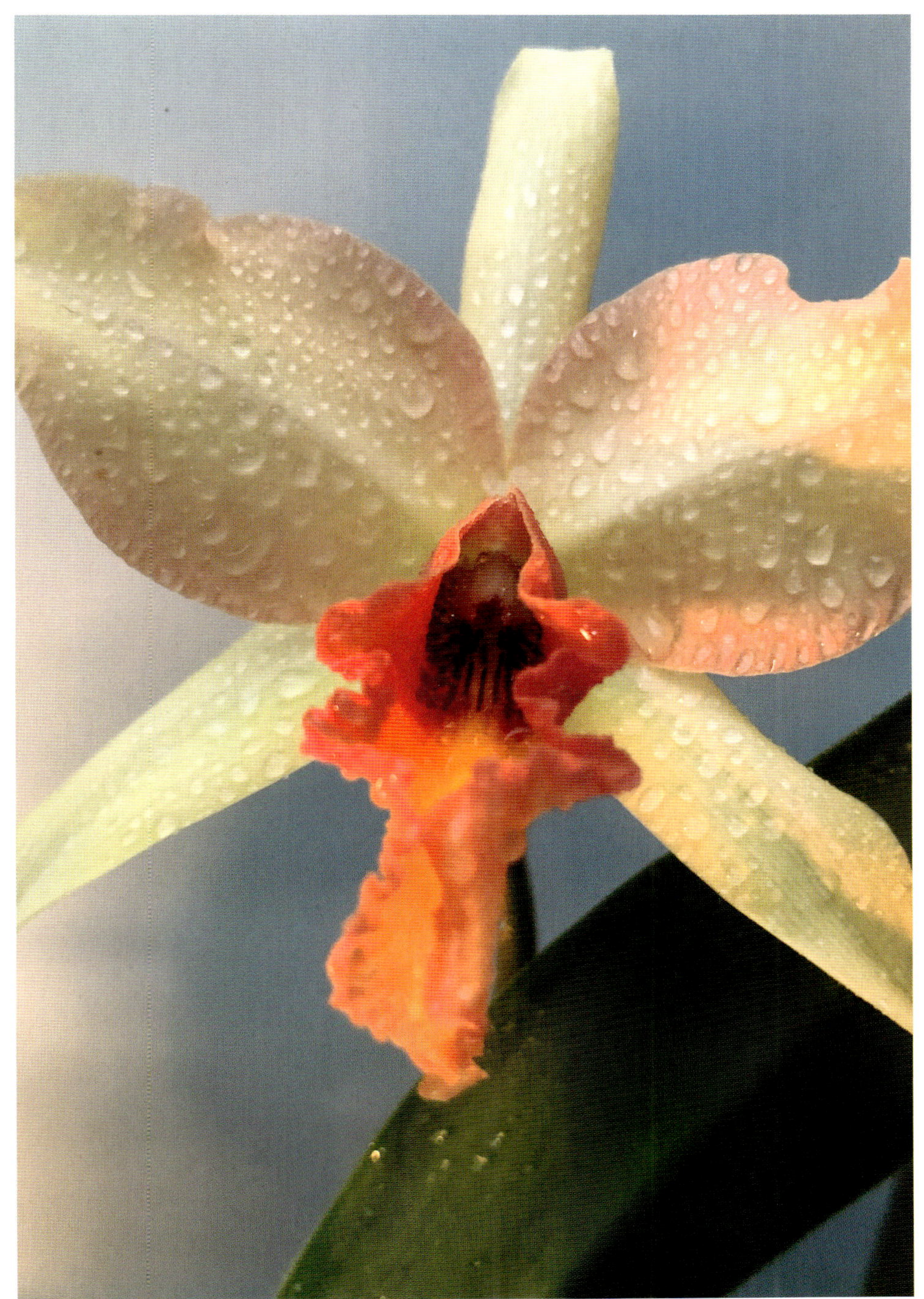

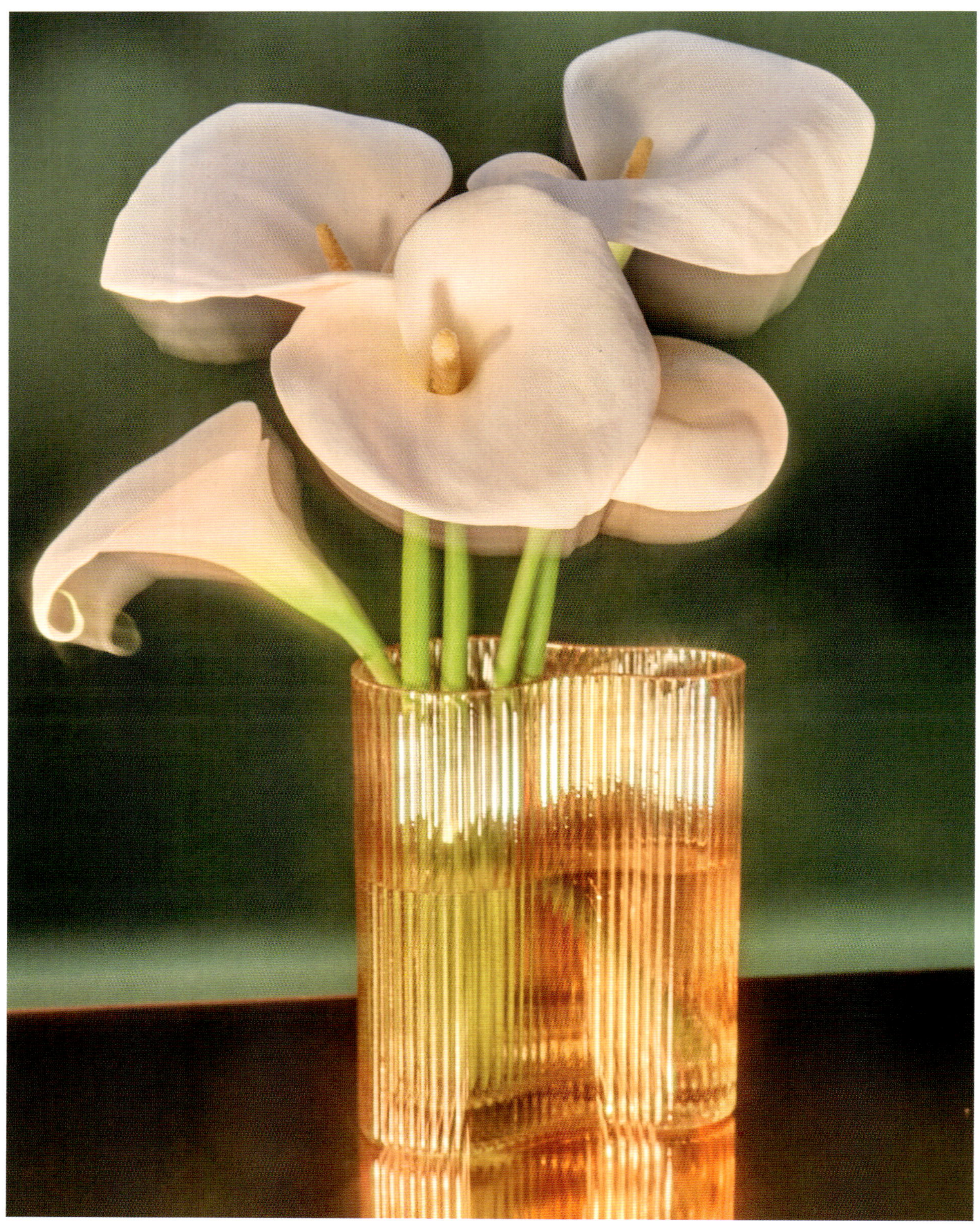

CALLA LILIES

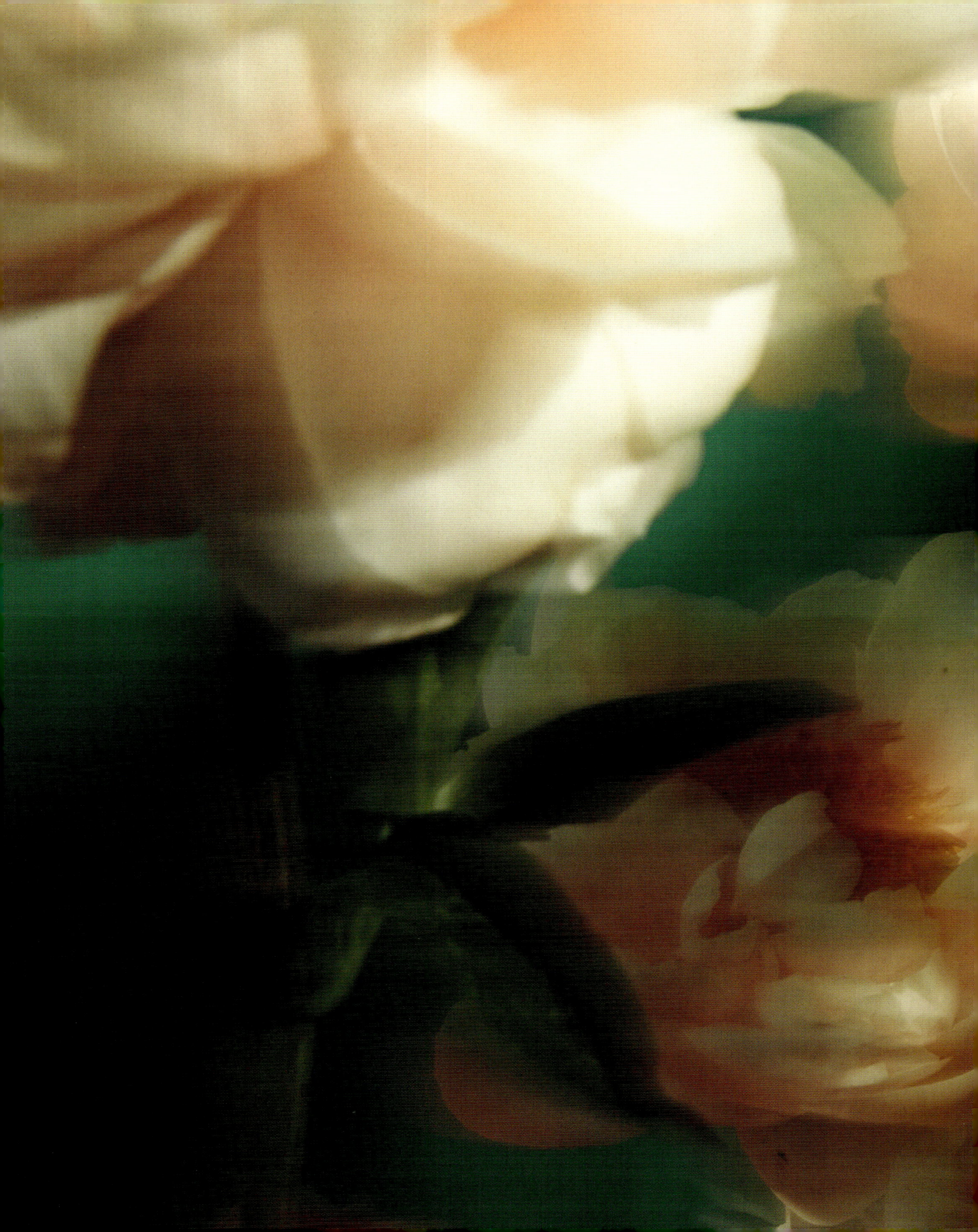

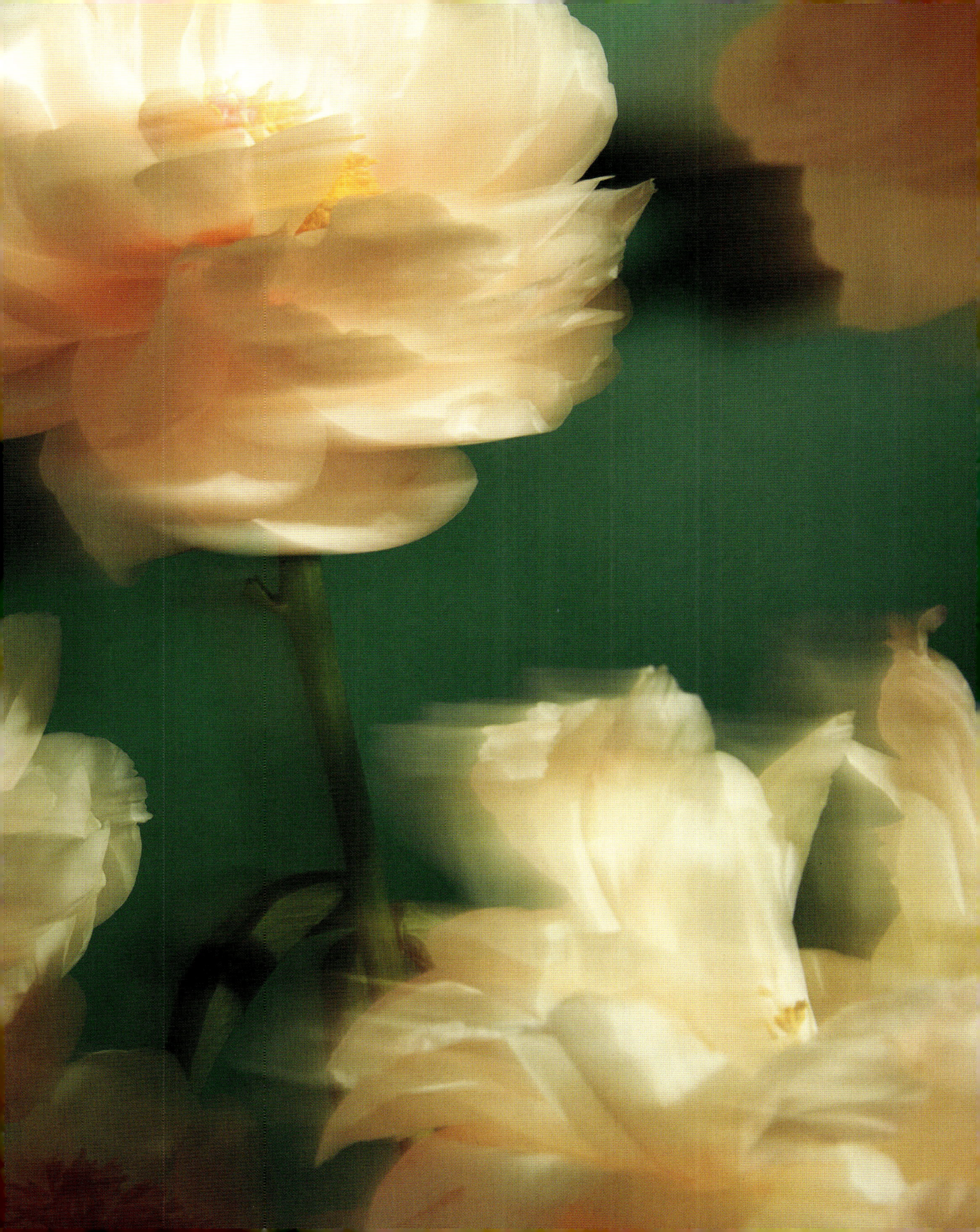

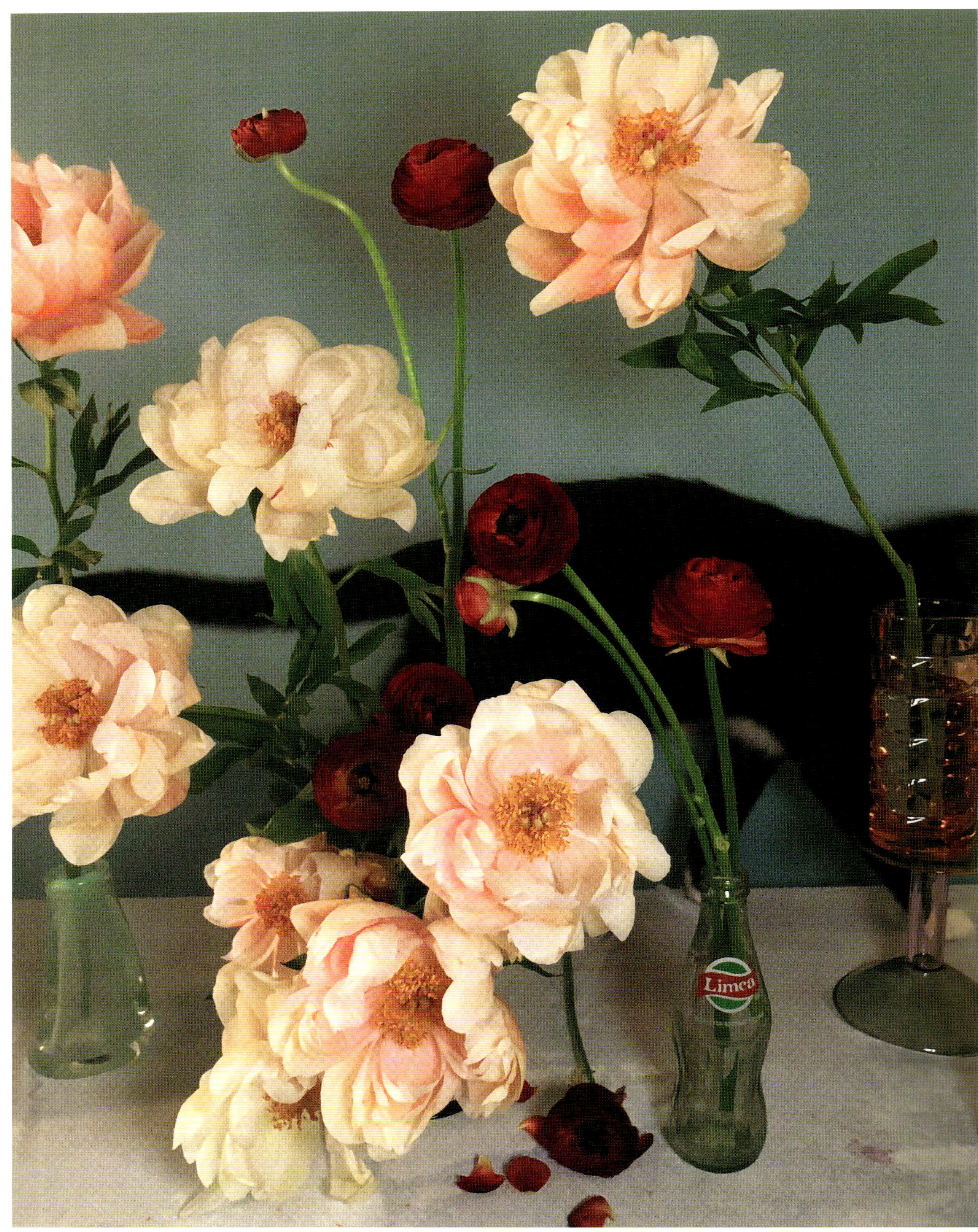

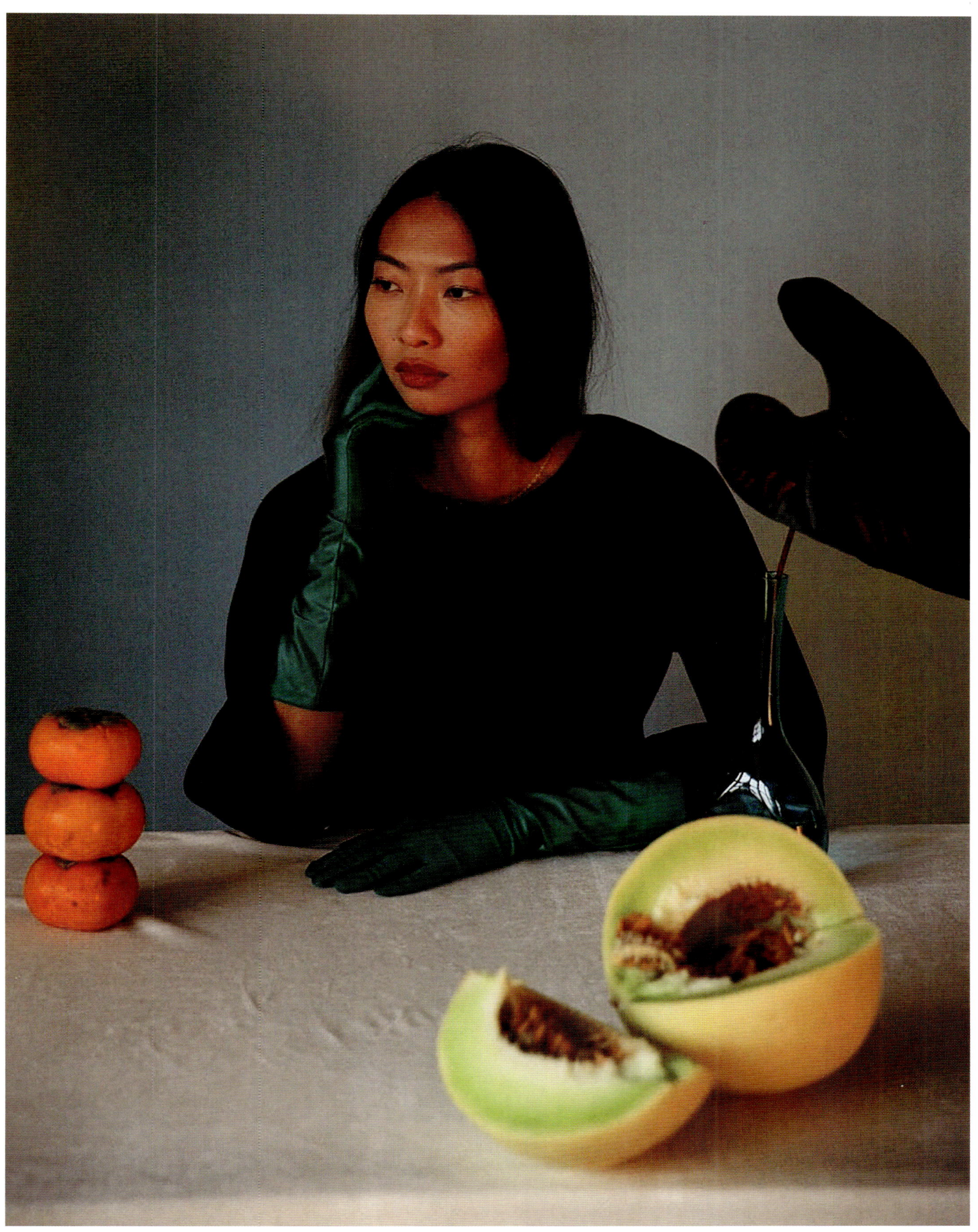

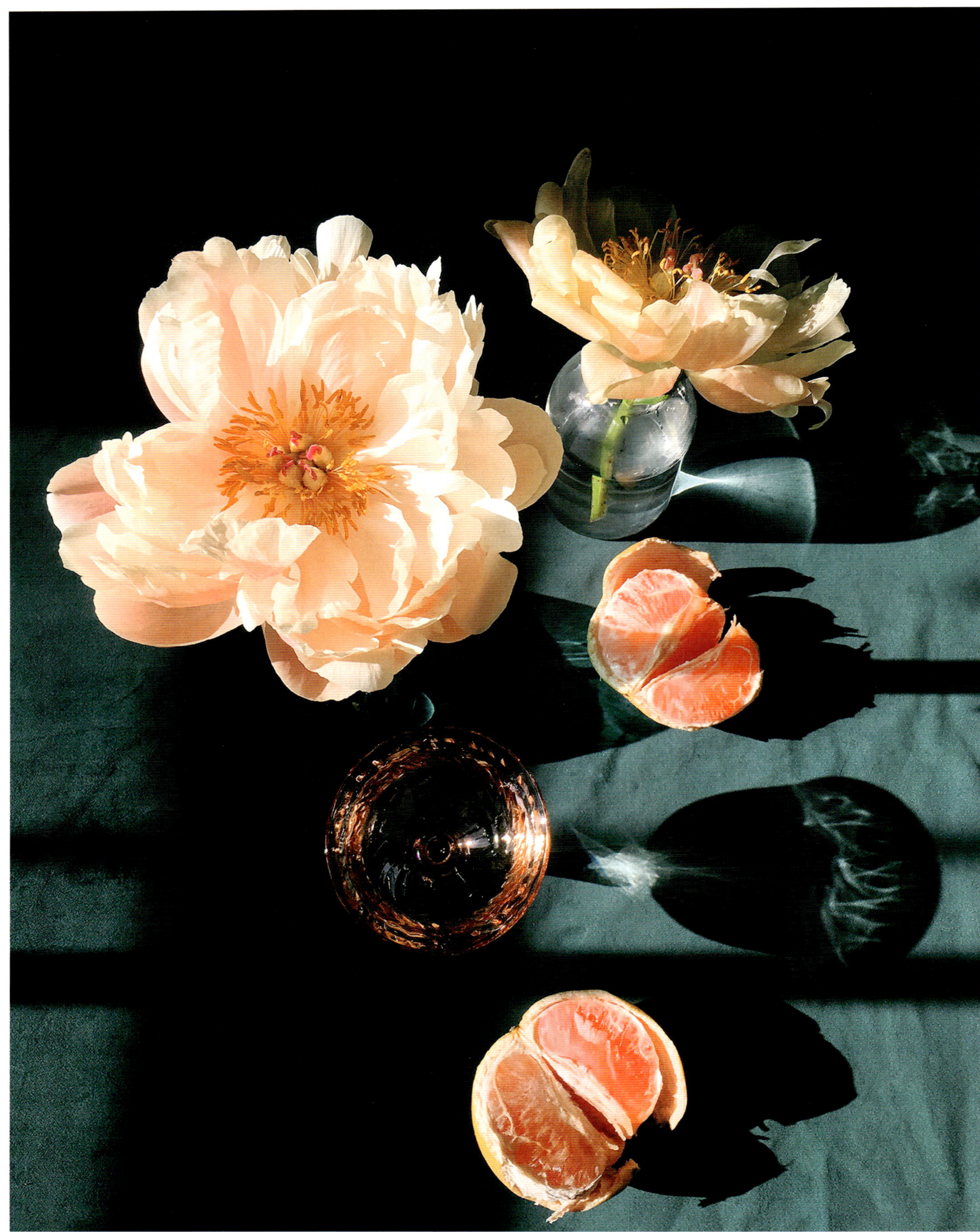

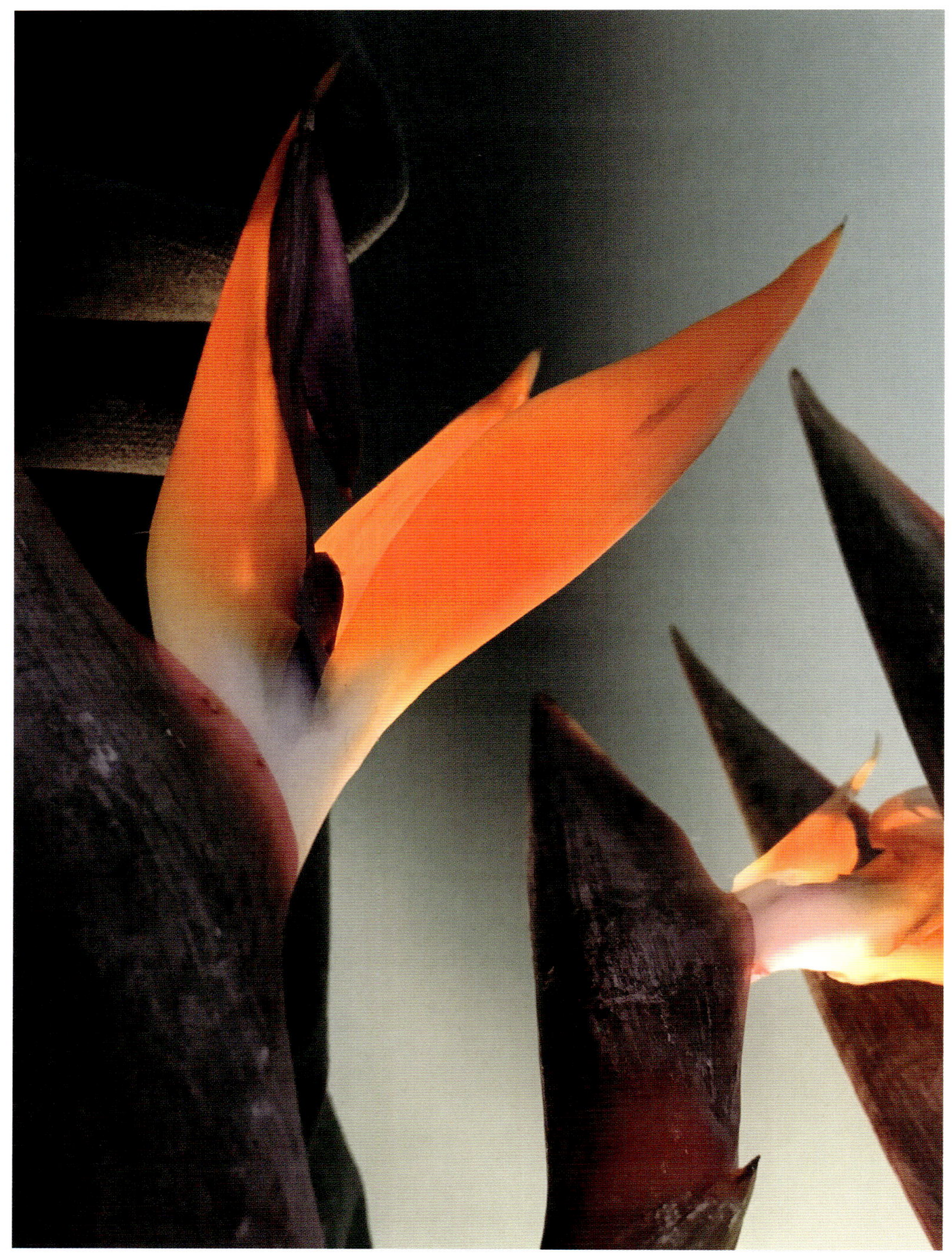

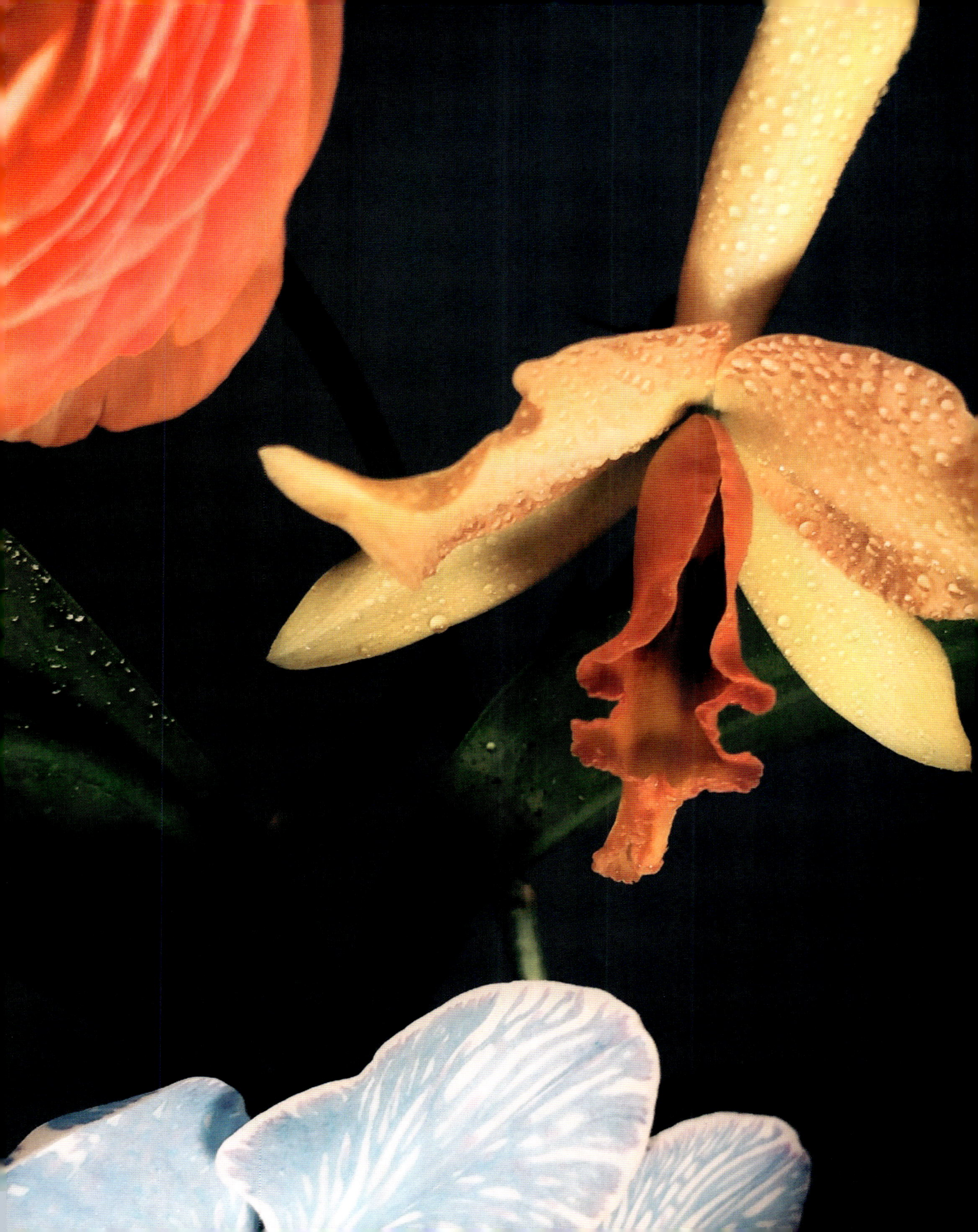

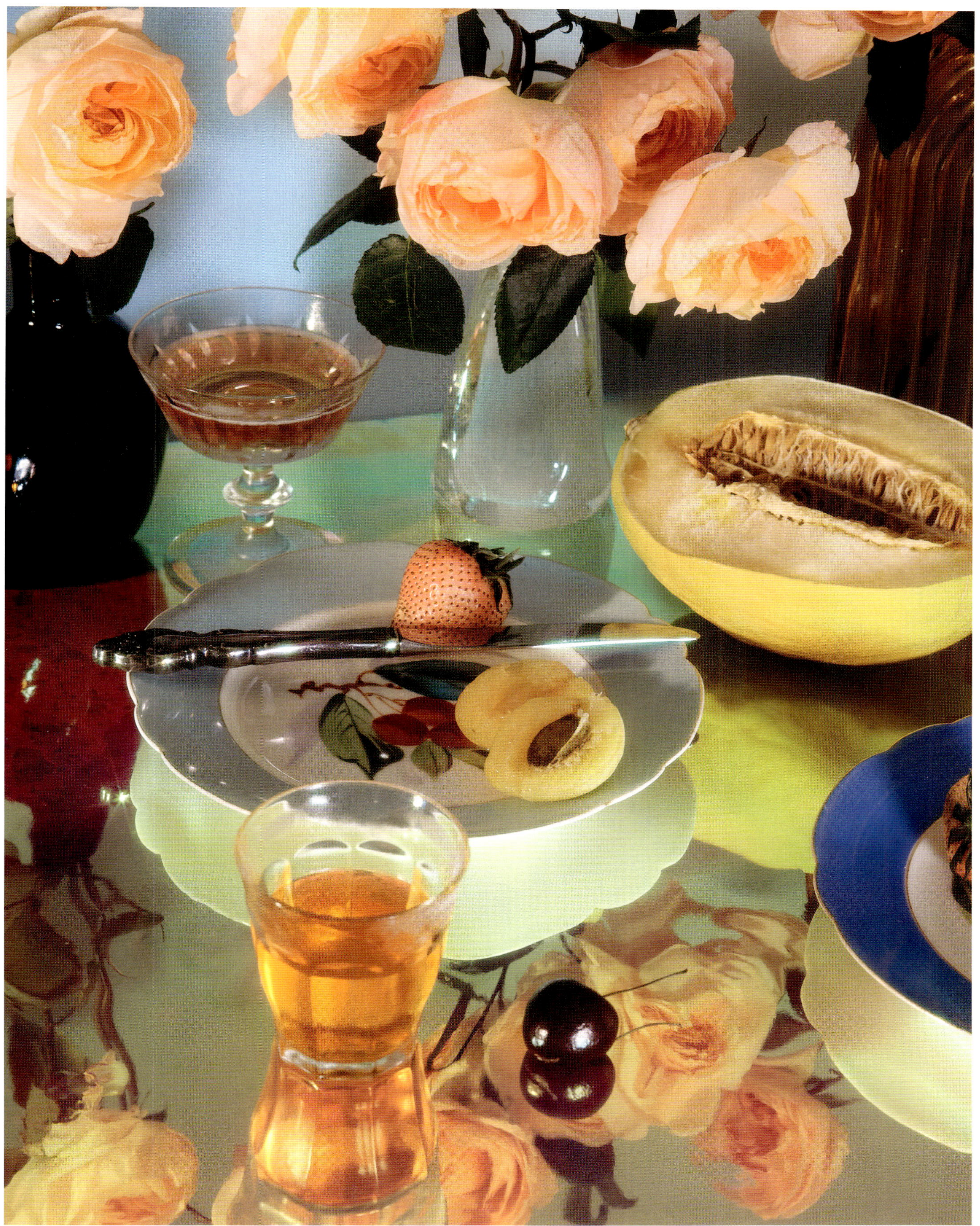

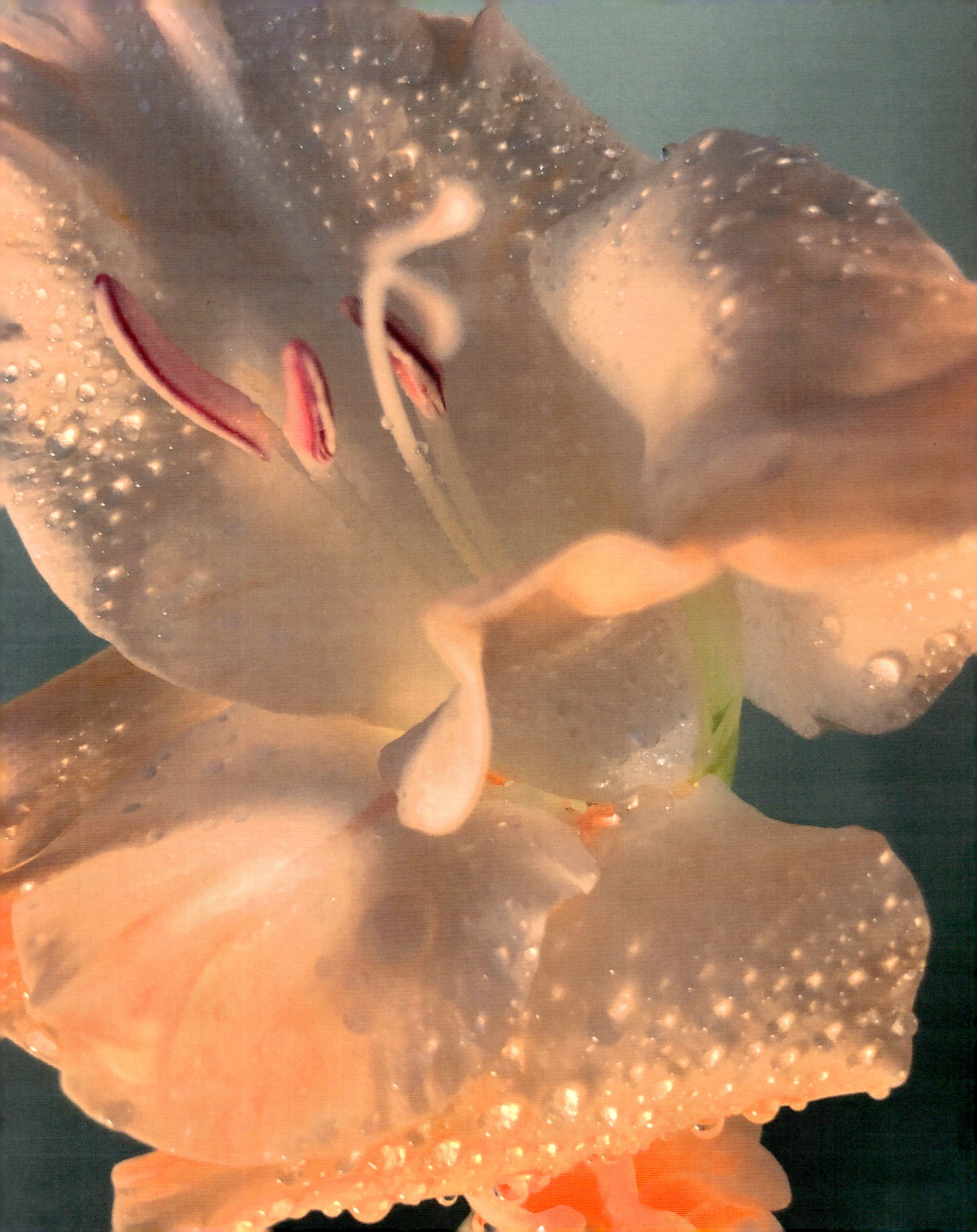

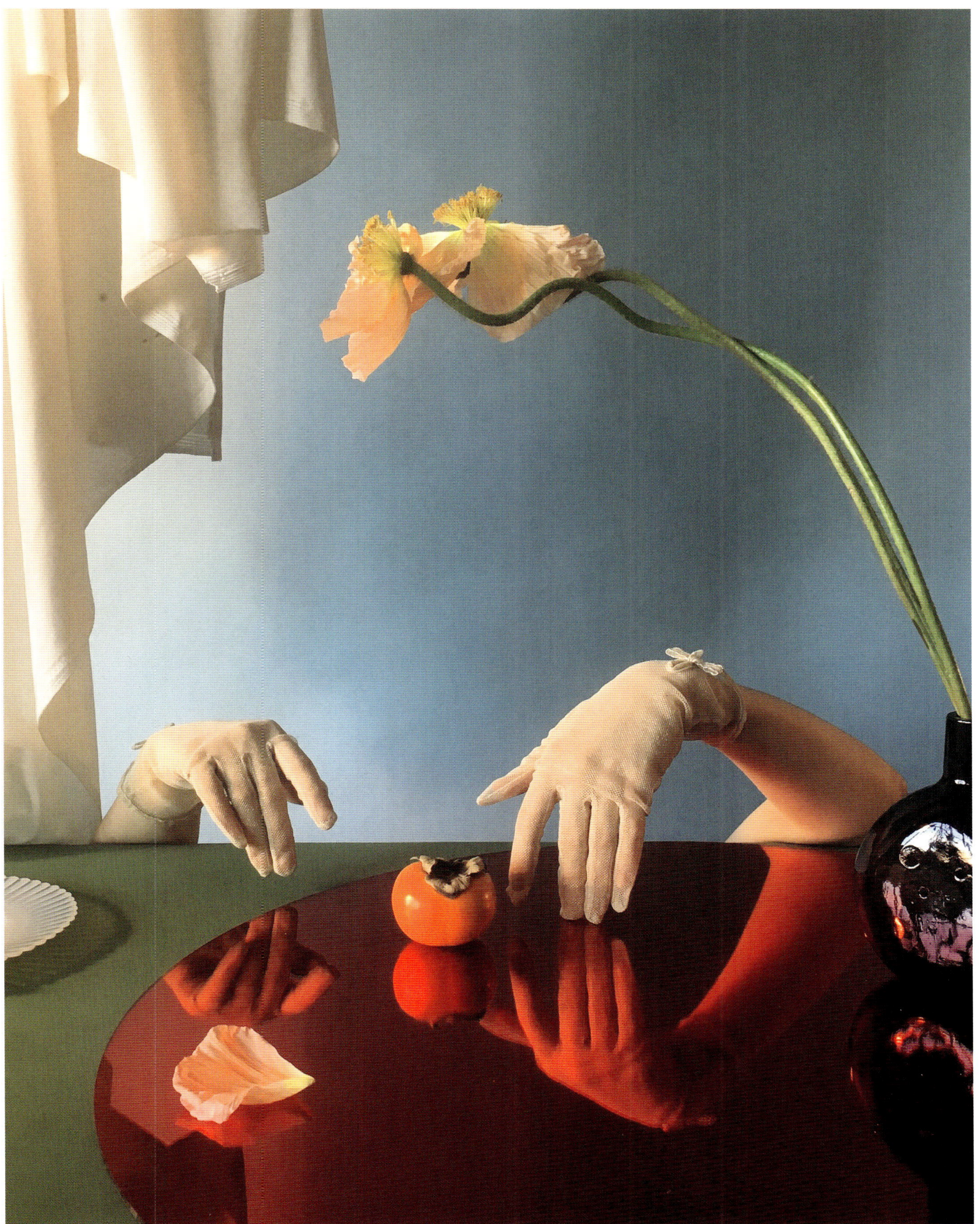

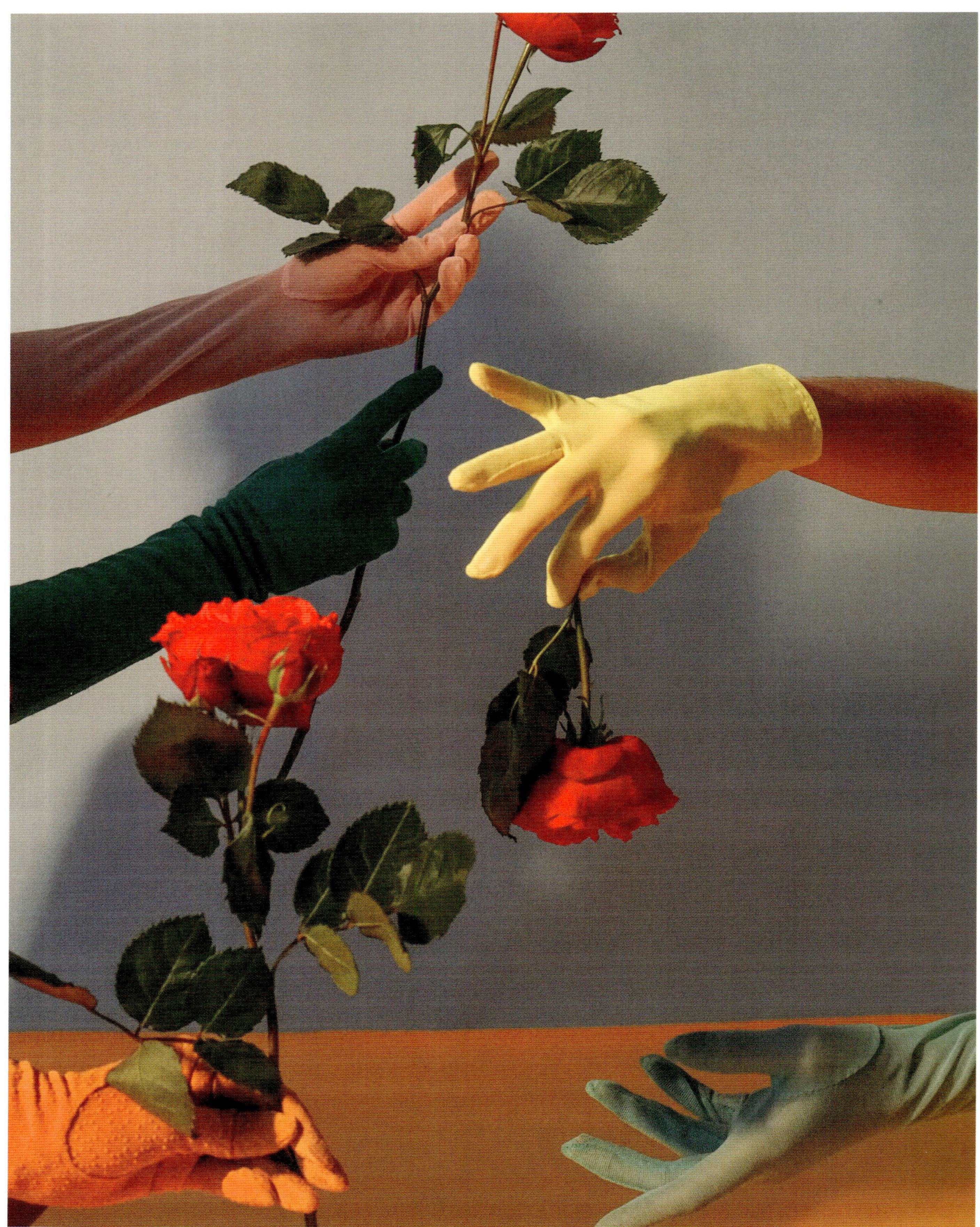

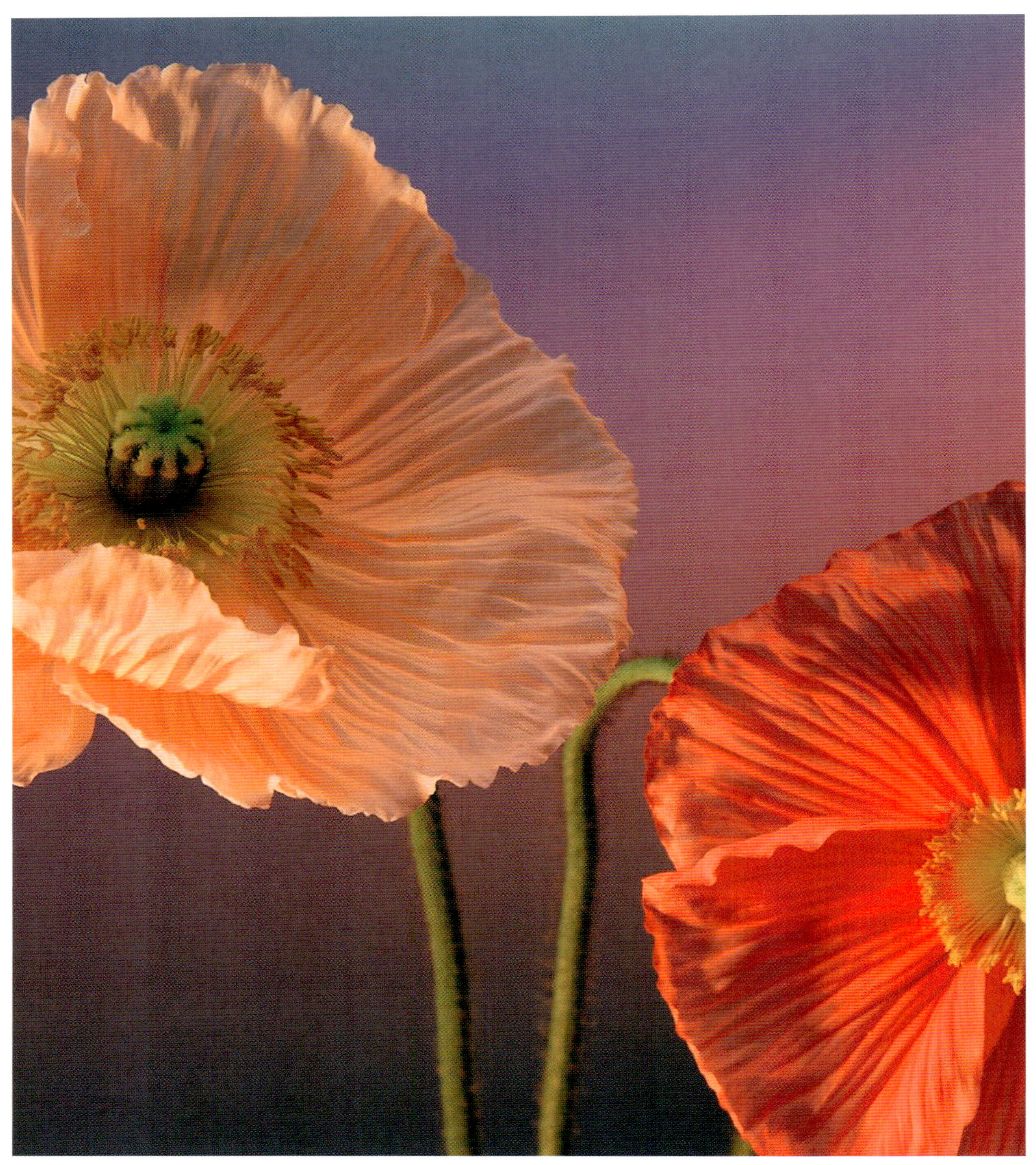

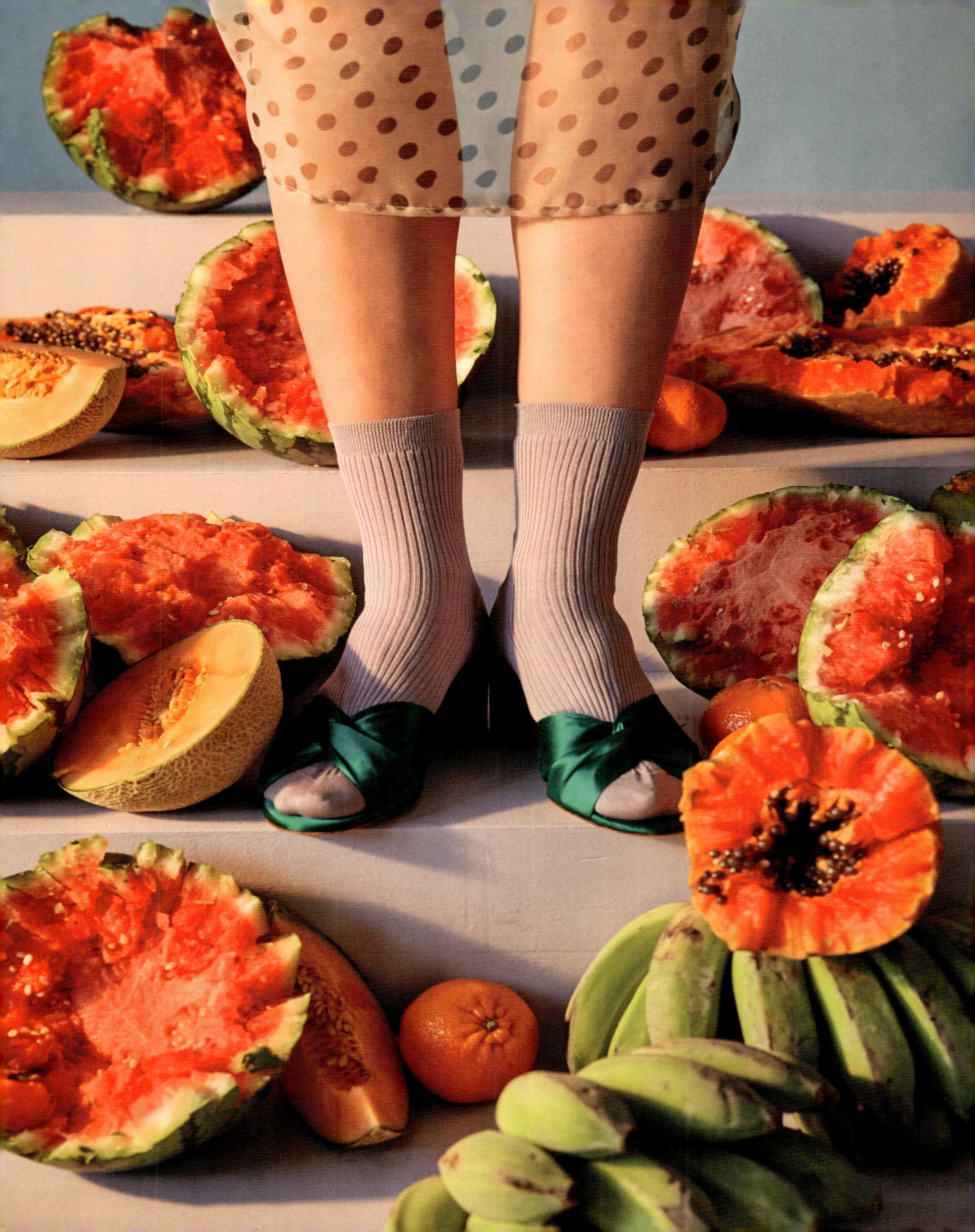

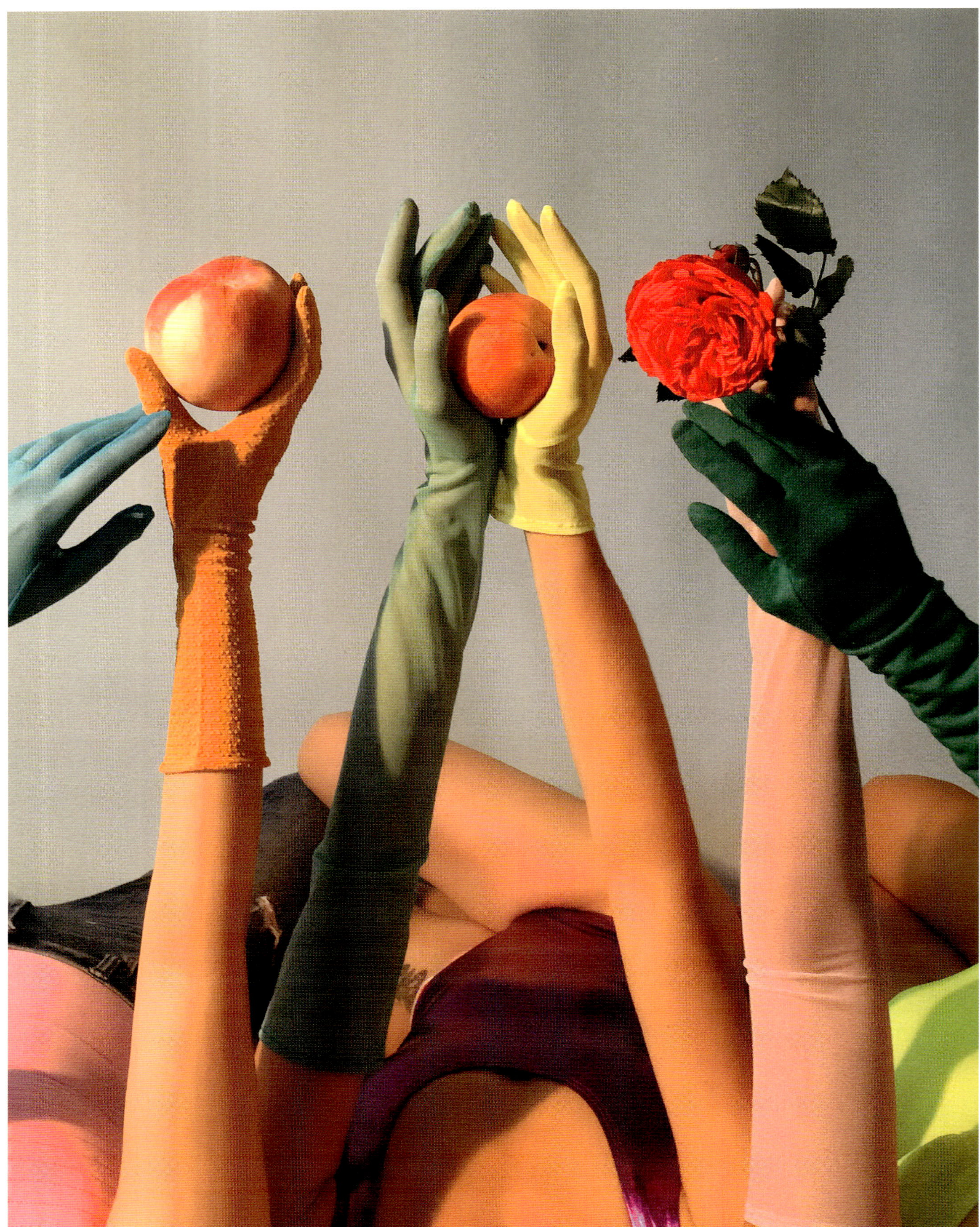

THREE MUSES

KRISTEN, DEVON, AND MAIKO—ORIGINAL ASSISTANTS WHEN
I FIRST STARTED THE COMPANY—POSED FOR THIS PHOTO. WE
HAD SO MUCH FUN.

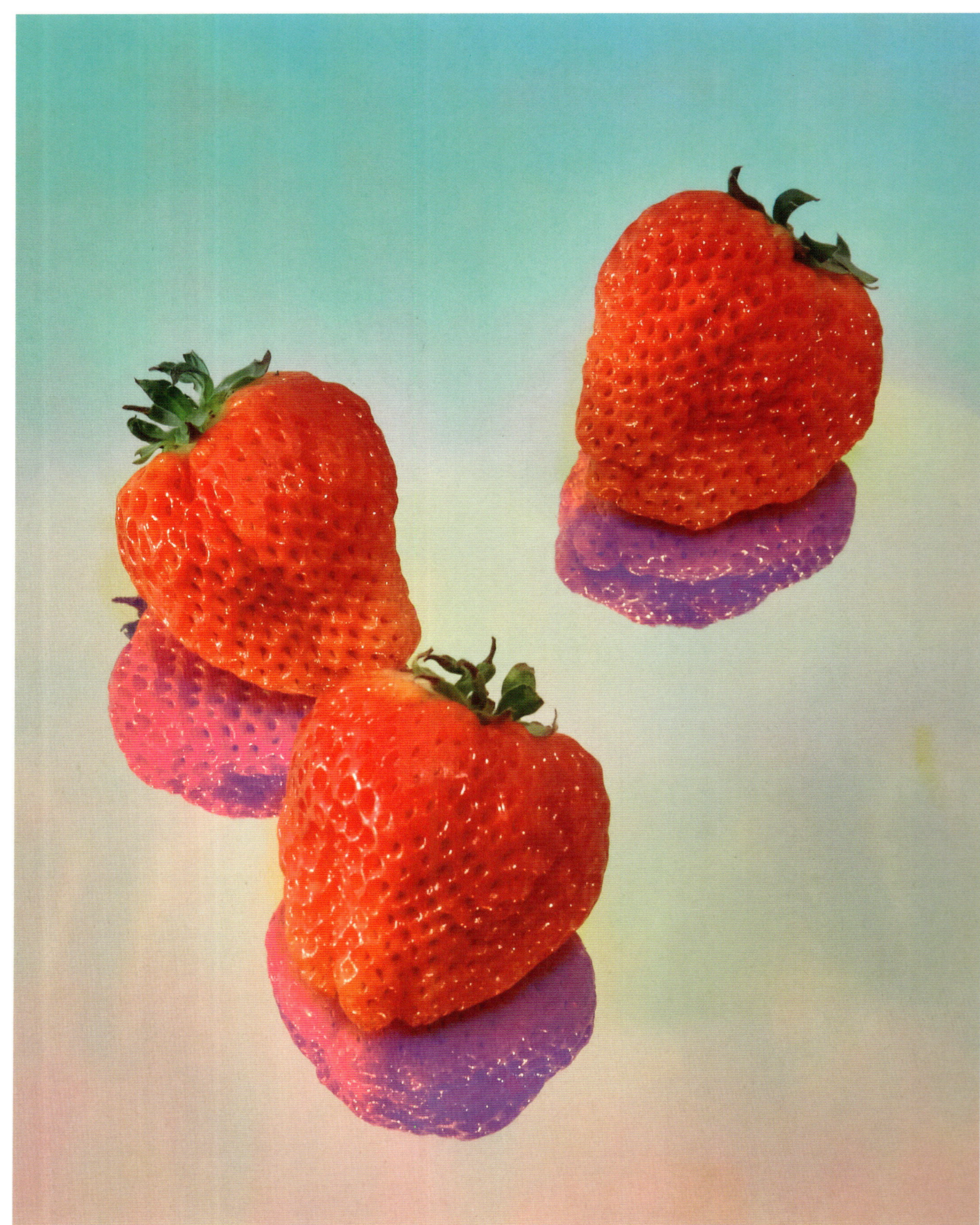

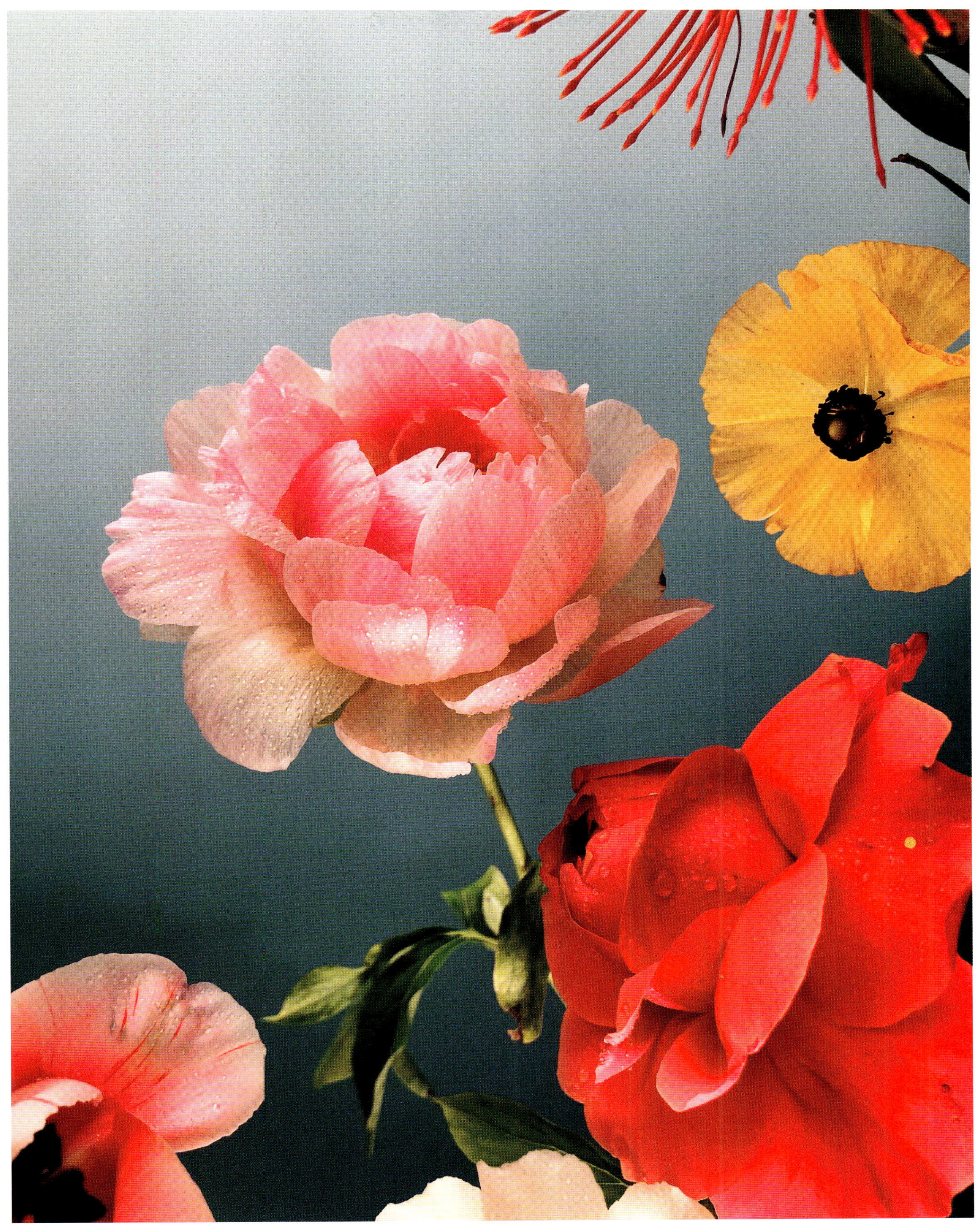

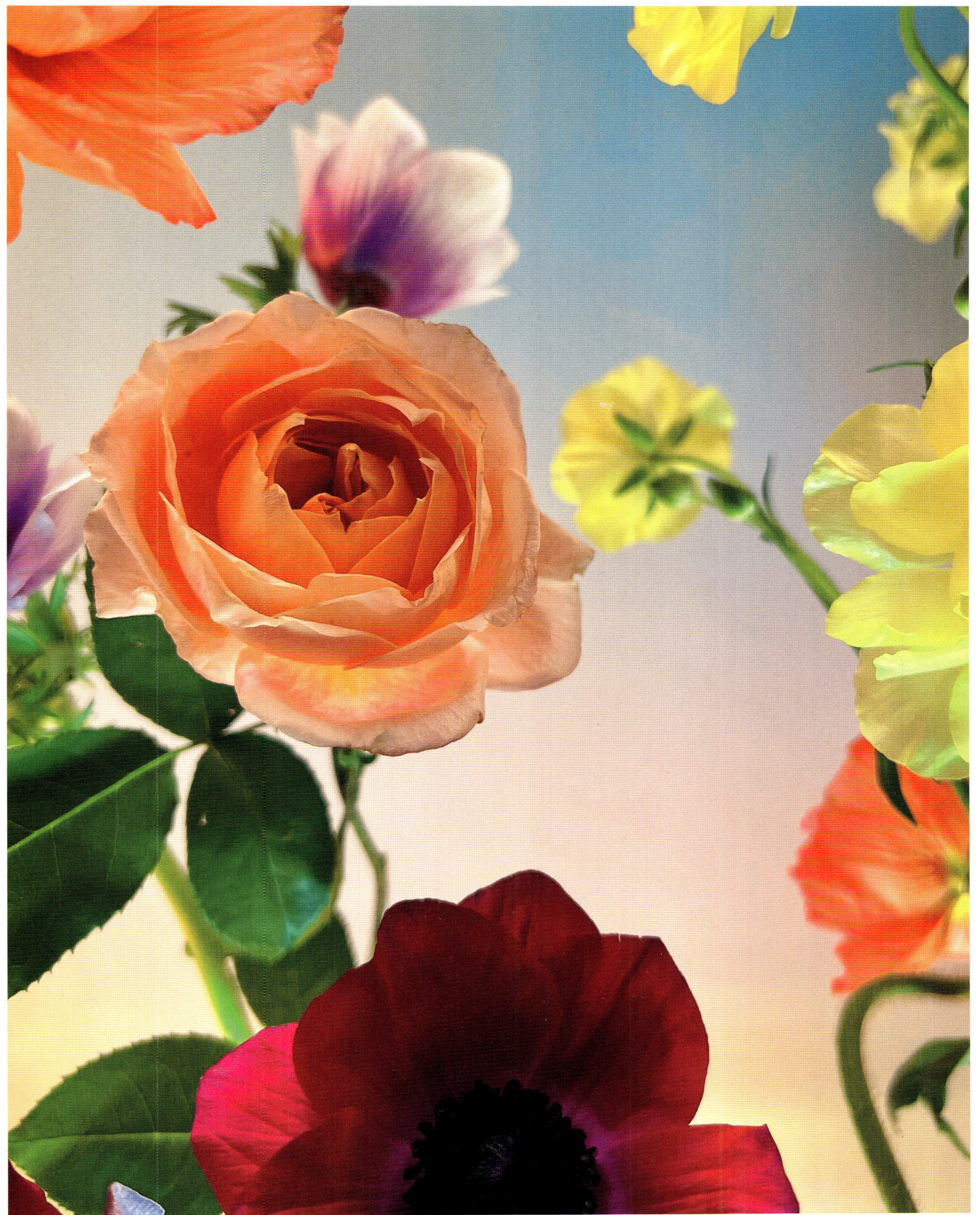

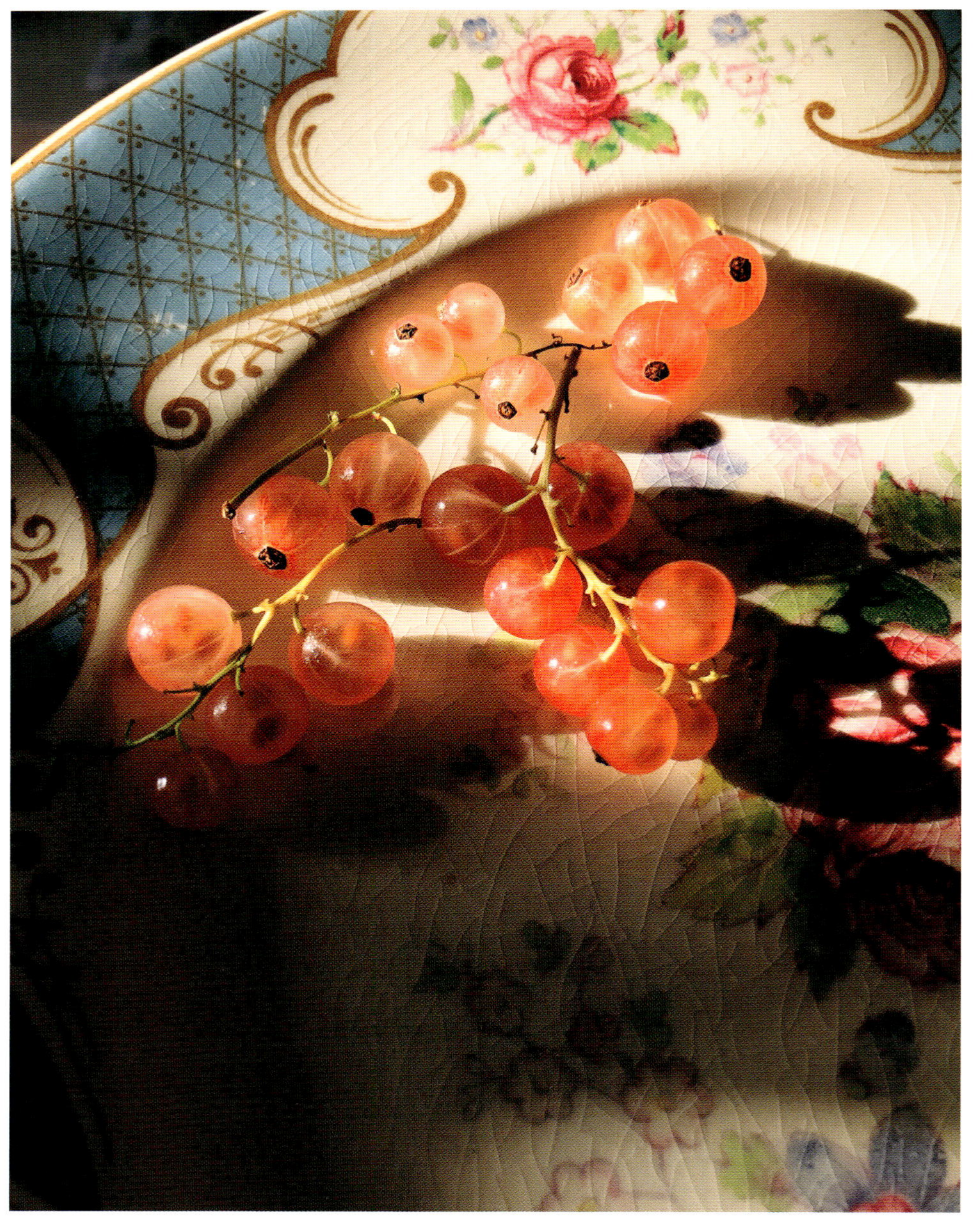

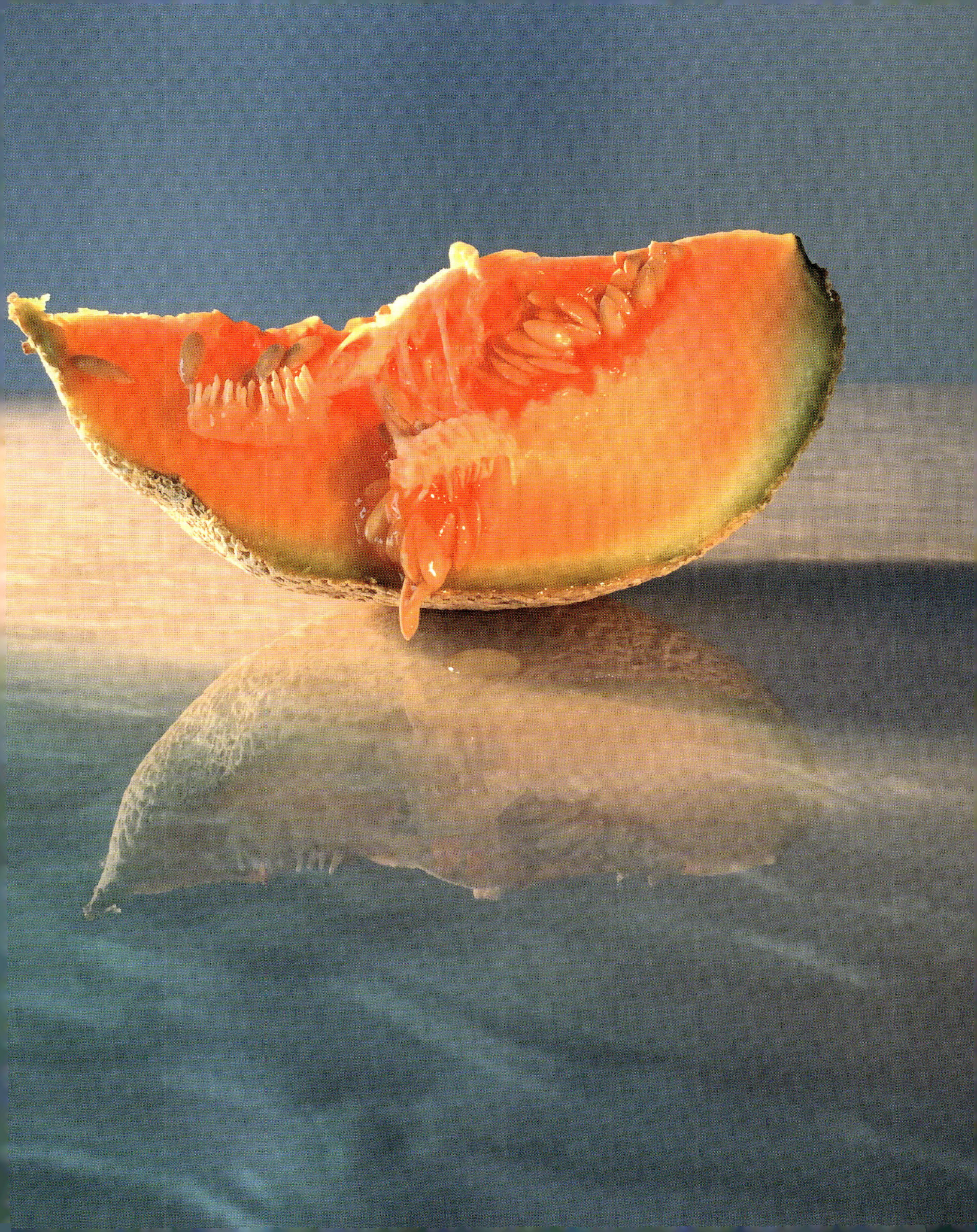

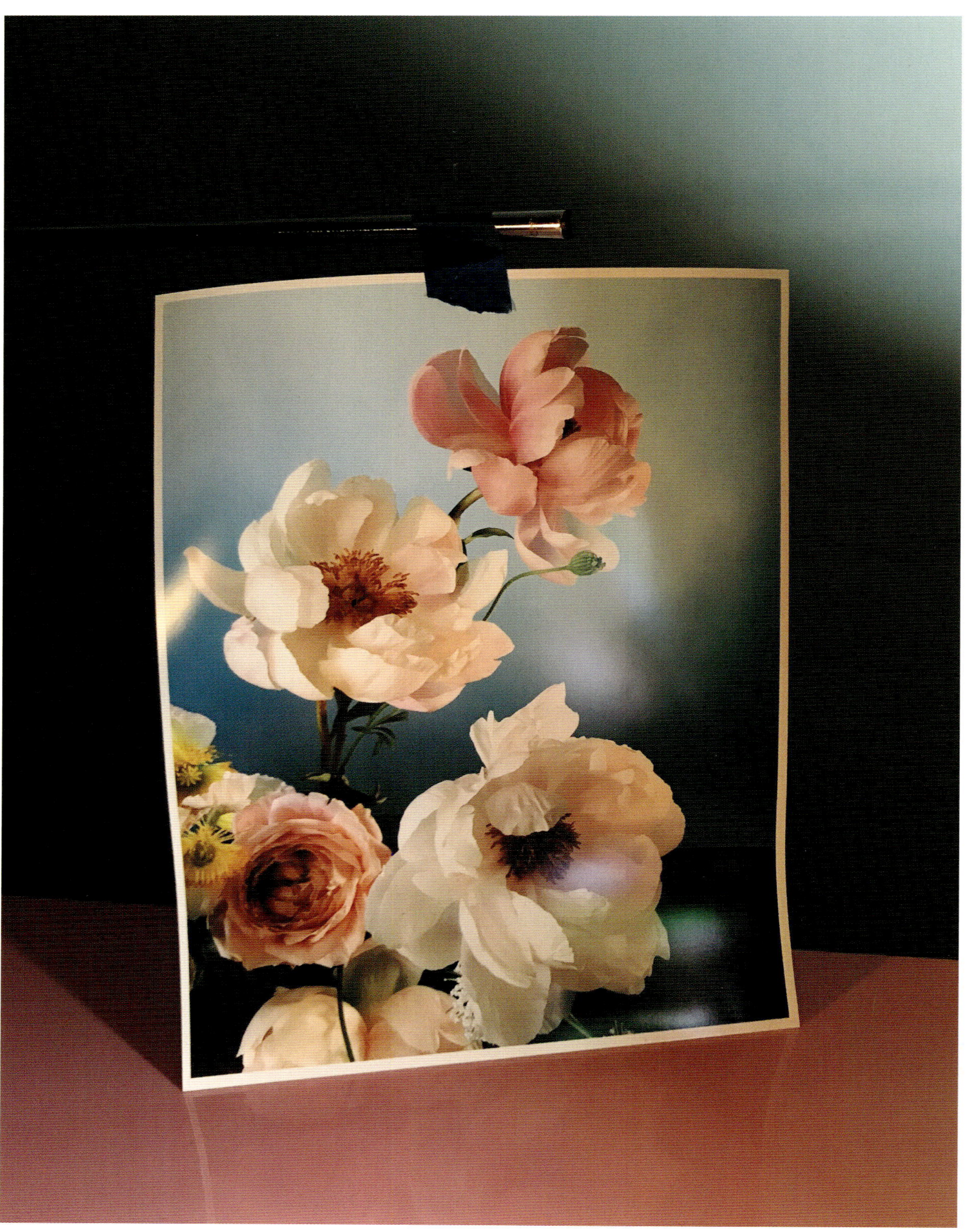

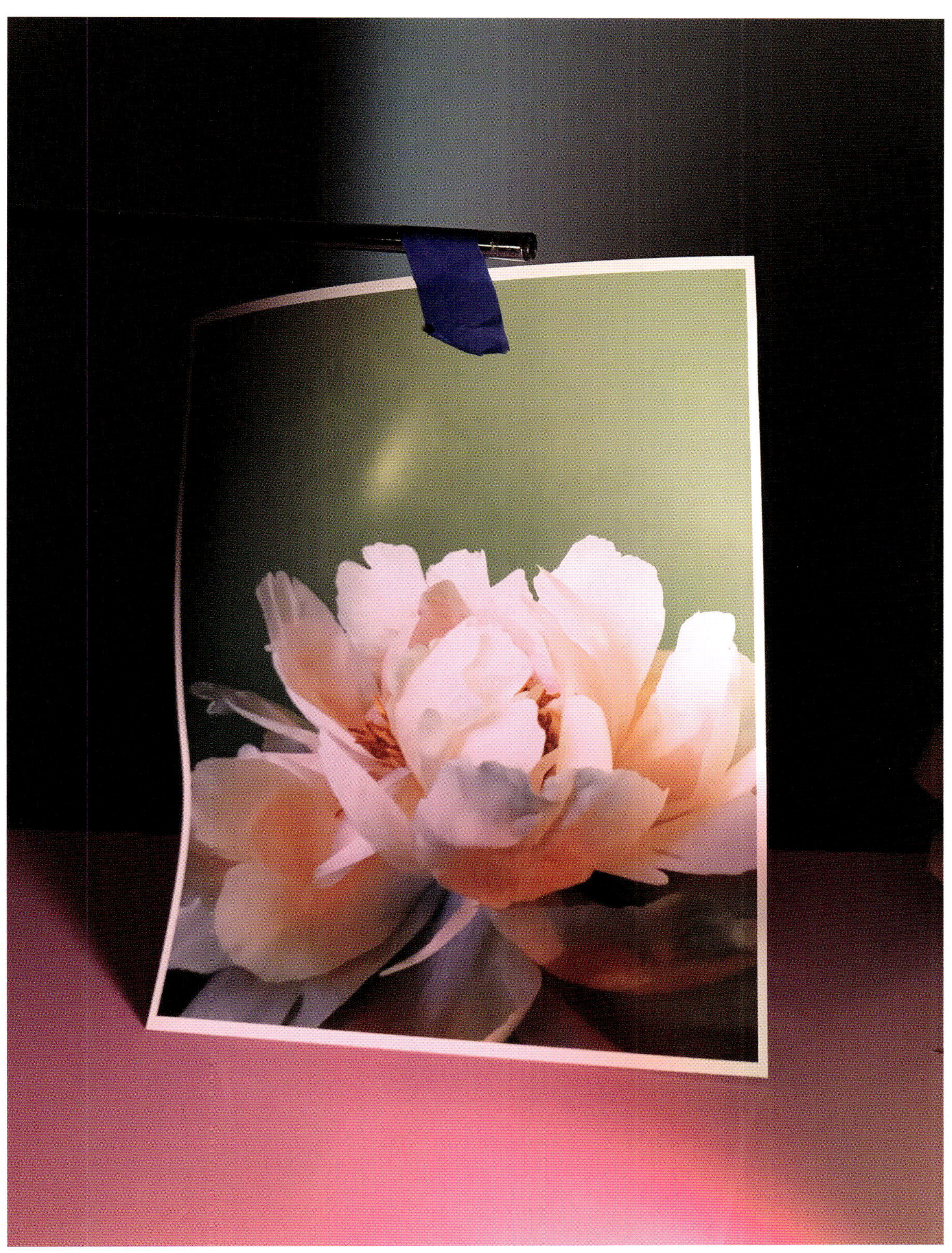

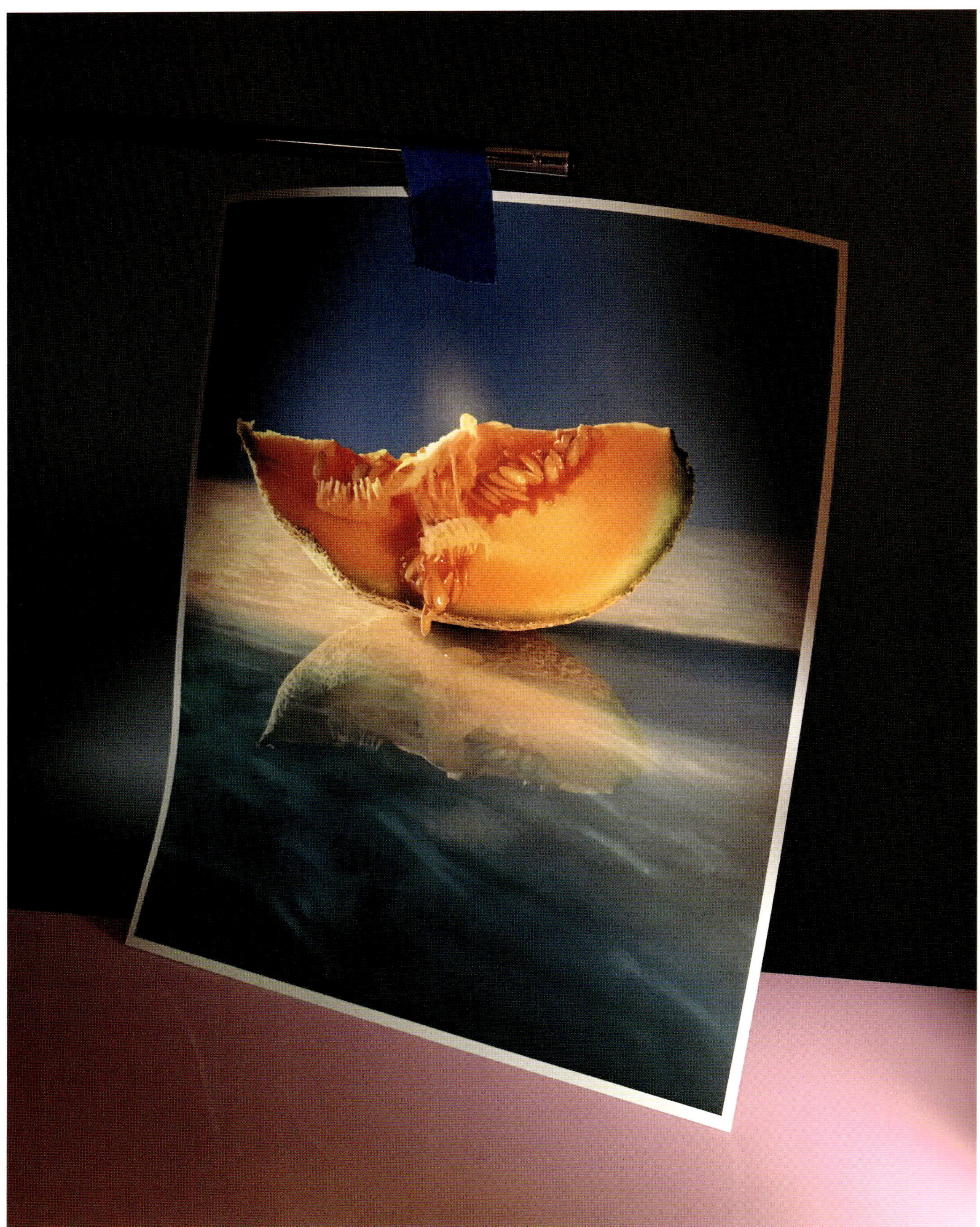

SOUNDS FAMILIAR

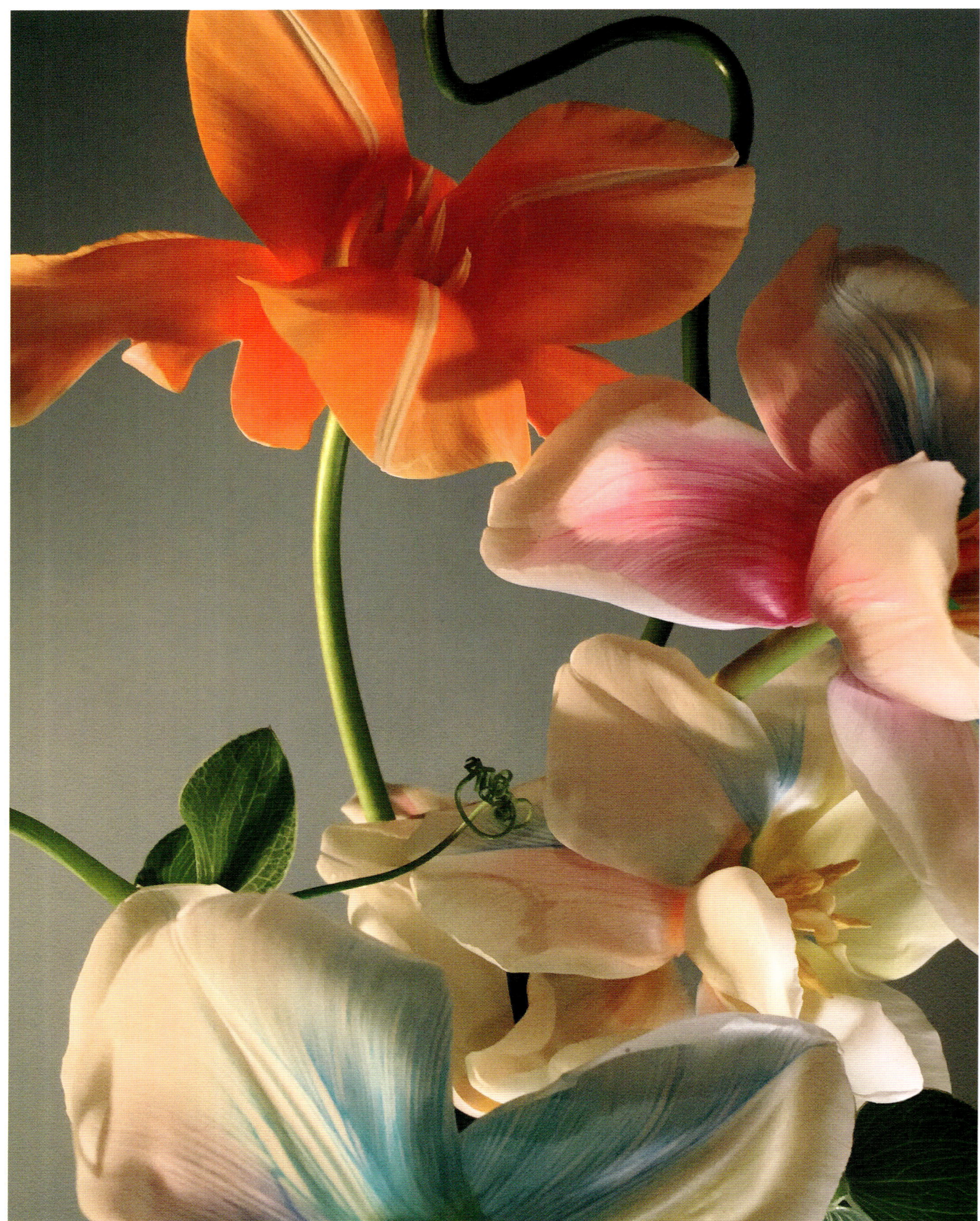

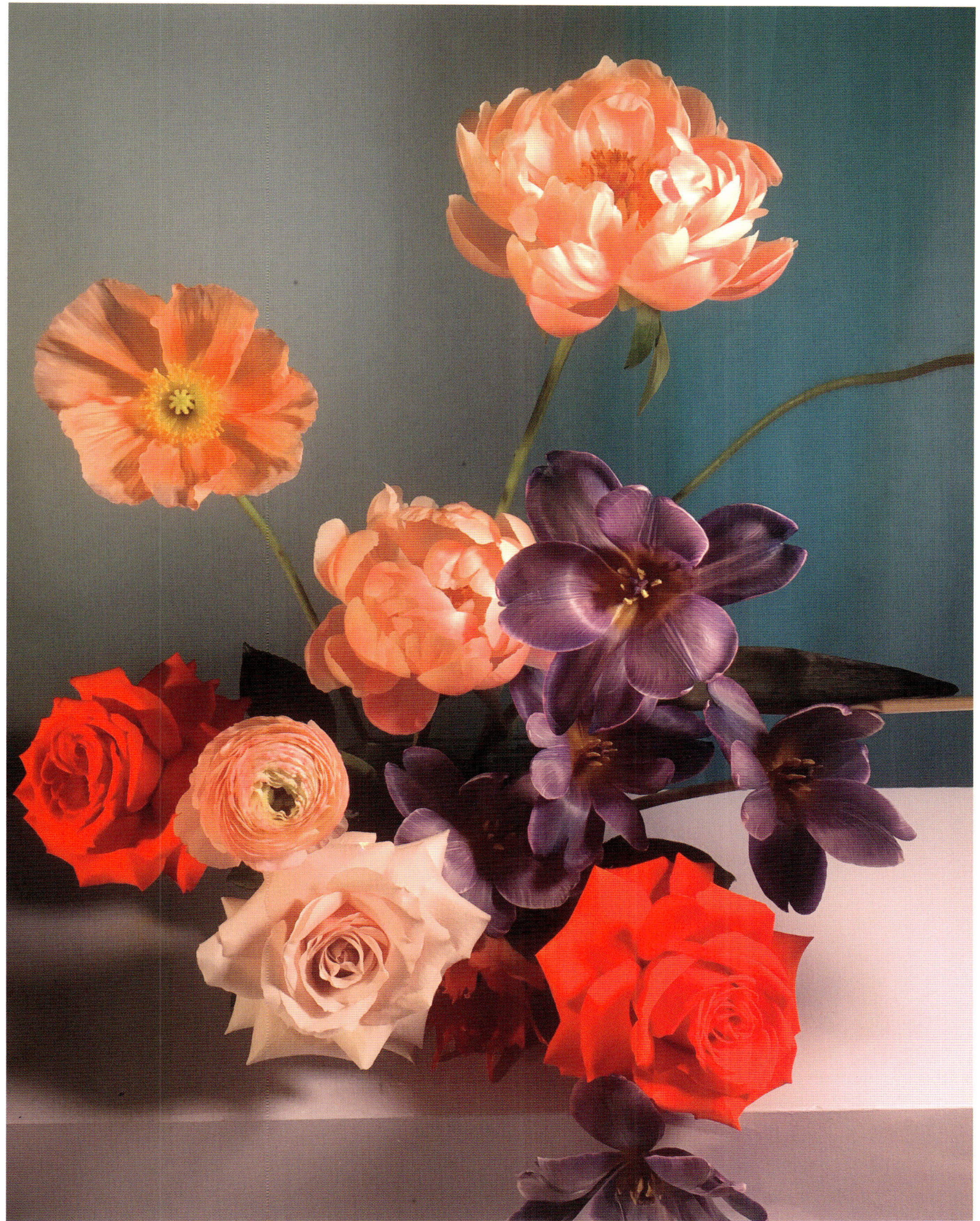

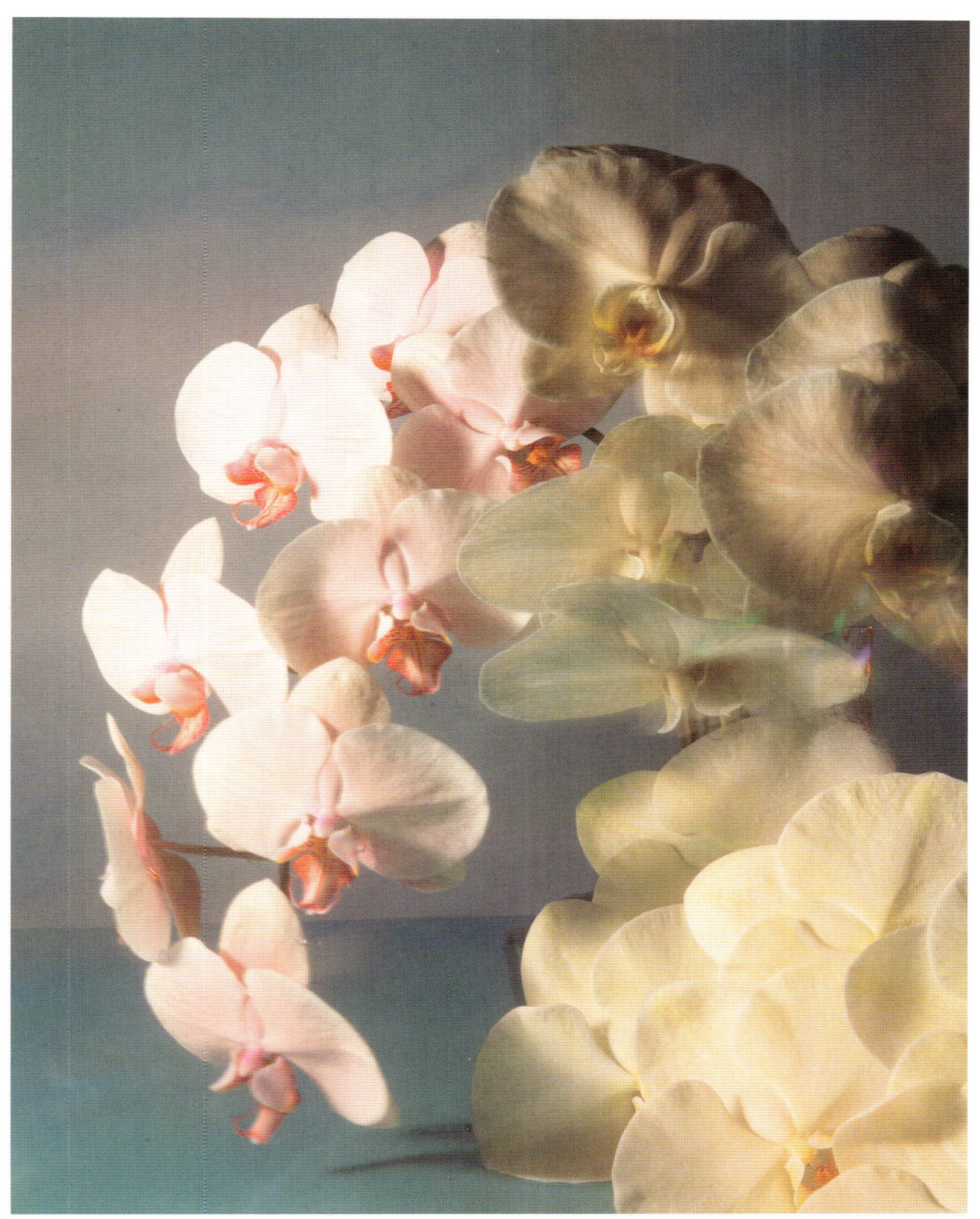

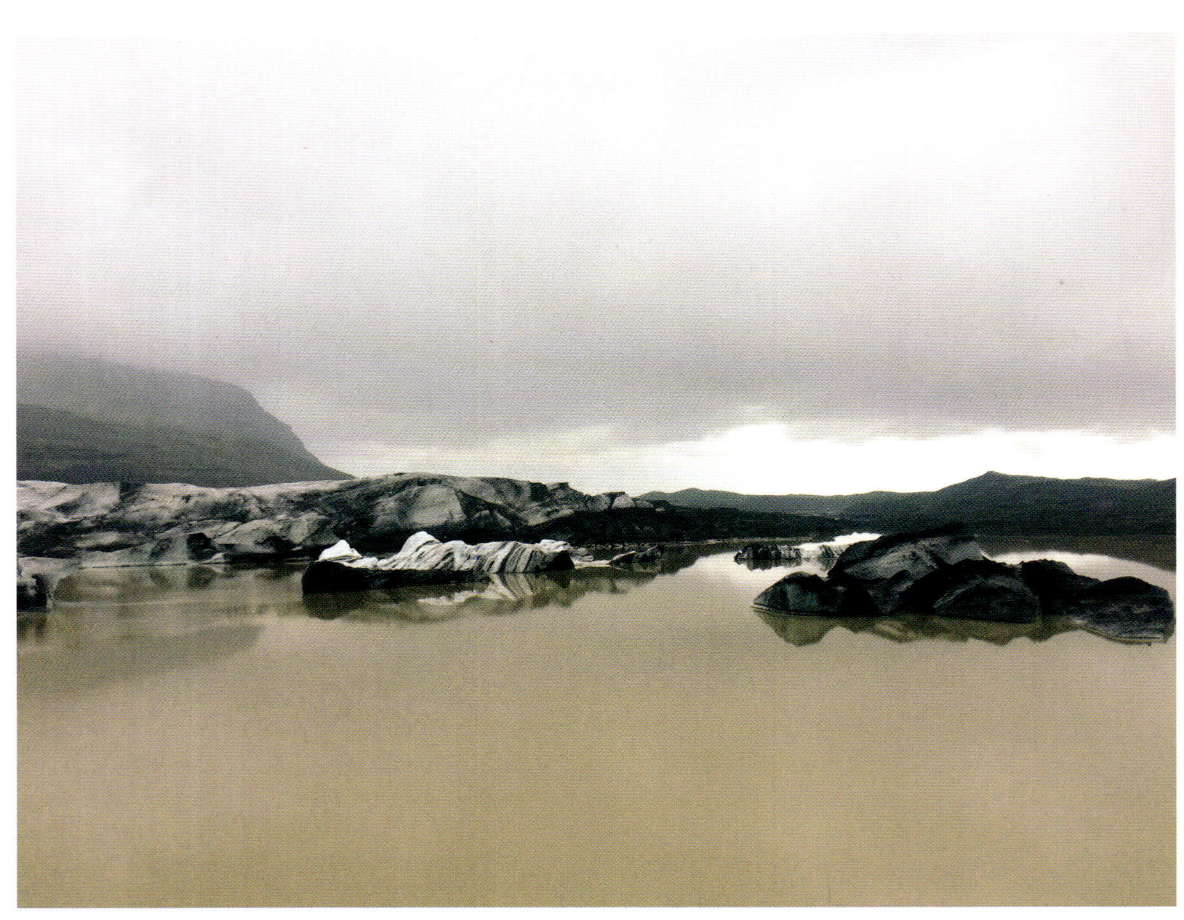

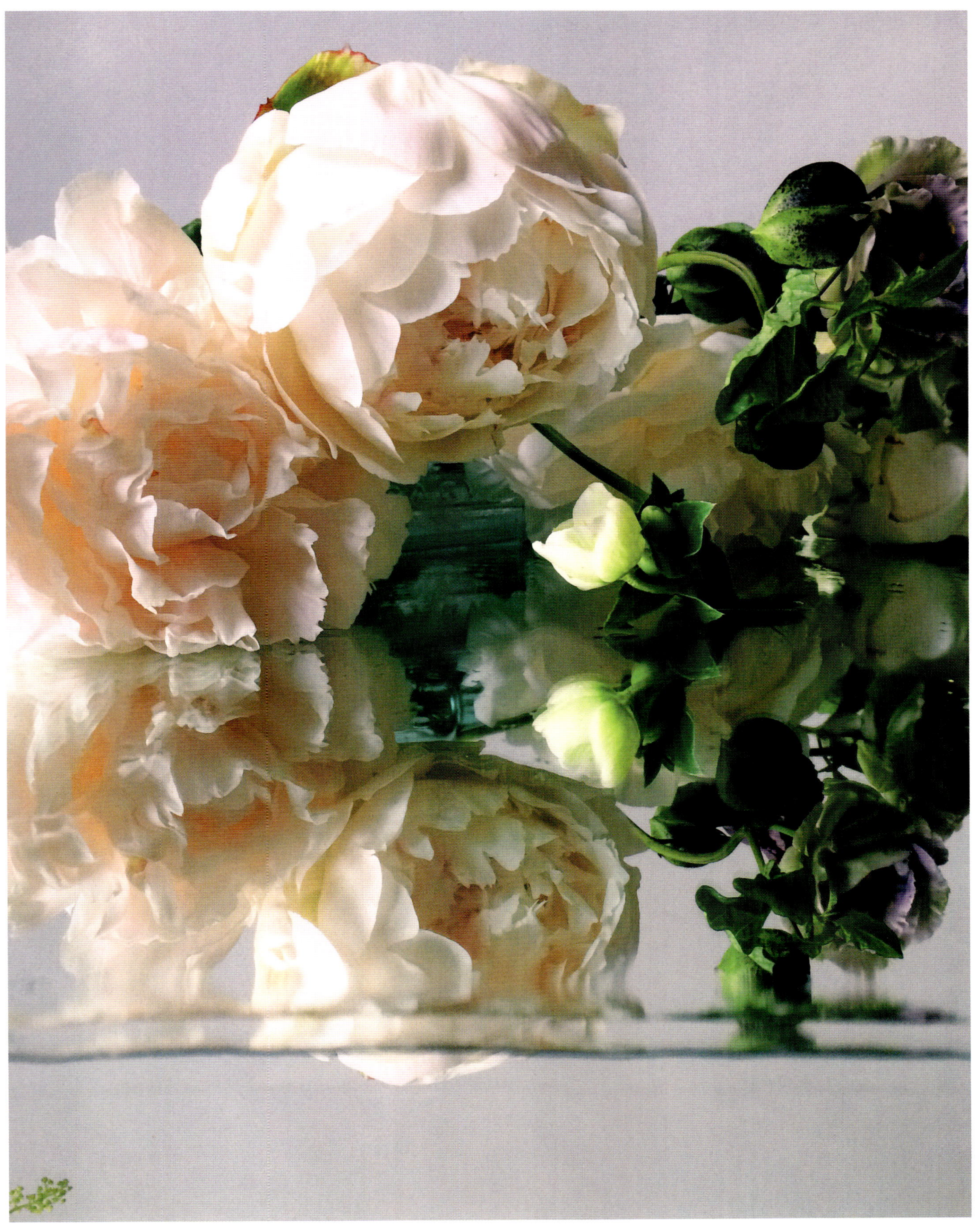

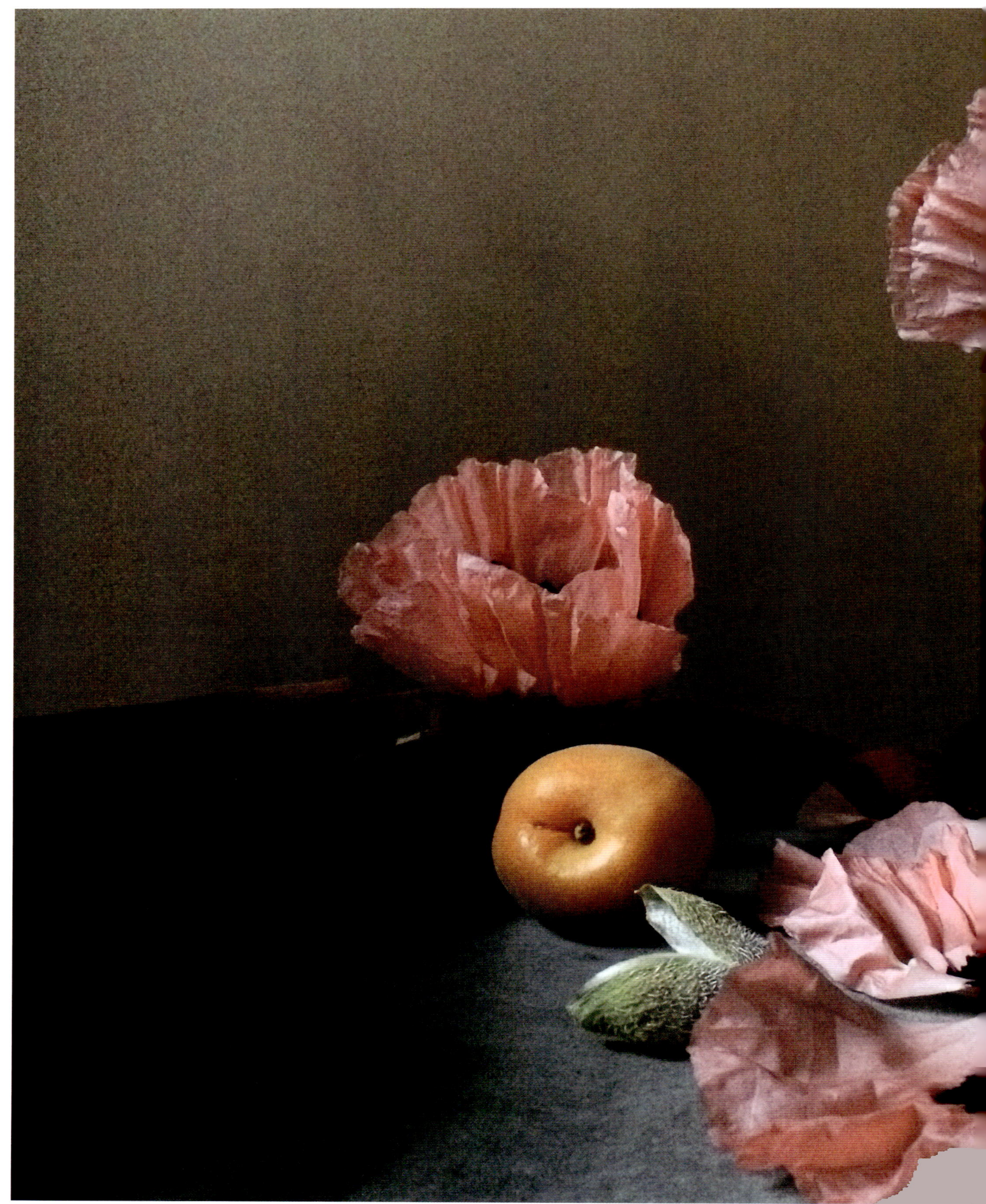

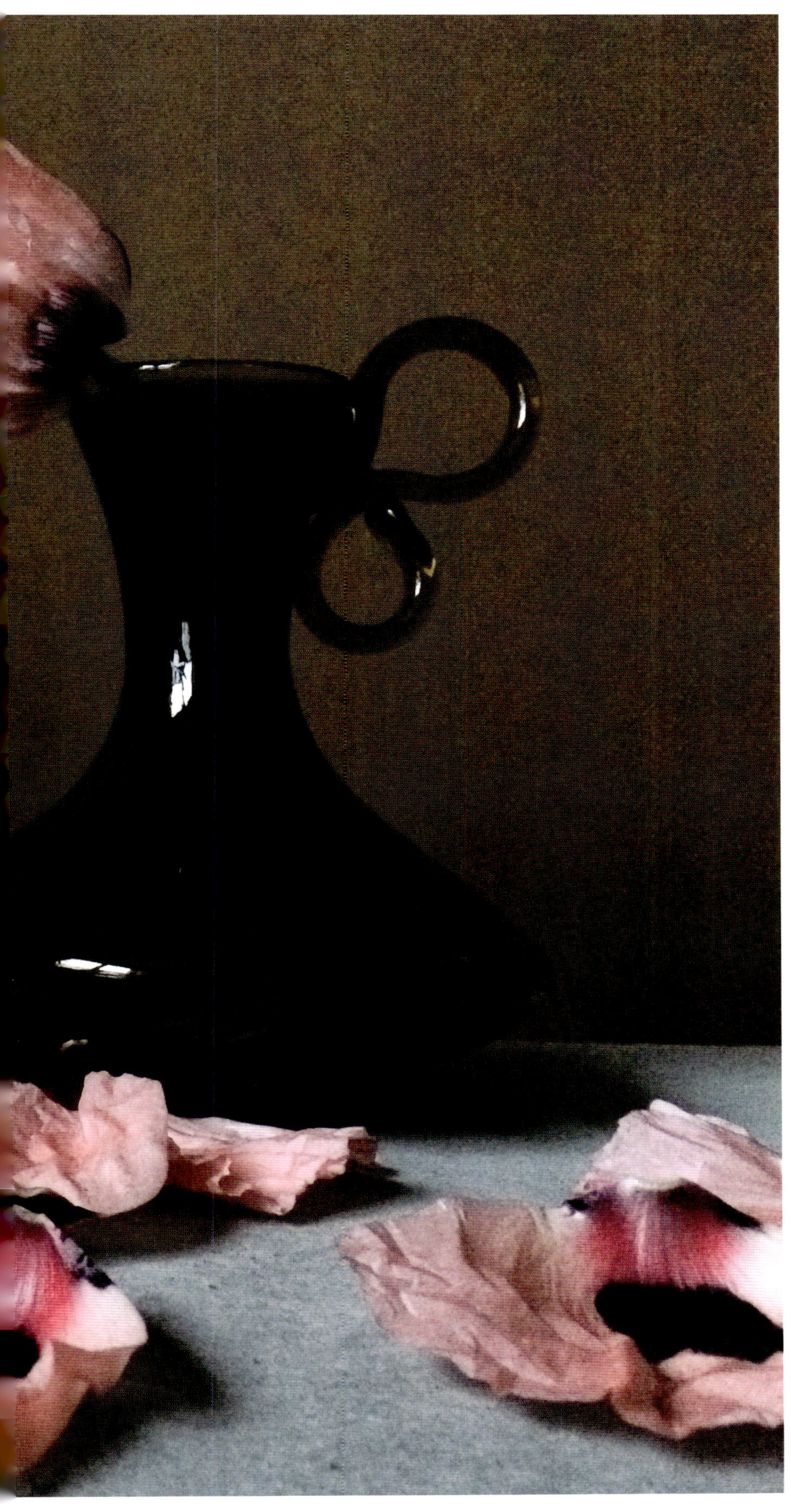

A LITTLE CRUSH

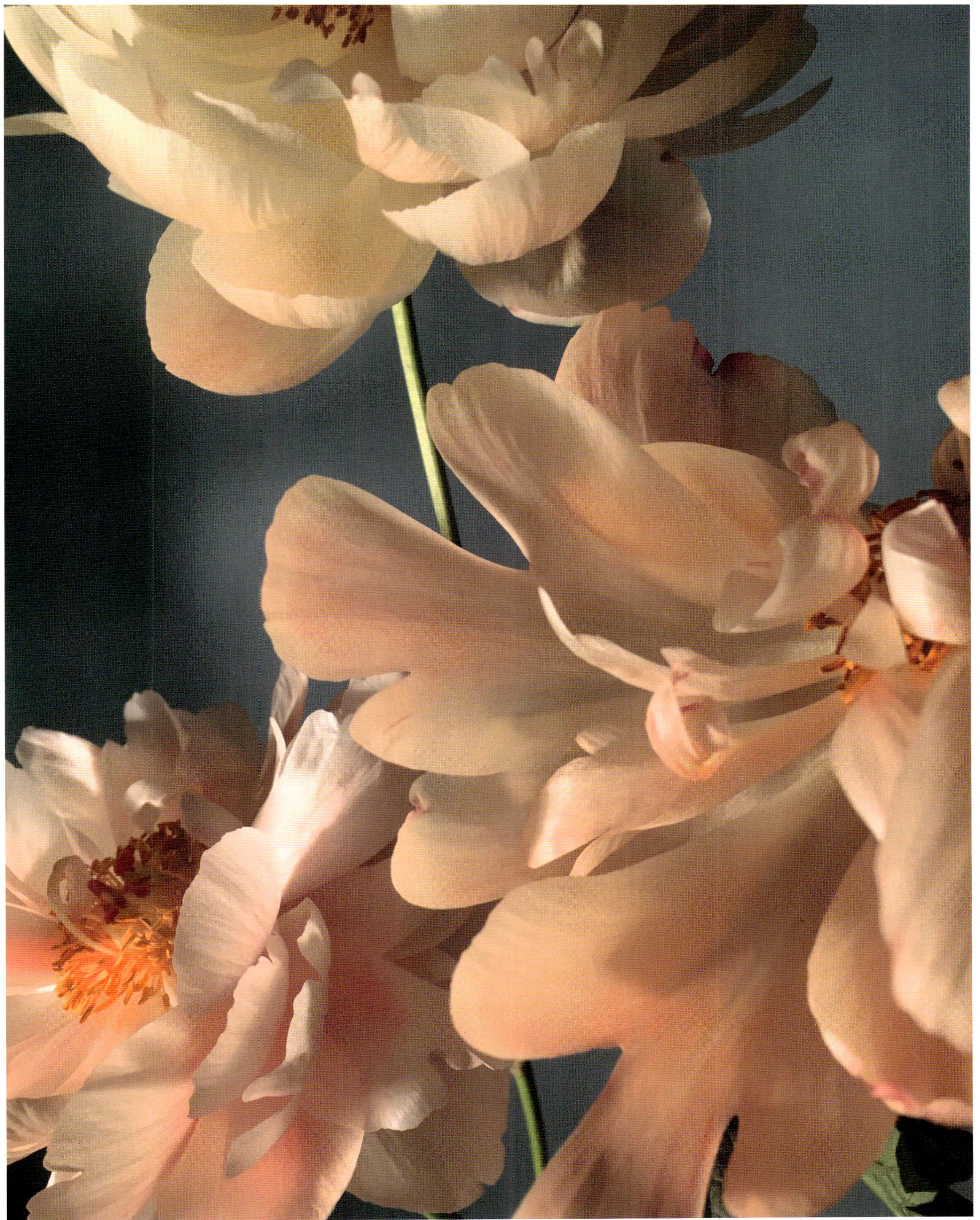

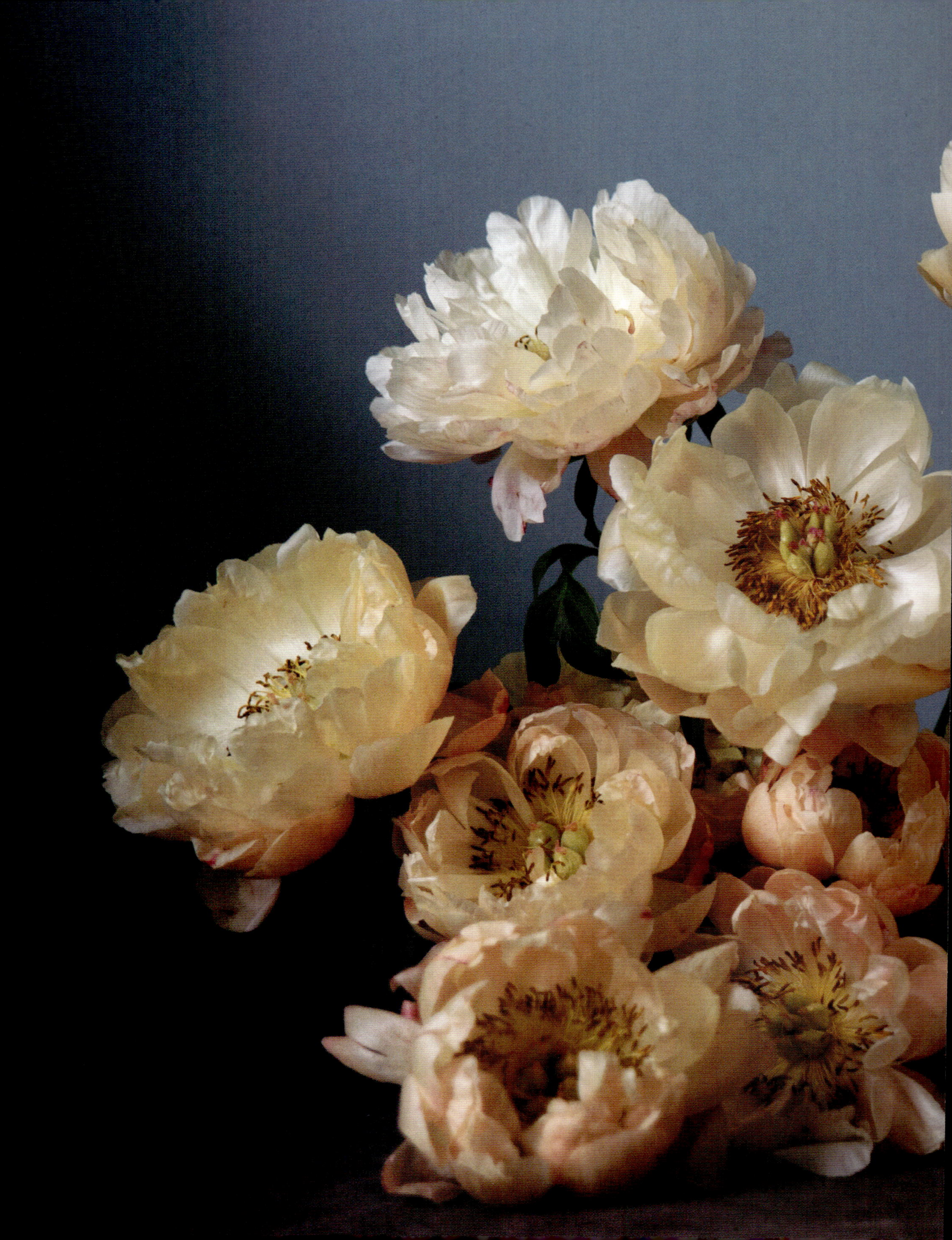

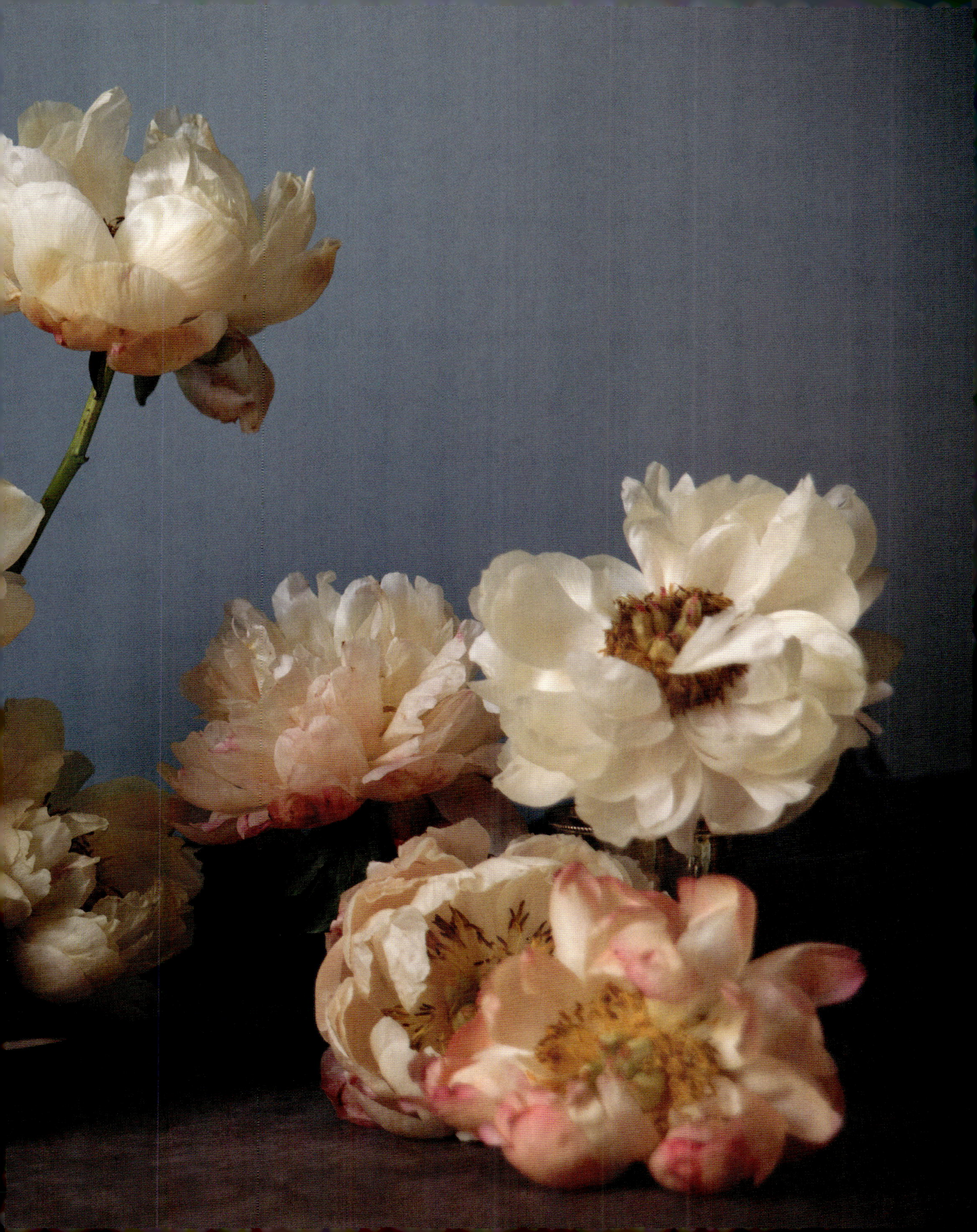

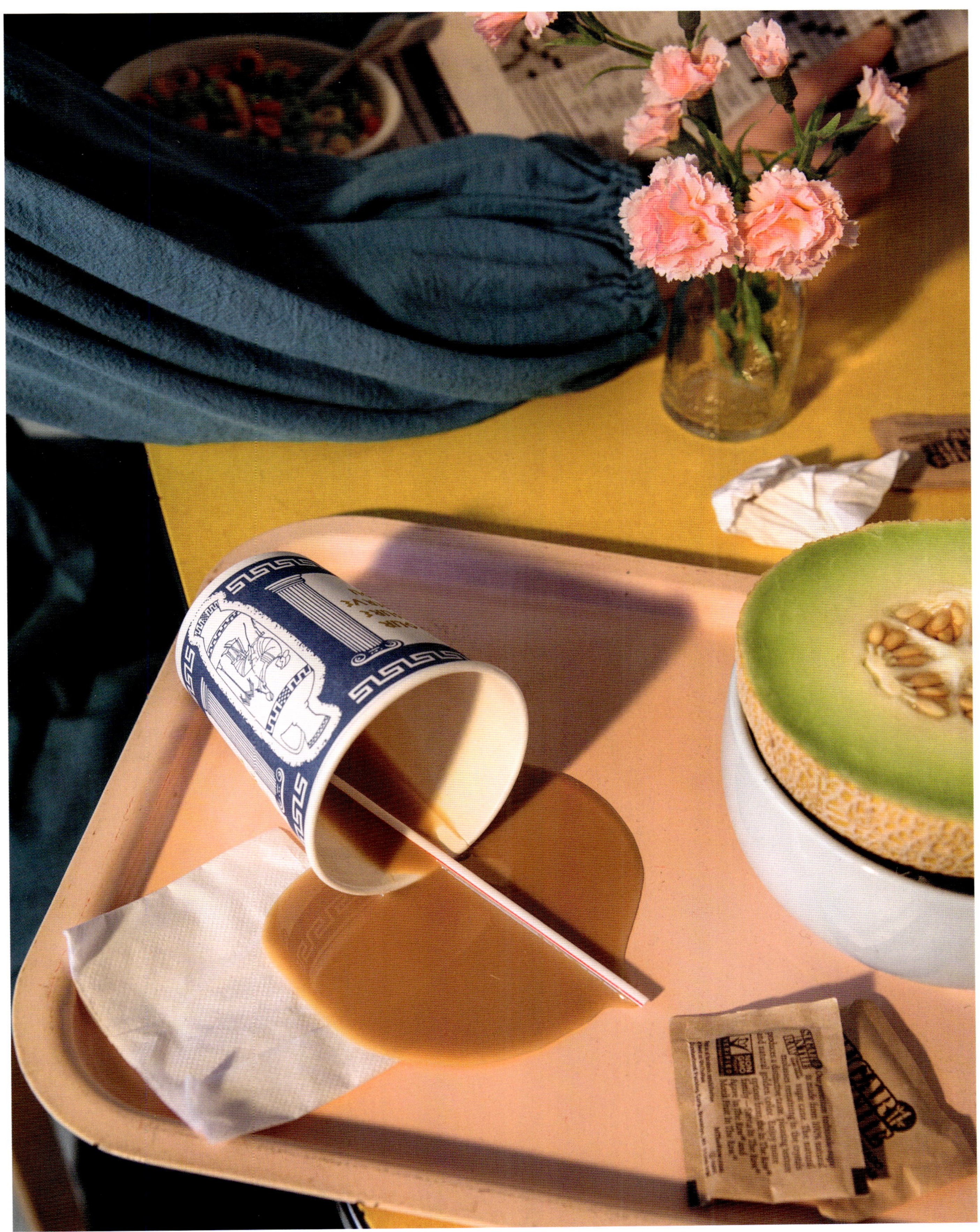

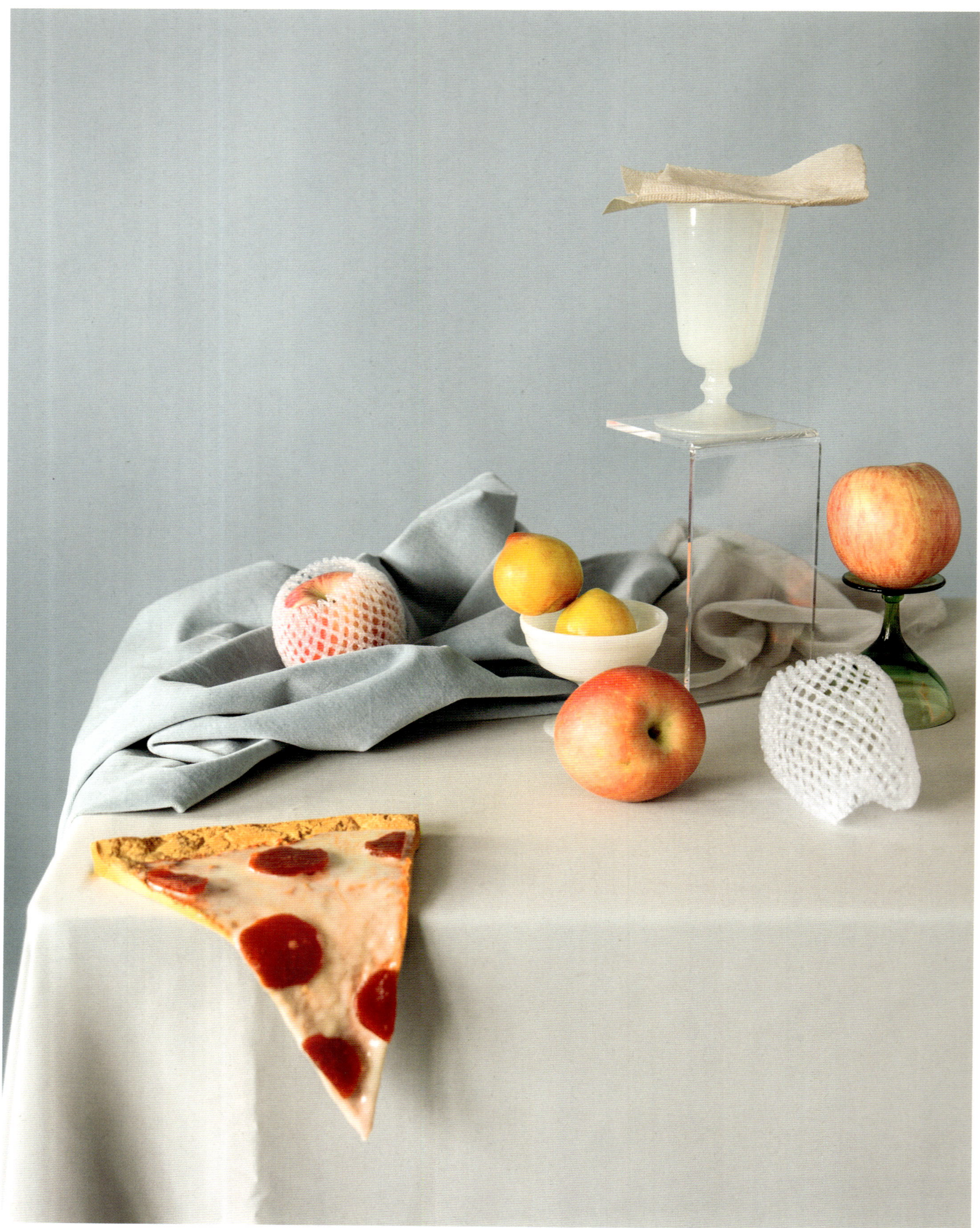

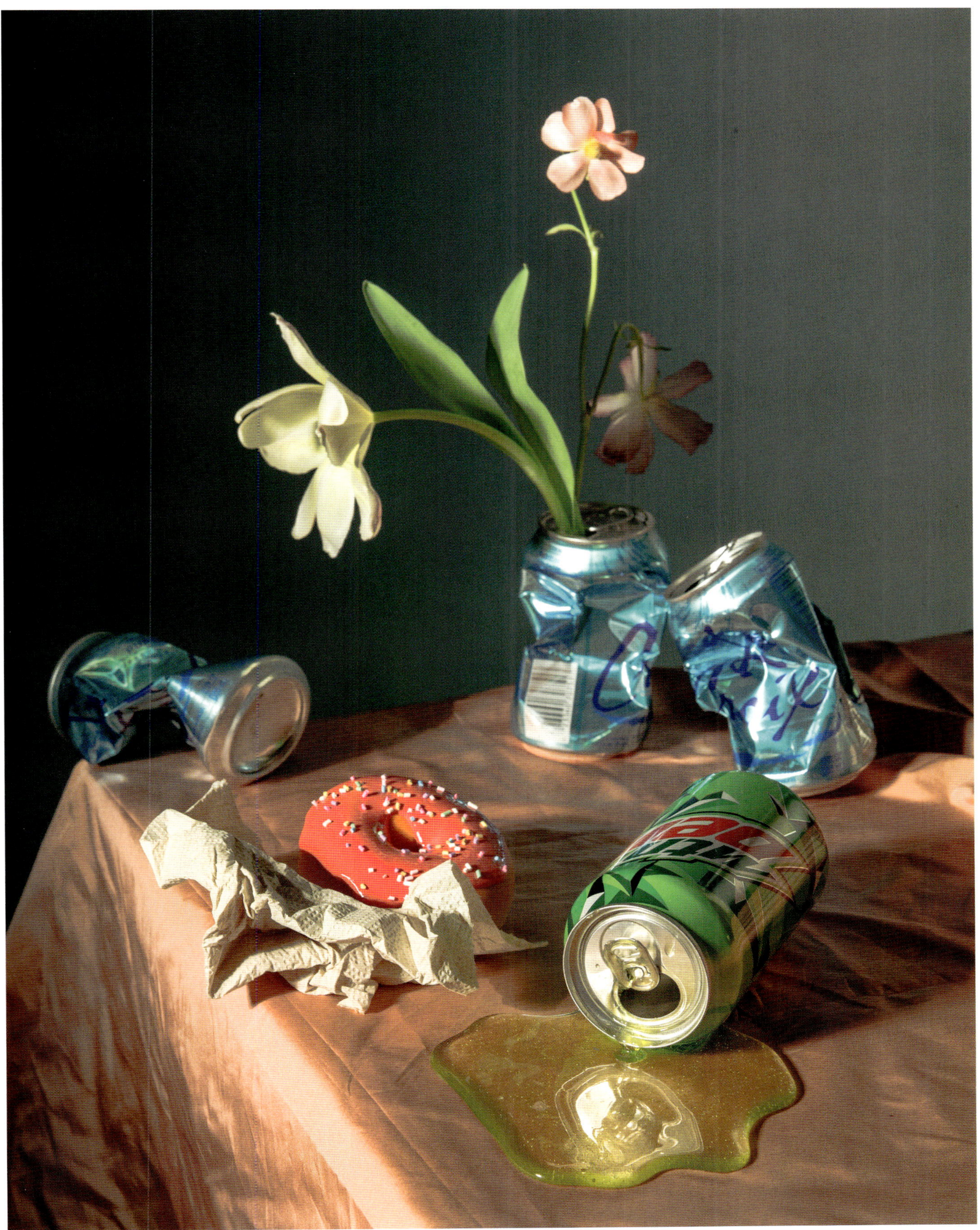

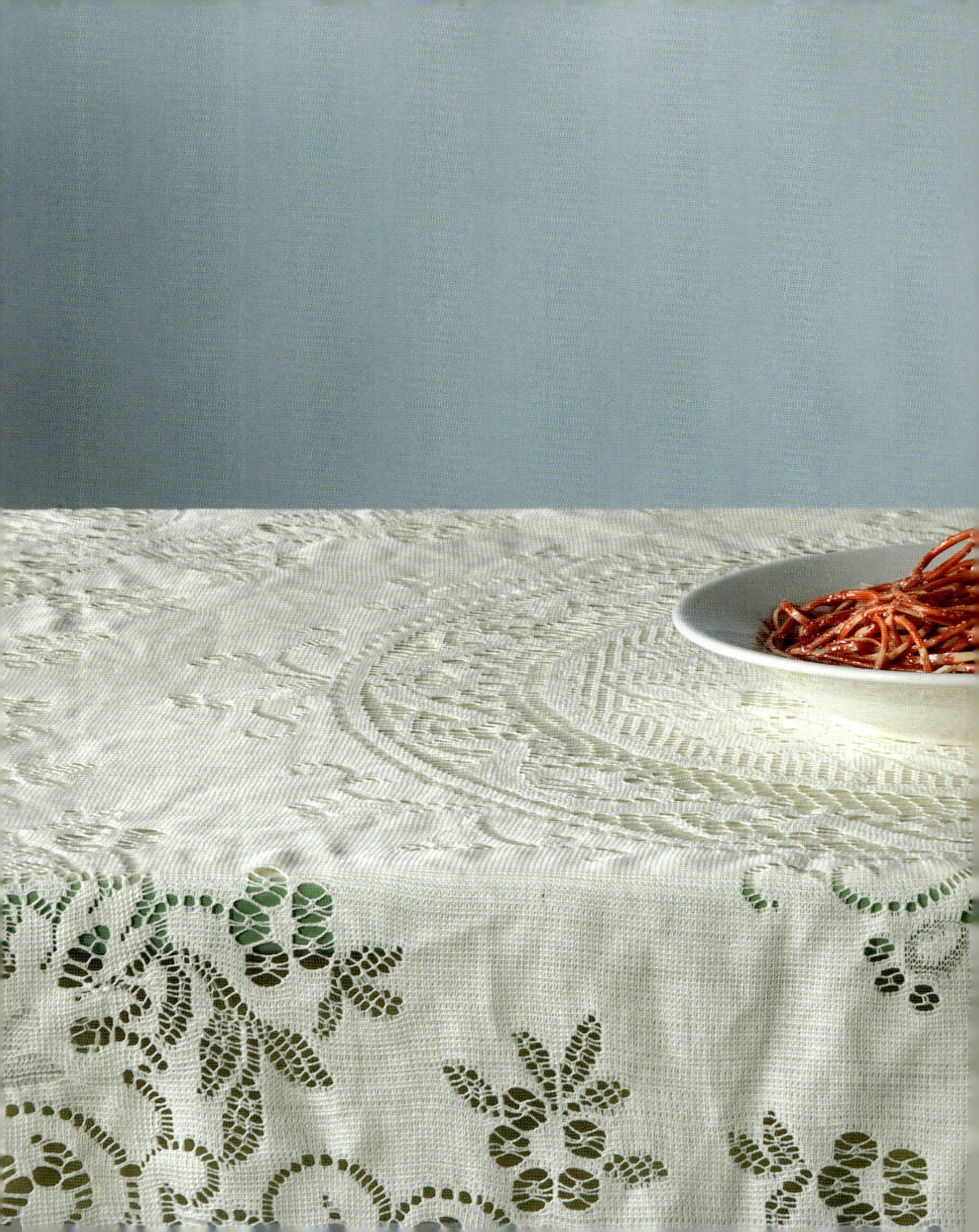

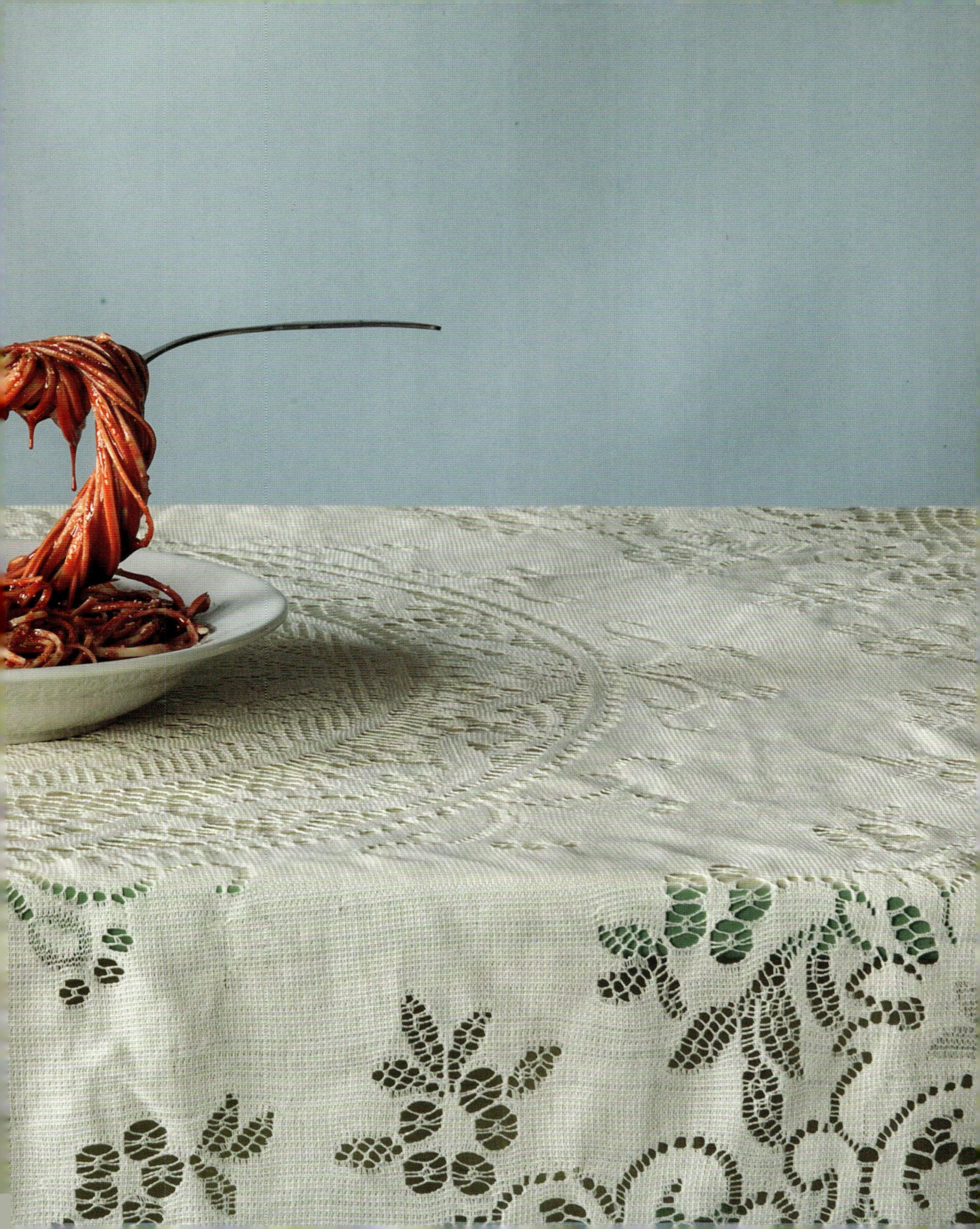

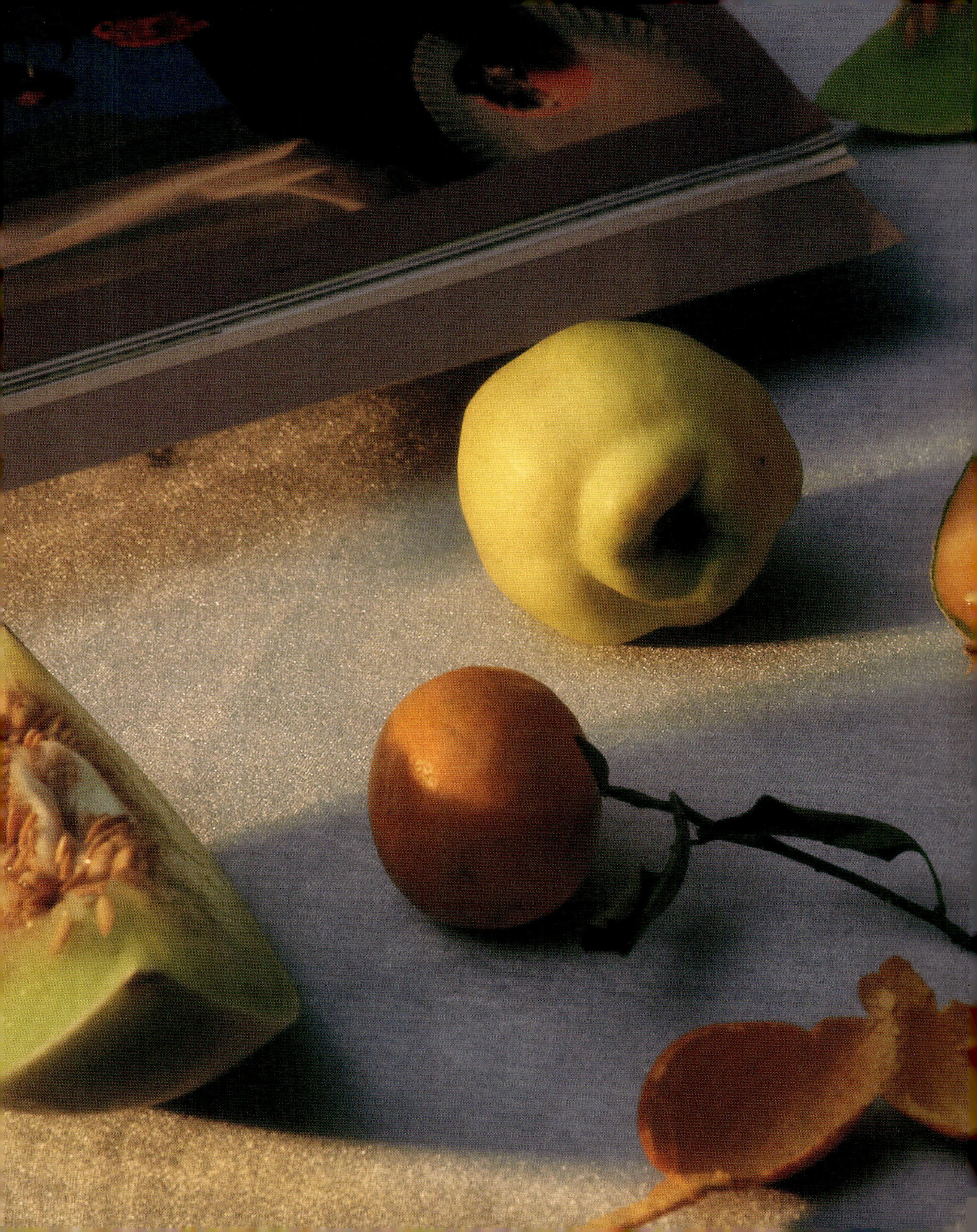

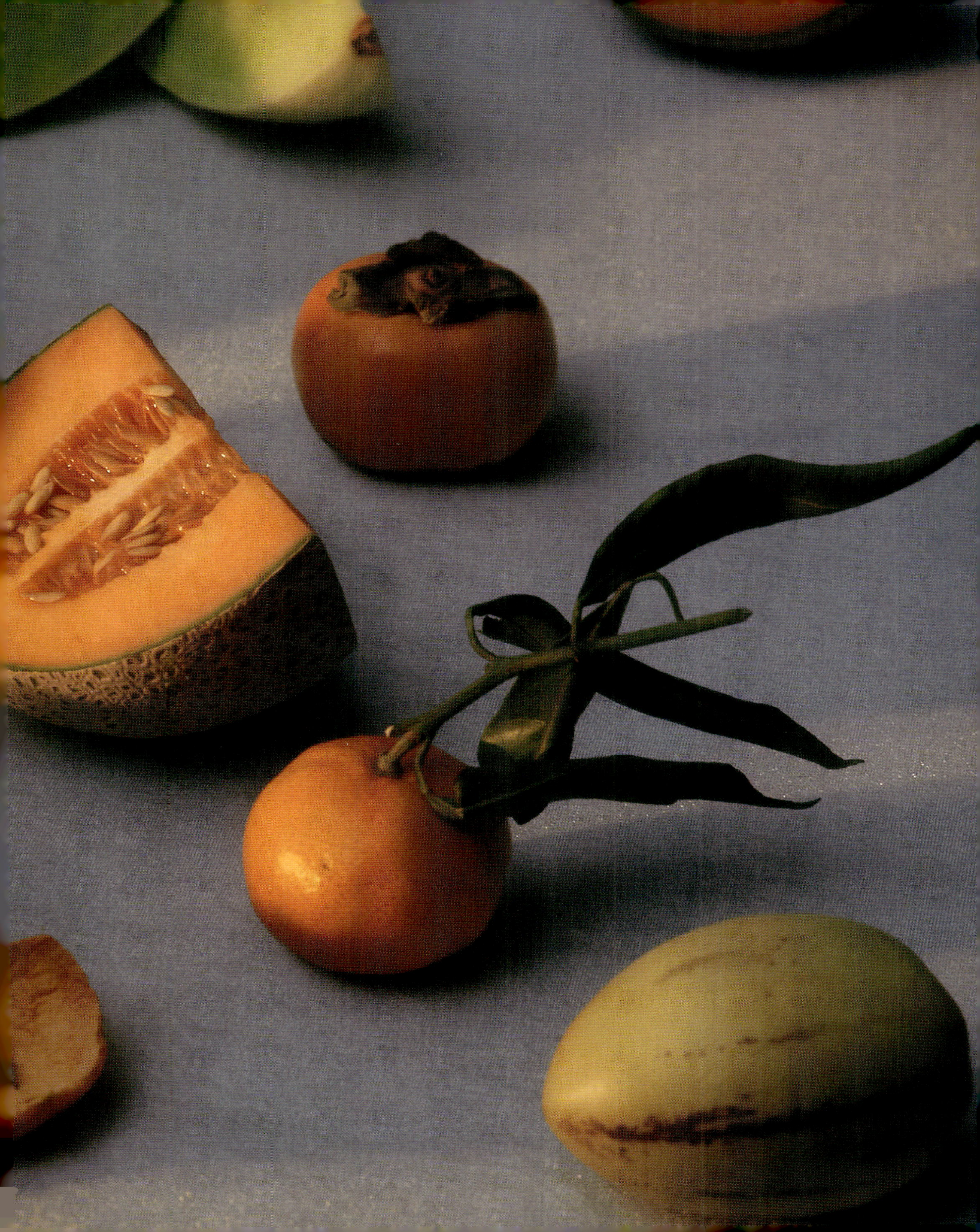

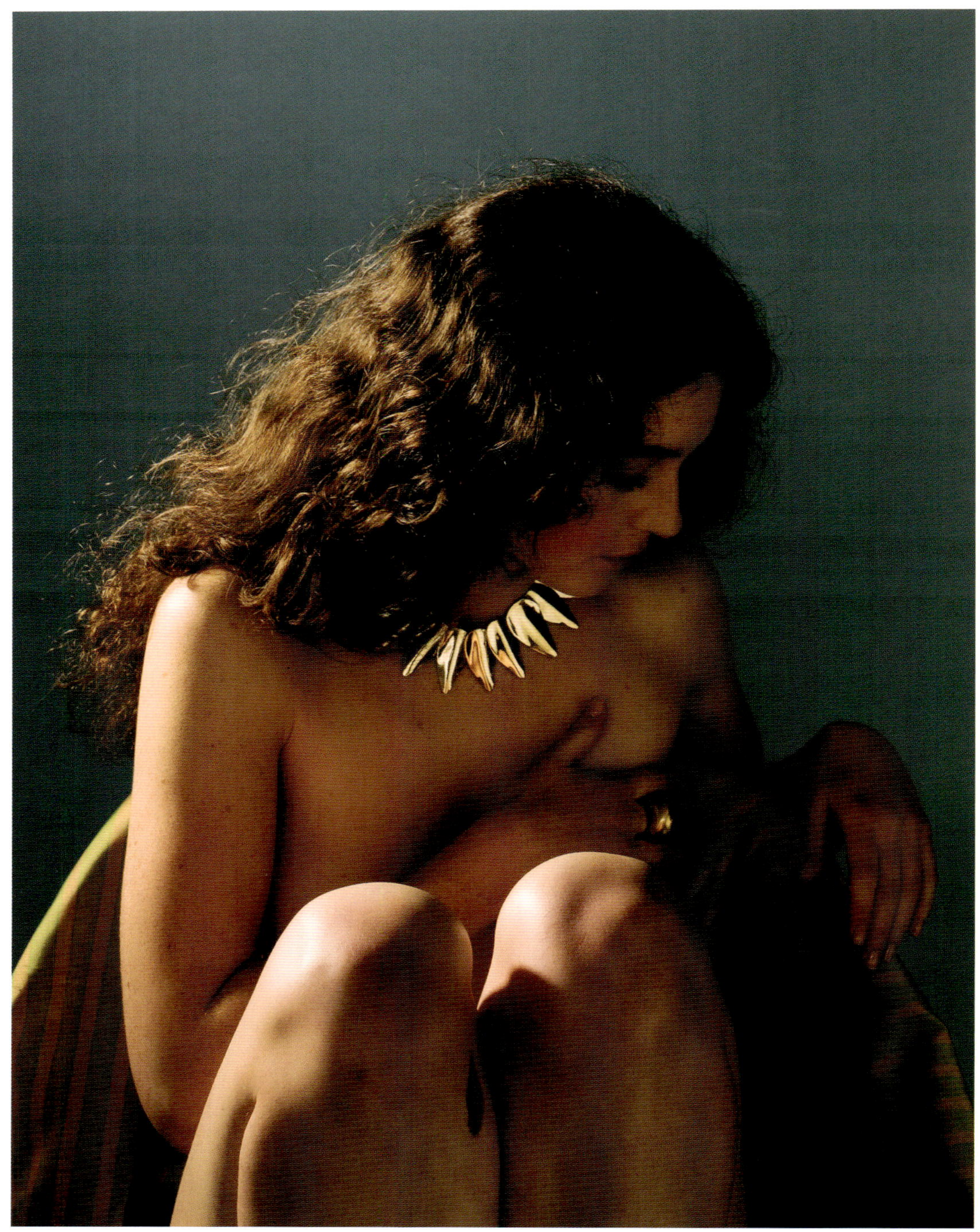

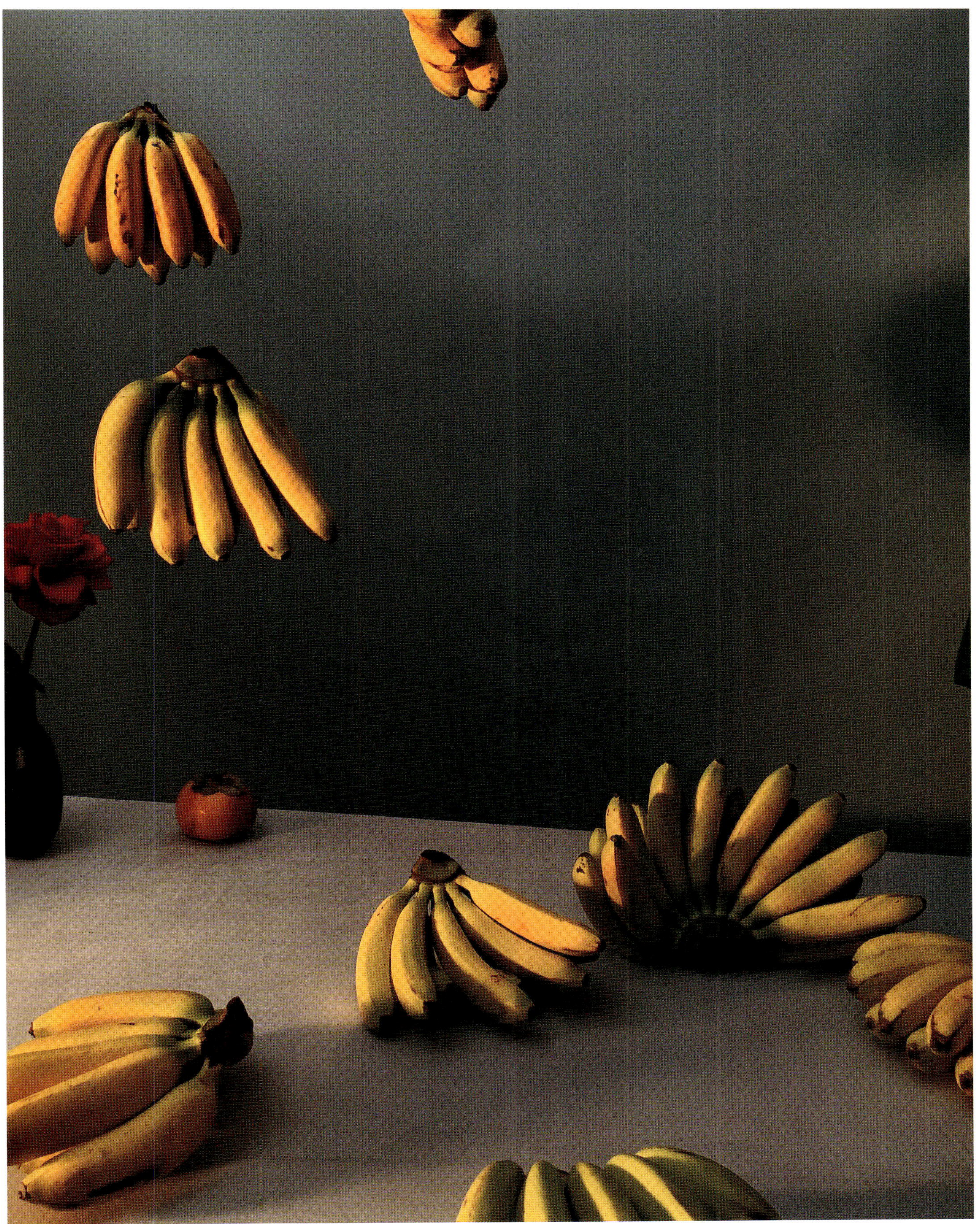

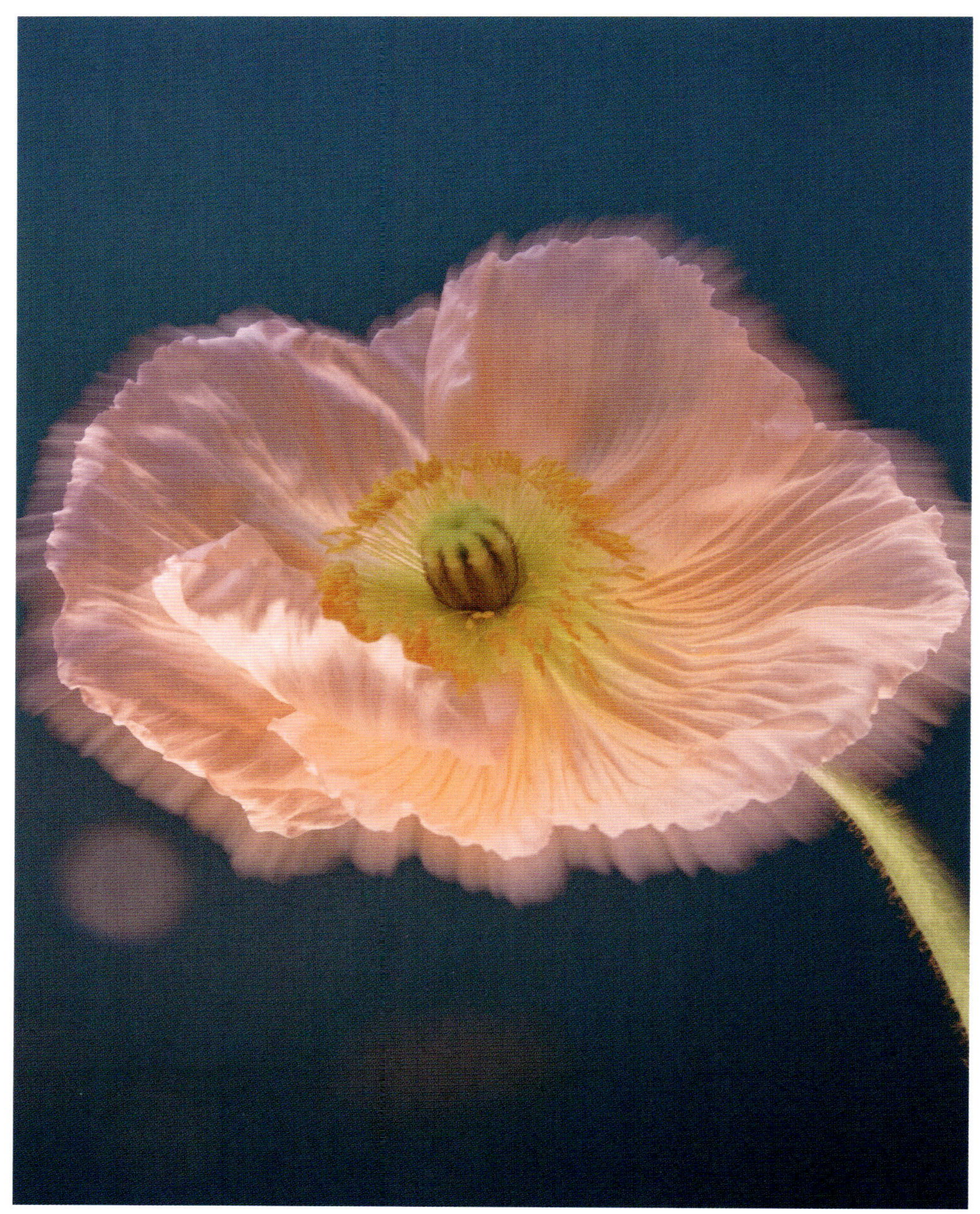

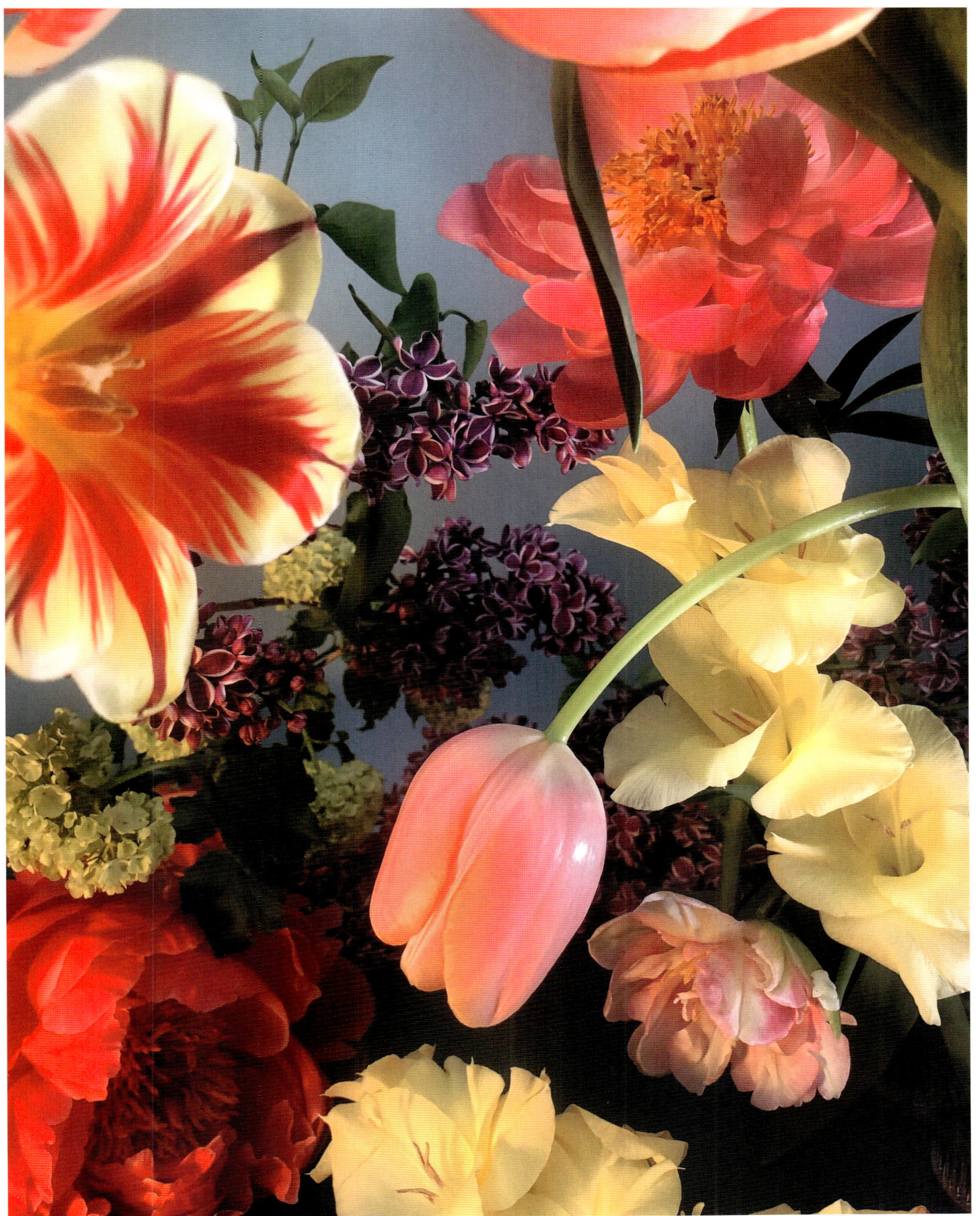

BUT IF YOU STAY

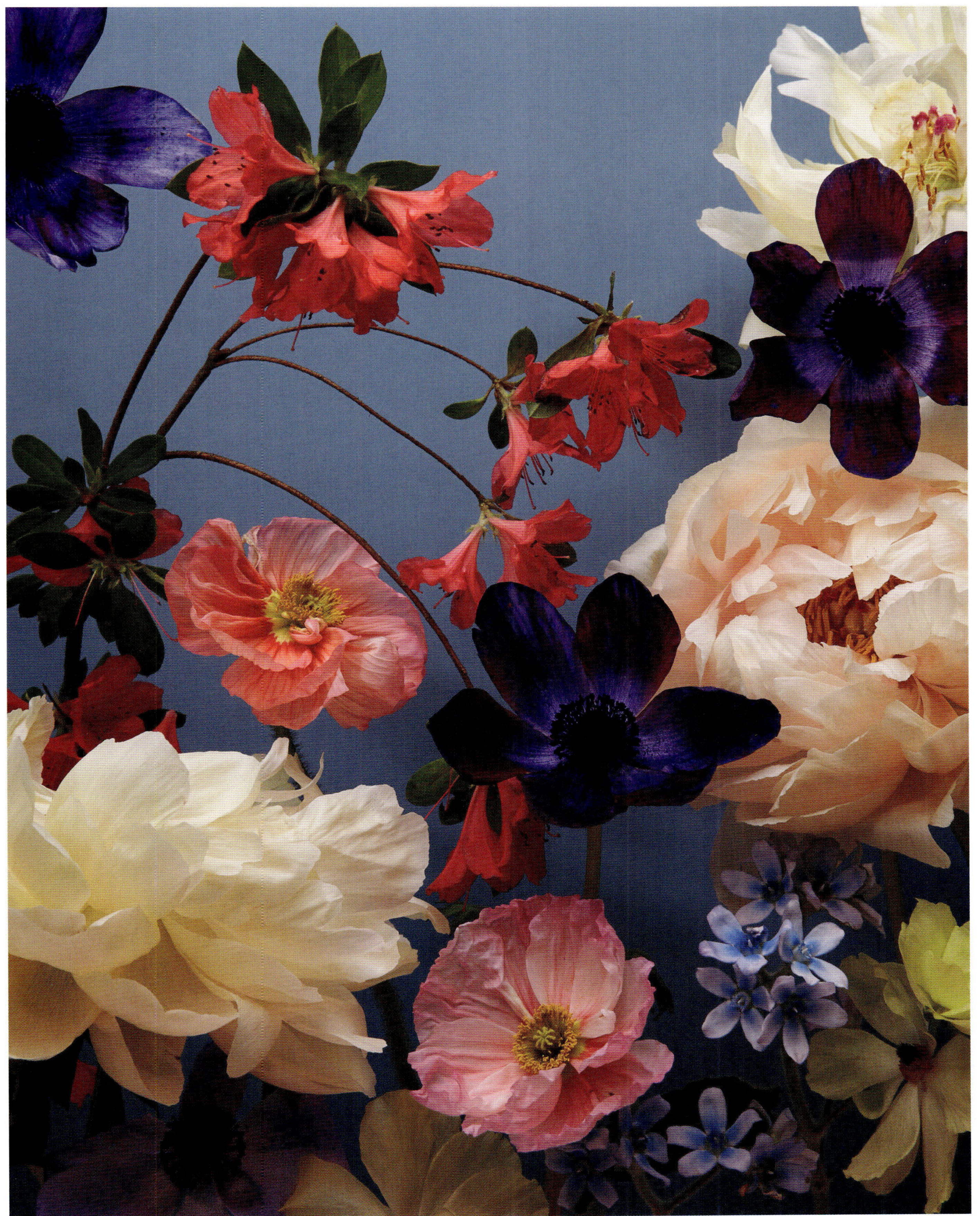

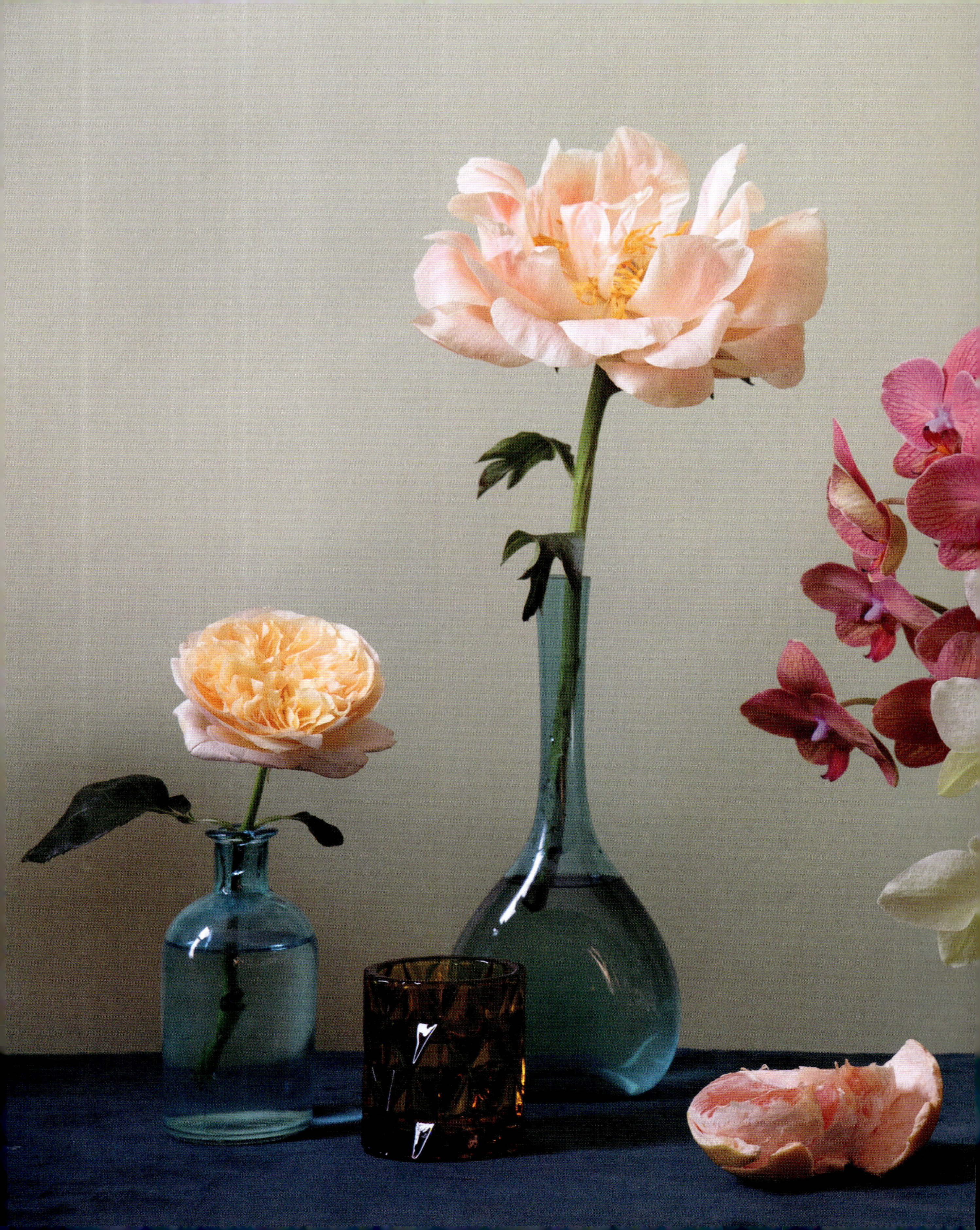

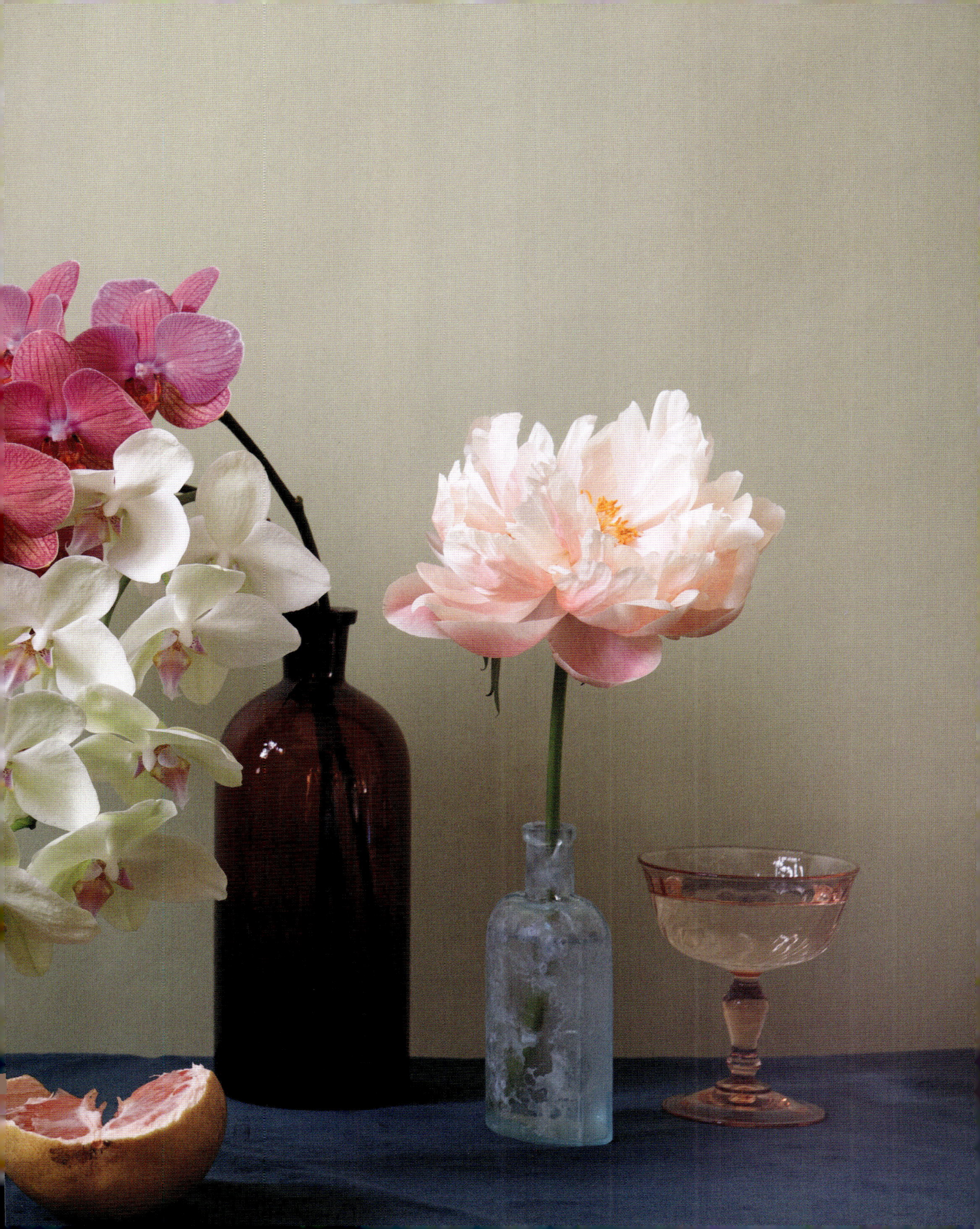

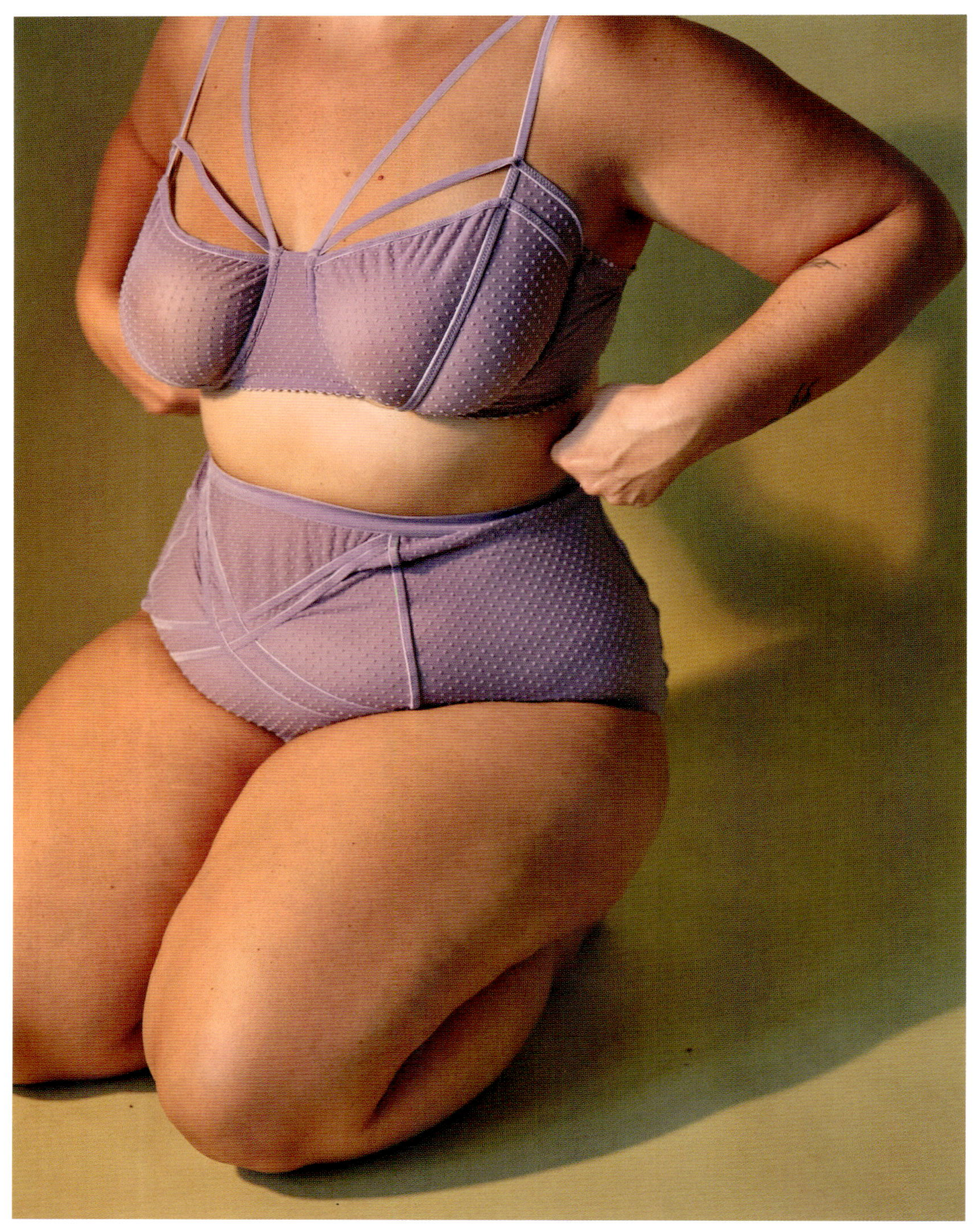

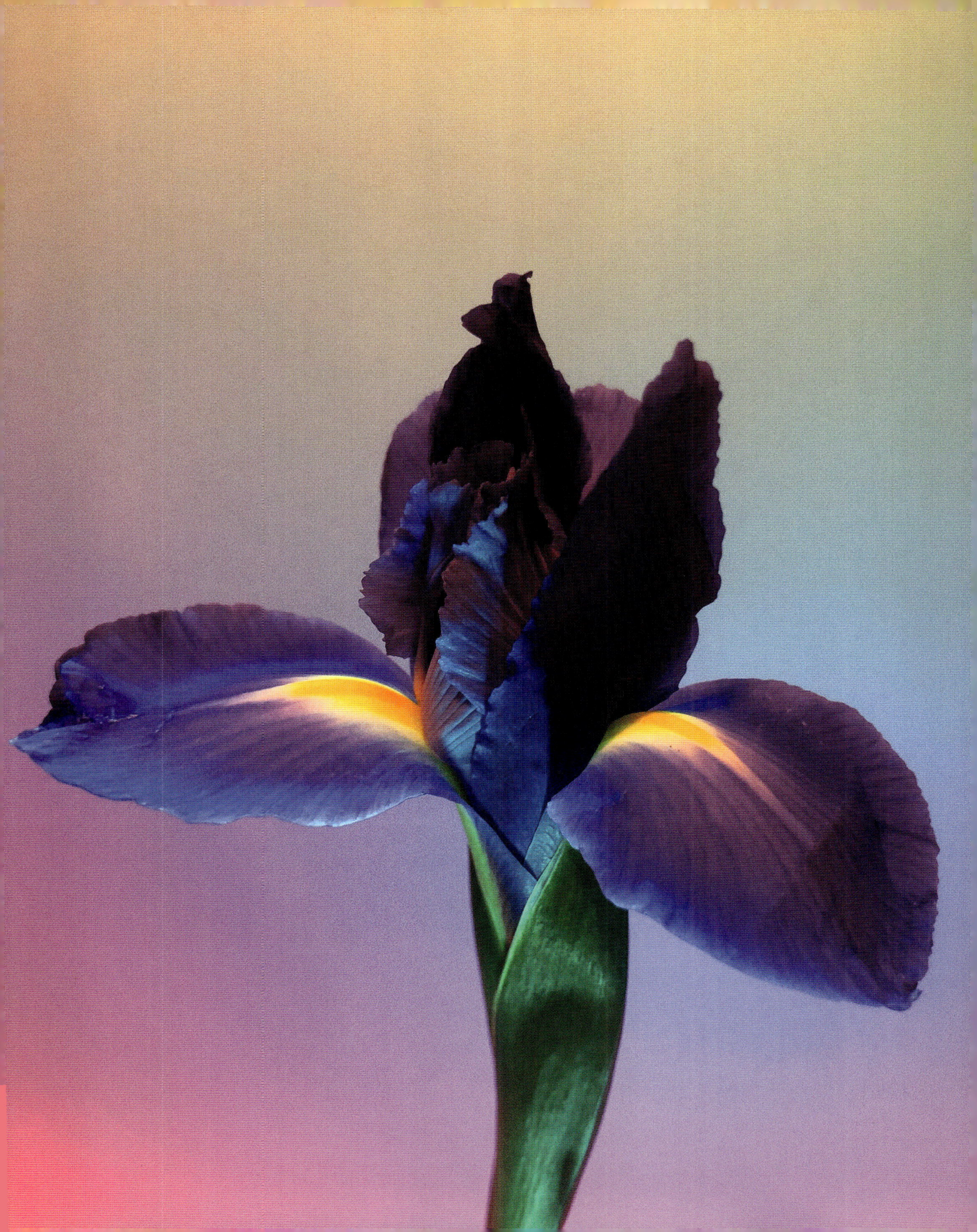

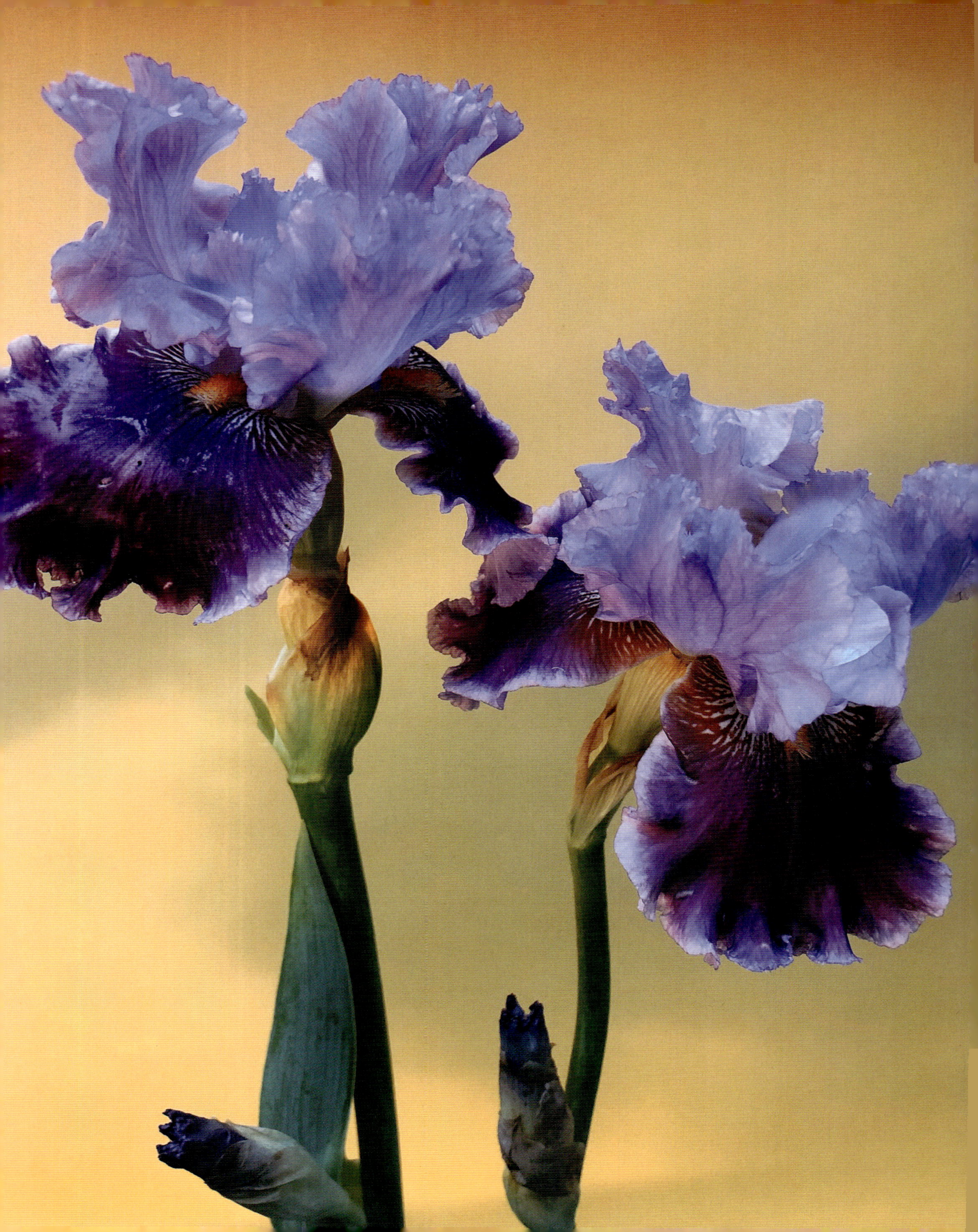

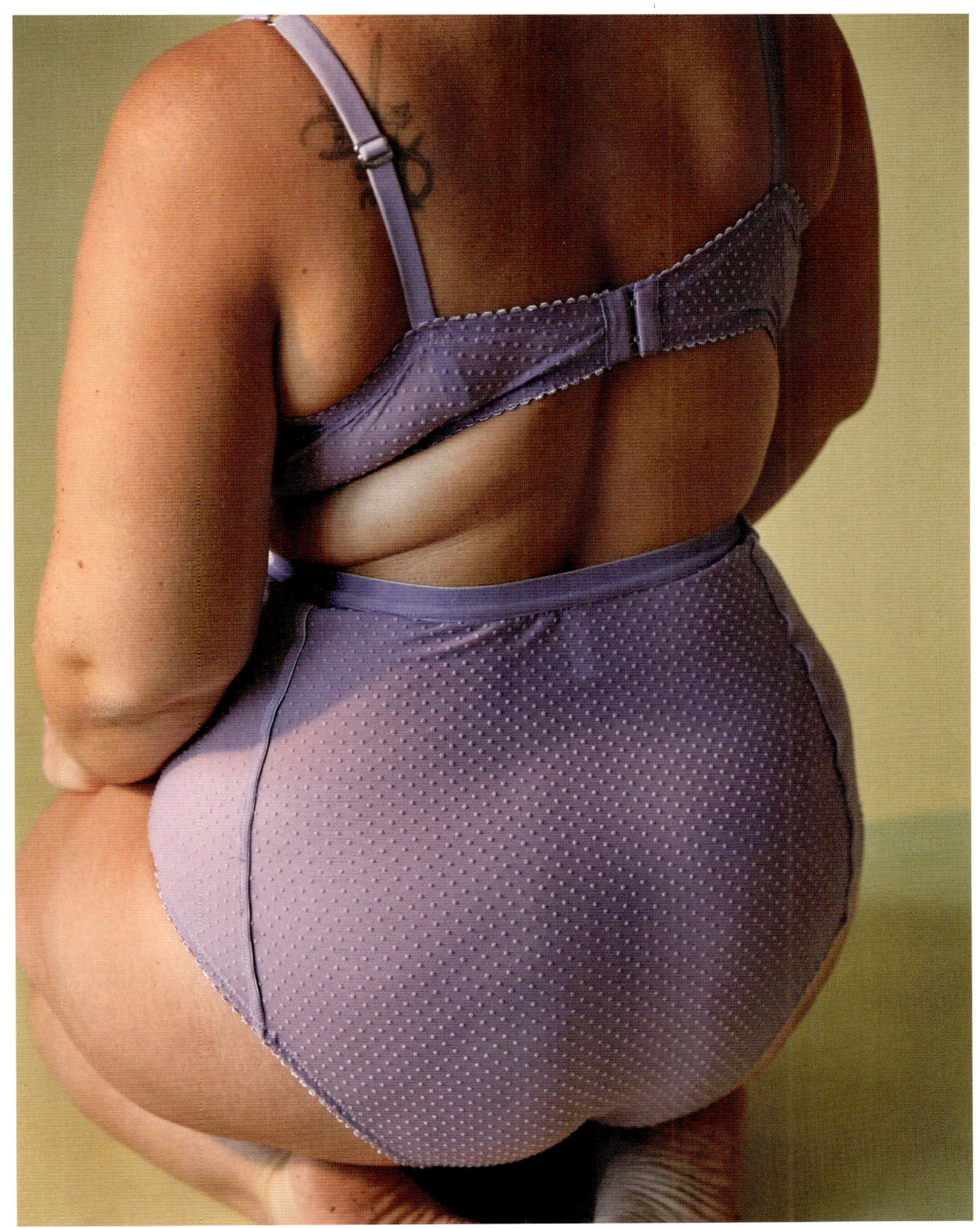

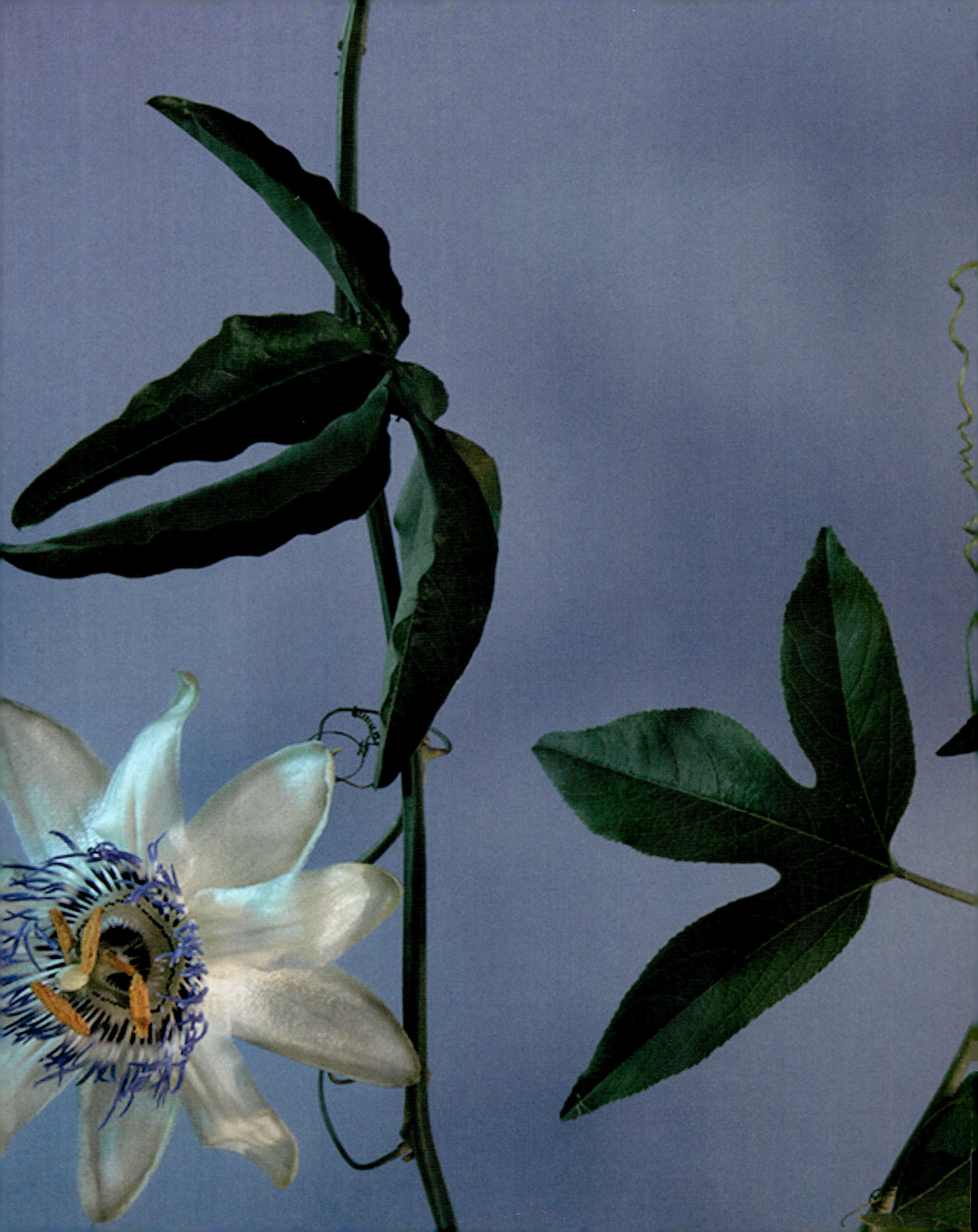

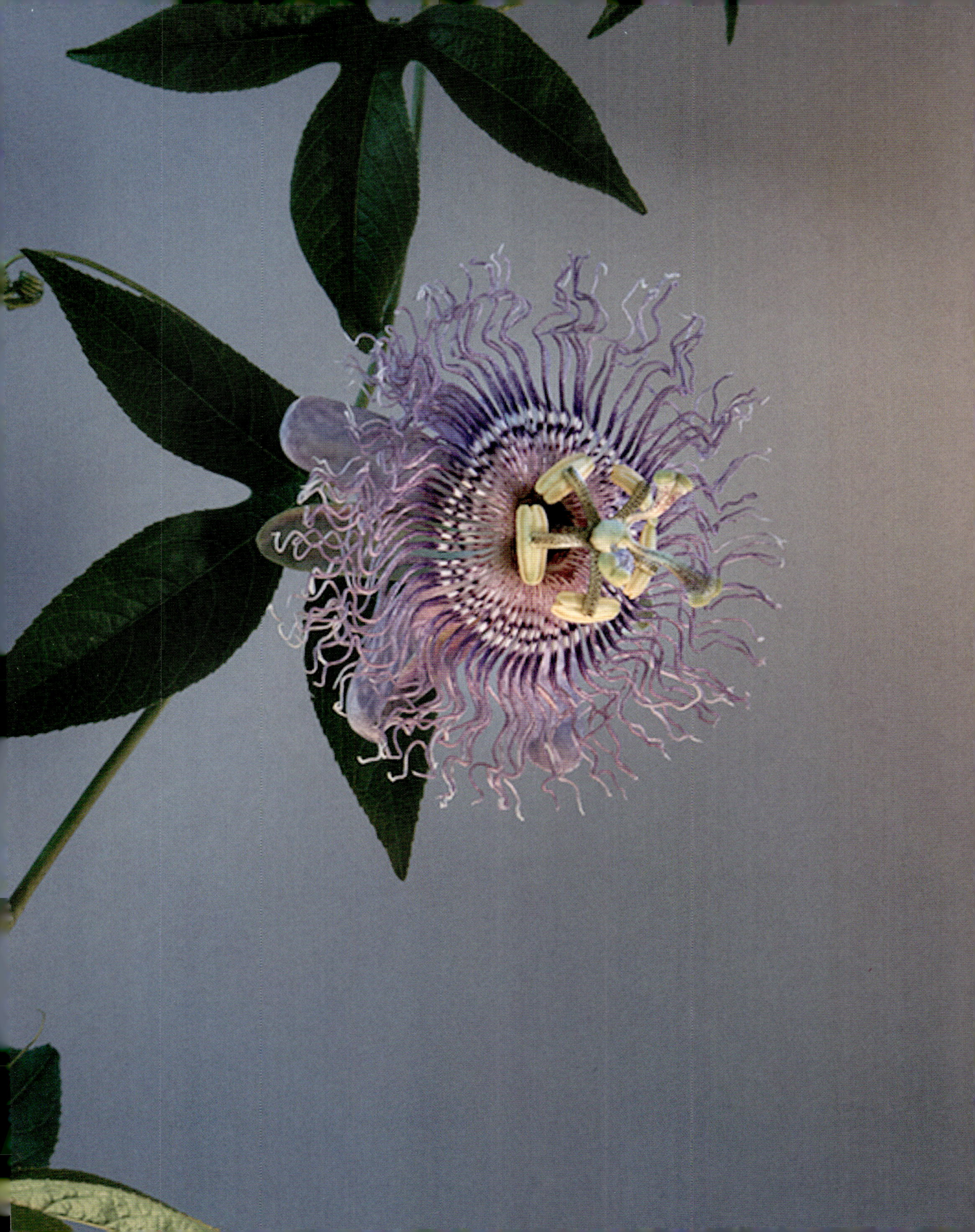

ACKNOWLEDGMENTS

Thank you to Gloria Fowler and Chronicle Chroma for believing in my work.

I am forever indebted to my inspiring models, Rachelle Rickert, Constance Tsang, Devon Grimes, Kristen Usui, Maiko Odaka, Annabella Mull, and Madeleine Macgillivray. You make it so fun. To my collaborators, Andy Lemmik, Pierce Harrison, Timor Raz, Sharlene Durfey, Danielle Ezzo, and Amelie Provosty, thanks so much for being a part of this journey. I am forever grateful. Rose Courteau, I loved our conversations together. Thank you for helping me find the words. Marisol Arteaga, you take such good care of me.

Mom and Dad! I turned out ok. I hope you're proud! I'm so proud of you!

And lastly, thanks to my ever, ever patient and supportive partner, Douglas Schall, for taking care of house and home while I work the long hours, for your impeccable eye, for always encouraging me to say what I believe, to say it simply, to say it with courage.

Still Life by Doan Ly
©2023 Doan Ly All Rights Reserved.

Publisher: Gloria Fowler, Steve Crist
Editor: Gloria Fowler
Introduction: Rose Courteau
Copy editor: Sara DeGonia
Designer and Production: Alexandria Martinez
Production: Freesia Blizard

© 2023 Chronicle Books LLC. All rights reserved.

No part of this book may be reproduced in any form without prior written permission from the publisher.

ISBN: 978-1-7972-2262-2

Library of Congress Cataloging-in-Publication Data available.

Manufactured in China

CREDITS:

Page 17, 202, 205: Rachelle Rickert
Page 27: Omono Okojie
Page 50–51: Devon Grimes, Imani Curry-Johnson, Kristen Usui, Constance Tsang
Page 55, 58–59: Imani Curry-Johnson, Devon Grimes, Kristen Usui
Page 57: Devon Grimes and Kristen Usui
Page 68–69, 79, 147: Constance Tsang
Page 130, 155: Annabella Mull
Page 156: Devon Grimes, Kristen Usui, Maiko Odaka
Page 159: Shawn Finlinson
Page 185: Danielle Ezzo
Page 194: Madeleine Macgillivray

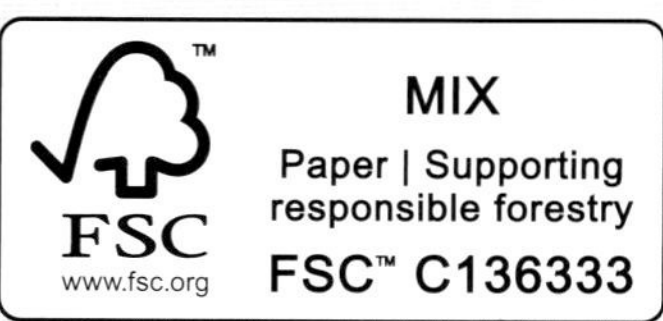

MIX
Paper | Supporting responsible forestry
FSC™ C136333
FSC
www.fsc.org

CHRONICLE CHROMA

Chronicle Chroma is an imprint of Chronicle Books.
Los Angeles, California

Follow us on Instagram @chroniclechroma

chroniclechroma.com